STATUTES & THEIR INTERPRETATION IN THE FIRST HALF OF THE FOURTEENTH CENTURY

BY

THEODORE F. T. PLUCKNETT

M.A. London; LL.B. Cambridge

Choate Fellow (1921–22) in Harvard University

Late Research Student of Emmanuel College, Cambridge

THE LAWBOOK EXCHANGE, LTD.

Clark, New Jersey

ISBN-13: 9781584774853 (hardcover)
ISBN-13: 9781616190712 (paperback)

Lawbook Exchange edition 2010

The quality of this reprint is equivalent to the quality of the original work.

THE LAWBOOK EXCHANGE, LTD.
33 Terminal Avenue
Clark, New Jersey 07066-1321

Please see our website for a selection of our other publications and fine facsimile reprints of classic works of legal history:
www.lawbookexchange.com

Library of Congress Cataloging-in-Publication Data

Plucknett, Theodore Frank Thomas, 1897-1965.
Statutes & their interpretation in the first half of the fourteenth century / by Theodore F.T. Plucknett.
p. cm.
Originally published: Cambridge : University Press. 1922. (Cambridge studies in English legal history).
Includes bibliographical references and index.
ISBN 1-58477-485-1 (cloth: alk. paper)
1. Law—England—Interpretation and construction—History—To 1500. 2. Statutes—England—History—To 1500. 3. Law, Medieval. I. Title: Statutes and their interpretation in the first half of the fourteenth century. II. Title. III. Cambridge studies in English legal history.

KD691.P59 2005
348.42'02—dc22 2004052706

Printed in the United States of America on acid-free paper

STATUTES & THEIR INTERPRETATION IN THE FIRST HALF OF THE FOURTEENTH CENTURY

BY

THEODORE F. T. PLUCKNETT
M.A. London; LL.B. Cambridge
Choate Fellow (1921–22) in Harvard University
Late Research Student of Emmanuel College, Cambridge

CAMBRIDGE
AT THE UNIVERSITY PRESS
1922

CAMBRIDGE UNIVERSITY PRESS
C. F. CLAY, MANAGER
LONDON : FETTER LANE, E.C. 4

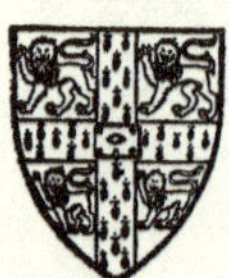

LONDON : STEVENS AND SONS, LTD.,
119 and 120 Chancery Lane, W.C. 2
NEW YORK : THE MACMILLAN CO.
BOMBAY, CALCUTTA, MADRAS } MACMILLAN AND CO., LTD.
TORONTO : THE MACMILLAN CO. OF CANADA, LTD.
TOKYO: MARUZEN-KABUSHIKI-KAISHA

THE INTERPRETATION OF LAW BY ENGLISH MEDIEVAL COURTS

I

THE study of statutes and their interpretation in the time of the first three Edwards (1272–1377) discloses a field of research in English medieval history which has received but scant attention on the part of scholars. We know as yet all too little of the medieval relation of enacted or written to unenacted or unwritten laws; we have even less knowledge of the influence of the judicial power of interpretation upon that part of the law which is legislative and written. These are subjects upon which our legal histories shed only a faint light. Within this sphere of study there is opportunity—and opportunity of no common kind—for exploration and discovery.

Mr Plucknett has entered one particular part of this medieval no man's land and made it his own; and in his choice of the Edwardian century he has shewn wisdom and foresight, wisdom by reason of the special importance of this formative period, foresight by reason of the guidance which the intensive culture of this one limited period will give to future studies of other epochs. He has also made a happy choice of his principal materials, the early year books; for these medieval reports give us better than any other class of historical sources, better even than the plea rolls, an insight into the attitude of the common law courts towards statutes. Previous scholars have dealt with certain aspects of judicial interpretation in this special period; and some of their writings Mr Plucknett has carefully considered. But he is the first scholar to study an important class of original materials from the sole standpoint of interpretation. His results, now embodied in this monograph, reveal for the first time certain processes and tendencies in legislation and adjudication; and, even when his results coincide with those of other students of the period, they bring to us valuable cumulative evidence.

The author's main object has been to study the methods and the principles of interpreting legislation which were evolved by the common law courts during the Edwardian reigns. The justices interpreted the enacted law of earlier reigns; but they were called upon to devote special attention to the statutes of their own time, more particularly those of Edward I. Some of the judges, as the king's counsellors, had taken part in the drafting of statutes which they later interpreted. This is one particular reason why their interpretation now illumines for us the meaning and scope of the acts and the relation of the acts to the unwritten common law. The maxim of the law, *contemporanea expositio est fortissima in lege*, has significance for the historian as well as for the lawyer. Especially in the late thirteenth and early fourteenth centuries, when the judges are closely identified with the council and the parliament, contemporary interpretation is a priceless key to the statutory law. His use of this key forms one of Mr Plucknett's main contributions to the history of his subject.

II

If the study of this century inspires other scholars with the purpose of investigating the history of interpretation in other periods, it might be well for them to begin with the time before Edward I. In approaching this earlier development they must bear in mind many things, and not least of all the wise dictum of Hobbes that "all laws, written and unwritten, have need of interpretation." Nor will they be well advised to overlook the historical teaching of the preface dedicatory to the Reports of Sir John Davies (1613), that "all men at all times and in all places do stand in need of justice and of law, which is the rule of justice, and of the interpreters and ministers of the law, which give life and motion unto justice." The judicial interpretation of the enacted or written and the unenacted or unwritten laws of political societies has ever been one of the principal factors not only in legal administration, but also in legal growth. In his Juridical Society paper "On the Principles of Legal Interpretation" Mr Hawkins has drawn attention to the fact that "Jurisprudence itself is defined by Heineccius [in his *Elementa Juris Civilis*, sec. 26] to be the art of interpreting the laws: 'habitus practicus leges recte interpretandi, applicandique rite speciebus quibusvis obvenientibus.'" In the civilized communities of history judicial interpreters of the law have given "life and motion unto justice." They have found, declared, and applied the law; they have, at the same time, adapted and fashioned the law to meet the claims of justice; they have been legislators as well as judges. In no country has this creative force of judicial interpretation been more marked than in England. All too often our historical vision has been obscured or blurred by the theories of lawyers. One particular dogma of the lawyers has concealed the actual working of the process of interpretation, the dogma which Bacon expresses in his essay *Of Judicature*, when he declares that "judges ought to remember, that their office is *ius dicere*, and not *ius dare*; to *interpret law*, and not to *make law*, or *give law*." Lord Kenyon repeats this maxim in *Geyer* v. *Aguilar*, 7 T.R. 696, where he says: "I am bound to decide according to the law; it is my duty *ius dicere et non ius dare*." However true Bacon's words may be as a theory of the judicial function in his day and in Kenyon's, they are not true as a statement of the historical part which the judges have played in legal development. The more one examines the historical processes by which the judicature interprets the written and the unwritten laws, the laws that are enacted and the laws that are unenacted, the more clearly one sees that the office *ius dicere*, to interpret law, involves also the office *ius dare*, to make law.

The detailed study of early English interpretation in its two separate but closely related aspects—the interpretation of enacted and of unenacted laws—would enable us, therefore, to observe the law-making processes of the courts at close range and, as a consequence, to trace the lines of institutional and legal evolution as from a new angle. Some of the well-known stages of growth would thus appear to us in a different light; while features of growth that are now hidden to us by lapse of time and by neglect might reveal themselves and illumine the past. If, furthermore, the history of English interpretation of laws be compared with the history of interpretation in foreign legal systems, the student would gain valuable points of contrast and of similarity; he would be able to view the English development from the higher altitudes of historical jurisprudence. When, moreover, he traces the history of the interpretation of written law, his vision must extend beyond the written law itself. His eye of scholarship must embrace not only the public and authoritative writings of the enacted law, such as the ordinances and the statutes, it must embrace also the private writings interpreted by the courts, such as the contracts, deeds, and wills of parties. Nor will the student of interpretation forget that in the middle ages the written law includes not only the king's assizes and charters, the king in parliament's statutes, and the like; it embraces also the private written agreements of parties, which, no less than local *consuetudines*, are regarded by medieval lawyers as sources of special law in derogation of the general or common law. In Bracton's words (f. 17 b): *modus tenendus est contra ius commune et contra legem, quia modus et conventio vincunt legem*. For the interpretation of contracts, deeds and wills, the courts have evolved, however, separate sets of axioms and canons differing in many respects from the principles applied in the interpretation of the written law of royal and parliamentary legislation. The one who studies the English historical development of interpretation of laws will need to bear this in mind; and from the judicial axioms and canons applicable to private writings he will be able to draw, for the illumination of his own particular line of research, some of his most instructive parallels.

III

The historian of the interpretation of laws is met, at the very beginning of his studies, by a problem in definition. The jurisprudential division of the law into the *ius scriptum* and the *ius non scriptum* does not correspond in all respects with popular ideas as to what is written and what is not written. Nor are the jurists of different ages and countries agreed as to the meaning of these terms. The Roman lawyers took the phrases *ius scriptum* and *ius non scriptum* literally. By *ius non scriptum* they meant customary law; by *ius scriptum* they meant all the rest of the law, whether enacted or unenacted. In the *ius scriptum* they included the enactments of the supreme legislative bodies and the constitutions of the emperors, and also the *edicta magistratuum*; they held that even the *responsa prudentium* were part of the written as distinct from the unwritten law. Both in medieval and in modern times juristic notions in all European communities have been influenced by this Roman division of law; but, from age to age, the Roman terms have been given meanings at variance with their sense in Roman days. In medieval France *ius scriptum* meant the Roman law in contrast with customary law: in the *pays de droit écrit*, where Roman legal influence was especially strong, the Roman law was the common law, whereas in the *pays de coutumes*, where Germanic influences were more potent than the Roman, the common law was custom. A survey of continental legal history shows us that one of the primary meanings of *ius scriptum* has always been that of written legislation as distinct from unwritten custom; and in theory, even if not always in practice, the written law of enactments and codes has generally held a place of superiority over the unwritten law of custom and cases. The explanation of this striking feature of continental legal systems lies partly in the fact that the written codifications of Roman law by Theodosius and Justinian spread over continental Europe and influenced law and ideas as to the nature of law; while, at an early stage, the Germanic peoples themselves put their own customary folk-laws in writing *juxta exemplum Romanorum*. The revival of legal studies at Bologna in the twelfth century furthered the growth of the notion that enactment in written form is the normal type of law. For upwards of five centuries, at least within the empire, the *corpus iuris civilis*, as the embodiment of Justinian's imperial legislation, was treated as obligatory statute law.

In England the course of development stands in marked contrast with that in continental countries. The early English kings, like other Germanic rulers, put the customs of their folk in writing *juxta exemplum Romanorum*. But in England, where the civil and canon law has had less influence upon the growth of secular law than in other European countries, except possibly

Scandinavia, the ancient Germanic notion that law is unwritten custom declared by the courts has held firmer sway. The fundamental English distinction in the middle ages is not between the "unwritten" and the "written" laws, but between the customs and the king's enactments, between "customs" and "laws"; and, at least until the statutes of the king in parliament acquire a position of prominence in relation to common law, neither customs nor the various forms of royal legislation are viewed as "written law." Ine, in his dooms, directs ecclesiastics to obey God's law and his people to observe both custom (*ryht aew*) and the king's ordinances (*ryhte cynedomas*); and, in general, the main contrast in the time of the Saxon and Danish kings is between the customary folk-law (*folc-riht*) and the enacted king's law of doom and charter. Even this line between folk-law and king's law cannot always be sharply drawn: many of the dooms of the king and his wise men are in large measure custumals as distinguished from enactments. Sir Paul Vinogradoff, in his *Historical Jurisprudence*, has drawn attention to the similarity of the old English *witan* to the *laghman* of ancient Norse and Swedish institutions and to the *lögsögu-madhr* of Iceland. In the case both of the *witenagemót* of the English kingdoms and the *folkmót* of the shires, "it was not only their chief duty to decide particular cases, but they were also required to give verdicts in regard to general customs of the land."

After the Norman Conquest, as before it, the main division of the law is nevertheless into "laws" and "customs," the laws of the kings and the customs of the communities, both of them being treated equally as unwritten. In this matter, as in so many others, our legal history preserves Germanic ideas, rejecting the Roman. The so-called "Leis Willelme," a private compilation composed sometime during the period 1090–1135, probably between the years 1100 and 1120 in Mercia, speaks of the *leis* and the *custumes*: "les leis e les custumes, que li reis Will. grantad al pople de Engleterre aprés le cunquest de la terre, iceles meimes que li reis Edward sun cusin tint devant lui." "Les leis e les custumes" of the French texts are the "leges et consuetudines" of the Latin and the "laws and customs" of the English texts. Glanvill and Bracton both write their treatises "de legibus et consuetudinibus Angliae." Both jurists are conversant with the civilian's distinction between the *ius scriptum* and the *ius non scriptum*; and both of them take pains to explain that, although the English *leges*, the laws enacted by the king on the advice of his counsellors, are not *ius scriptum*, they are nevertheless true laws. "For," says Glanvill, "if from the mere want of writing only, they [the *leges*] should not be considered as laws, then, unquestionably, writing would seem to confer more authority upon laws themselves, than either the equity of the persons constituting, or the reason of those framing, them." To reduce all of the laws of the realm into writing, declares Glanvill, would be impossible. It is his purpose to put into writing certain of the laws which "more generally occur in court and are more frequently used": and, in essentials, his treatise is a custumal, a written collection of those unwritten *leges* and *consuetudines* which have worked their way into the custom of the king's court. Nor is Glanvill's the only custumal composed in the Angevin dominions at this time; for we learn from Dr Powicke's *Loss of Normandy* that "under the shadow of Henry II's government, in all parts of the empire, from England to Gascony, legal principles and customs are reduced to writing in response to the pressure of local forces."

In process of time the *leges* and *consuetudines* of Glanvill's and Bracton's age develop into the system which Coke describes in his *First Institute*, 110 b, as "the maine triangles of the lawes of England; those lawes being divided into common law, statute law, and custome." The growth of parliamentary statute law has gradually resulted in the drawing of a sharper line of distinction than existed in earlier days between the customary and judge-made common law and the law embodied in legislation. The case-law of the common law courts and the statute-law of the parliament now stand opposed to each other as the two most important "maine triangles of the lawes of England." *Consuetudo*, originally the most important and almost the sole source of the law, is still one of its three "maine triangles," but, both in Coke's order and in fact, it now holds the third place and not the first or the second. Coke's words are an epitome of English legal history up to his time.

Only when parliament becomes the power which Sir Thomas Smith, the Elizabethan, describes as "the most high and absolute power of the realme of Englande," do English jurists finally adopt the Roman terminology of "written" and "unwritten" laws. To Hale, to Blackstone, who follows him, and to later jurists, the statute law is the English "lex scripta," the common law is the English "lex non scripta." In this use of Roman terms we may see one of the influences of the legal renaissance upon English jurisprudential thought. But this particular Roman influence, like most of the others, touches only the surface of the law; it does not substitute the *corpus iuris civilis* for the *corpus* of the year books, the plea and statute rolls, and the books of Coke; it merely decks out the English cases and the English statutes in Roman garb. Maitland has taught us that the Inns of Court, where the year books were read and taught, "saved English law in the age of the Renaissance." Other factors, we may suspect, had also a share in preserving the Englishry of the law; and not least of all Westminster and the statutes of the king in parliament. The "Nolumus leges Angliae mutare" of the barons in 1236 persists throughout the ages as a living maxim of legislative conservatism. Even the Roman garb of the "lex scripta" and the "lex non scripta" has never settled down comfortably upon the shoulders of English *consuetudines* and *leges* and of English case-law and statute-law. Present-day English jurists dispute as to the meaning of these foreign terms; some of them at least state their distinctions under the influence of the modern doctrine—and a doctrine, too, far from general acceptance—that law is the command of the sovereign power. In his *Nature and Sources of the Law* Gray proposes that, in view of the uncertainty of the meaning of the phrases and their "inaptness to any of the supposed meanings except that of the Romans," the best way is to discontinue their use.

The historian of English interpretation has need, therefore, of caution; he must not carry back into the middle ages distinctions and refinements based on terms of Roman jurisprudence and adopted only when common law and statute law have clearly emerged as distinct divisions of the legal system. For the earlier periods it is better to adhere to the native English distinction most commonly found in the sources, the distinction between the *leges* and the *consuetudines*, the king's *enactments* of various sorts and the many *customs* which have validity apart from and independent of royal legislation. As rough equivalents of "enacted" and "unenacted" laws the terms "written" and "unwritten" laws are, however, convenient. But if we use them in this sense we must be careful not to invest them either with their Roman or with their modern English meanings. We must at the same time remember that in the English middle ages not all of the enacted law is written and not all of the unenacted law is unwritten. Some of the king's legislation is oral and of an administrative character; it is not embodied in written form. Although the customs are unenacted, some of them are nevertheless embodied in written dooms and written custumals.

In medieval England there is more legislation than we sometimes assume; but, on the whole, it is of far less importance than the unwritten law declared and evolved by the courts. Continental communities in the middle ages are more Roman than Germanic in laying stress upon the enacted or written law; England is more Germanic than Roman in her adherence to the notion that the law is fundamentally customary and unwritten, the law of courts rather than the law of legislators. Remembrance of this vital point of contrast between the laws of the continent and the laws of England gives meaning and spirit to our studies of English judicial interpretation. Such studies bring out, into clear relief, the judicial nature of English medieval jurisprudence as its most characteristic feature. We see it in the processes of the courts when they interpret and apply customs and precedents; we see it in the judicial nature of many of the acts of legislation, as, for example, some of the enactments of the early high court of parliament; and we see it also in the attitude of the courts towards the various forms of enacted and written law, more particularly in their position as to parliamentary statutes in relation to the unwritten common law. There is deep historical significance in these words of Bacon: "For the common law of England, it appeareth, is no text law, but the substance of it consisteth in the series and succession of judicial acts from time to time which have been set out in the books which we term year books." Much of the enacted law remains "text law" to the very end; but much of it, on the other hand, does not. Much of the enacted law is rapidly absorbed, by judicial interpretation and application, into the general mass of the unenacted law; it is transformed by court processes, it loses its character as written law and acquires a new character as unwritten law. This happens to many of the Angevin assizes and ordinances; and it happens also, to a certain extent, as Mr Plucknett points out, to some of the Plantagenet statutes. Even Magna Carta is partly assimilated by the unwritten law of the courts.

IV

The history of the enacted law and its interpretation is, in some ways, more complex and more difficult to trace than is the history of the interpretation of the unenacted law during the same periods. Complexities and difficulties arise in part from the very fact that the law is embodied in authoritative written form and not in oral tradition or the precedents of courts. The written form of the law helps in general to produce certainty: and, as remarked by Serjeant Carus, when speaking of laws, in the case of *Stowel* v. *Lord Zouch*, 1 Plowden, 353, "certainty is the mother of repose, and incertainty is the mother of contention." Many texts of the written law are, however, "incertain" rather than "certain" in their wording and sense: and this uncertainty is sometimes increased by varying judicial interpretations. But complexities and difficulties are created chiefly by the fact that the written law is of later growth than the unwritten, that from the time of the emergence of written enactments the two kinds of law evolve side by side, and that the interpretation of written law involves also an interpretation of the law that is unwritten. One main aspect of this difficulty in Angevin and later times is to be found in the problem of the relation of unwritten common law and written statutory law; a problem that is solved, in nearly all cases of conflict, by the processes of interpretation. The difficulties incident to the history of the interpretation of written law are increased by the complexities of institutional evolution. These particular difficulties are not resolved by saying that the enactment of written law is the function of the legislature, while its interpretation is the function of the judicature. The fluidity of institutions and the fusion of powers in the middle age do not permit us to explain the matter so summarily.

The problems of the enacted law and its interpretation are vastly more complex in medieval times than they are in our modern age; and, as a consequence of this complexity, the medieval problems are vastly more interesting. Their solution will carry the student from medieval into modern times; and it will help him to reach sound solutions if he can survey the whole course of English legislation from the days of Aethelbehrt to our own time. One of the most valuable lessons which this survey will teach him is that royal legislation in the middle age assumes many different forms. The king legislates by doom and charter, by writ and provision, by ordinance and statute, and by other forms. This variety in the forms of the king's medieval legislation produces its own special problems in the matter of interpretation; and these problems are further complicated by the fact that the early common law judges who interpret the legislation have sometimes had a prominent part in drafting it and in giving it validity. The rise of the parliament —the king in parliament—as the sovereign legislative power in the state tends to a simplification of the processes of legislation by making the statute law supreme over all other forms of legislation: and the simplification of legislation simplifies at the same time the processes and principles of judicial interpretation.

V

Legislation, if under that term we include the several forms of royal enactment, steadily increases in importance during the two centuries before Edward I's accession. Even in the Norman reigns the enacted law is not unimportant. The time of Henry II, the first and the greatest of the Angevins, marks however a new epoch in the history of legislation; for in this reign the ordaining power of the king produces momentous changes in the processes of the courts and in the substantive rules and principles of justice. Much of Henry's enacted law is informal and administrative in character, for as yet the king of England is not checked by a parliament jealous of his power; and, although not all of Henry's important ordinances or assizes have come down to us, we possess nevertheless in the Constitutions of Clarendon, the Assize of Clarendon, the Assize of Northampton, the Inquest of Sheriffs, the Assize of the Forest, and in other extant acts of the king's ordaining or decreeing power the written evidences of a period of legislative reform comparable, in the whole of the English middle age, only to the time of Edward I.

As yet no one has studied Norman and Angevin legislation in England from the point of view of interpretation. Such a special study would bring much light to bear on the legislative and judicial processes of legal growth and on their relation to each other, and it would also help to make clear the early history of many rules of our substantive law. But it would be a study beset with its own special difficulties. One of them is the difficulty of finding any precise points of distinction that give individuality and character to each one of the several forms of royal legislation, such as the charters, writs, assizes, provisions, edicts, ordinances, and statutes. There is even the difficulty of sharply distinguishing between legislation and adjudication, of drawing the line between the written and the unwritten law. The search for distinctions between legislative and judicial acts, in the history of Norman and Angevin institutions, is prompted by our modern notions of the division or separation of powers: we read present-day ideas into the middle ages, and are surprised and puzzled to find that they do not square with the medieval facts. Medieval fusion of powers frequently results in an obliteration of any marked differences between the enacted and the unenacted law. Speaking of the law of Normandy in the time of Henry II, Dr Haskins assures us, in his *Norman Institutions*, that "now and then, in an age when no line was drawn between legislation and adjudication, there are instances of general enactments in the form of judicial decisions." This statement is true of English law at that time; and it is also true of English law throughout the middle age. The remark of Bereford, C.J. in *Venour* v. *Blund*, a year book case in the early part of Edward II's time, that "by a decision of this avowry we shall make a law throughout the land," represents an important aspect of medieval thought. Sharp lines are drawn between legislation and adjudication only when parliamentary statute law acquires, by gradual stages, a position of mastery.

VI

The century of the early Edwards, which Mr Plucknett has studied, possesses definite characteristics of its own, even a unity of its own. It is transitional, as every age is transitional; but, at the same time, it evolves out of its heritage from the past certain institutional and legal features which continue to be the permanent basis of all later development.

The first of the fundamental principles of the century is the supremacy of the crown as the representative of the omnipotence of the central government; and it is only very gradually that the growth of parliamentary powers as opposed to royal powers transforms, in a later age, the supremacy of the king in council into the sovereignty of the king in parliament. The second of the fundamental principles of the century is the rule or supremacy of law, the principle which brings even the king himself into subjection to law; and this is to-day, under the legal sovereignty of the parliament, the dominating feature of the English polity. Observance of the scope and the inter-relations of these two basic principles of the Edwardian epoch—the supremacy of the crown and the supremacy of the law—will throw a flood of light upon our studies of the interpretation of law.

The age of the early Edwards has an abiding significance in the history of the law. It draws somewhat more clearly than the Angevin age the main lines of distinction between the enacted and the unenacted law, the law of statutes and ordinances and the law of customs and cases. The transfer of the power to create absolutely new writs from the king's chancellor and justices to the king's parliament is one of the principal factors which make for this sharper line of difference. The

Edwardian period also draws the first wavy lines of differentiation between the unwritten common law and equity of the king's older courts and the unwritten equity of the council and the chancery. It marks, furthermore, the definite beginnings of the contrast between the two parts of the enacted law, the law of parliamentary statutes and the law of conciliar ordinances. The fact that during the reigns of the early Edwards these several jurisprudential divisions of the law of the land emerge more clearly than formerly gives to the century one of its main features of definition and progress. The relations of these different parts of the law create difficult historical problems. They are among those which Mr Plucknett studies in his history of judicial interpretation.

VII

The problems in regard to the nature of the early statutes and their relation to the common law still serve as the subject-matter of learned controversies among historians. Two main characteristics of the Edwardian statutes seem to be generally admitted. In the first place, they are the king's acts. The king is in and of his parliament; and the enacting power of the king in parliament is the king's power. As the year book of 23 Edward III expresses it: *Que le roy fist les leis par assent dez peres et de la commune, et non pas lez pares et la commune.* In this sense the statutes are the king's statutes; they are one form of royal legislation, conciliar ordinances are another. In the second place, statutes are generally framed by the king's justices. The justices are of the council and of the parliament, of the body described by Fleta as the king's "curia in consilio suo in parliamentis suis"; and this judicial element in the early parliament is by far its most important element, not only from the point of view of its adjudication, but also from that of its legislation. The fact that statutes are drafted by the king's justices helps to give them a judicial character and to bring them into close relationship with the unwritten common law administered by the justices when they sit in their several courts. Passing beyond these two points in regard to the character of the early statutes, we enter at once into the realm of controversy.

Controversy plays a rôle in Mr Plucknett's study. As an historian of interpretation he was obliged to deal with these problems as to the nature of statutes and their relation to the common law; and he has faced the problems boldly. At several places he has occasion to consider the views of scholars who have dealt with aspects of his subject. Especially with certain of the results of Dr McIlwain's researches, in so far as they concern the Edwardian period, he is not in agreement. Thus, Dr McIlwain holds, in his *High Court of Parliament* and his essay on "Magna Carta and Common Law," that common law is fundamental law, and that statutes are affirmations of common law and do not "make" law; while Mr Plucknett contends that statutes are legislative acts which create "novel" and "special" law, and that this statute law overrides and "defeats," on occasion, the common law itself. Another point of difference relates to the old dispute over statutes and ordinances. Dr McIlwain holds that by the time of Edward III some distinction exists between statutes and ordinances; that the former, as affirmations of common law, are viewed as permanent, while the latter are looked upon as merely temporary provisions. Mr Plucknett contends that in the period now in question "there is no contrast expressed or distinction visible between statutes and ordinances." There are other differences of view between the scholars; but these two are the most important. The controversies on these two points are very ancient ones; they run through the historical and juristic literature of medieval and modern times. Mr Plucknett's views are based almost exclusively on his careful study of the early year books; and, in this respect, his present monograph constitutes a fresh contribution to the subject. It is also worth pointing out that the differences between the positions of Dr McIlwain and Mr Plucknett seem to be due, in part at least, to differences in outlook and in the nature of the materials which they have consulted. Dr McIlwain has used the writings of foreign jurists for purposes of comparison, and has laid stress upon the light they throw upon the rolls of parliament; the year books he has used only occasionally and has approached them from the point of view derived from the rolls. Mr Plucknett, on the other hand, has studiously neglected foreign analogies as likely to bias his reading of the year books; he has likewise treated the rolls of parliament as sharing in some measure the same disadvantage and as representing political in contrast with legal views. As a result of this attitude, he has made the year books his main historical sources, finding in them the legal or judicial attitude, and has referred only occasionally to the rolls of parliament. It is possible that differences in opinion, based in large measure on differences in outlook and in materials, might be reconciled by looking at the subject from all points of view and by bringing into consideration all the available materials. Mr Plucknett's study points to the necessity of re-examining, upon such lines of treatment, those old but still unsolved problems as to the nature of the early statutes and ordinances and their relation to the common law. There are aspects of the subject in question which neither Dr McIlwain nor Mr Plucknett has considered; there are materials which neither one of them has examined. The study of the materials for administrative history, for example, is already bringing new light to bear on old problems. Thus, after an examination of such sources, Dr Tout holds that the administrative changes effected by the household and exchequer ordinances of the king in council during the years 1318–1326 mean that "we are in fact drifting towards the famous distinction between an ordinance in council and a statute in parliament."

In the history of English legislation the statutes of Edward I stand out in bold relief: the reigns of Edward II and Edward III leave us little to place beside them. Indeed, not until we reach the age of the Tudors do we find legislative activity comparable to that of Edward I's time. But the originality of Edward's statutes has been unduly stressed ever since Hale remarked, in his *History of the Common Law*, that Edward's reign was a period of "great advance and alteration of the laws of England." There is less in Edward's statutes that is new and revolutionary than is sometimes assumed. We seem to come nearest the truth when we view his legislation as the work of a statesman who is bent upon arranging and systematizing, with the help of his justices and other counsellors, the legal growths of the period of rapid development which followed Henry II's earlier work of centralising royal justice and making it vigorous. Stubbs has taught us that Edward I's reign is an age of definition: and this is as true of legislation as it is of other aspects of the reign. We seem to be justified indeed in viewing much of Edward's legislation as declaratory of the common law; but, at the same time, we must not forget that his legislation also adds new elements to the law. Some statutes embody both old and new law. We ought not to be too dogmatic in our views with regard to the nature of the early statutes; we ought not to place them—all neatly tied together—in one single pigeon-hole. We do not do this in the case of the king's charters; nor do we do it in the case of the king's writs. There is equal reason for our not doing it in the case of the king's statutes.

VIII

The reader of the present monograph will be impressed with the fact that the justices in the first part of the fourteenth century are still wielding the wide discretionary powers of the king. These powers enable them to deal with statutes not only on legal but also on equitable grounds: and the freedom which the justices exercise in respect to statutes shews us clearly that they are still very closely associated with the crown as its instruments of prerogative power. Certain of these earlier practices of the justices the common law courts retain throughout their history; other practices in course of time fall into desuetude and pass to other courts, more particularly the council and the chancery.

One of the practices which the common law courts retain is the search for the intention of parliament. In the history of Roman law interpretation passes through two main stages. In the period of the *ius strictum* the interpreter feels bound by word and form; in the period of *aequitas* he seeks for the intent that lies behind the word and form of the law. Celsus (D. 1. 3. 17) expresses this in the well-known words, *scire leges non hoc est verba earum tenere, sed vim ac potestatem*, words which become in time the common possession of all modern systems of law.

Likewise in the history of English interpretation we seem to see that reliance on word and form is associated with the period of strict law and the search for intent with the period of equity; although literal and strict interpretation shews us also that, even in the age of equity, the older attitude of judges persists. It is the wide discretion which the judges of the early Edwardian period possess that enables them to administer equity as well as law; and their search for intent is one of the most striking illustrations of their equity. The Elizabethan reports prove to us that equitable interpretation is retained by the common law courts as one of their practices. In the words of Plowden (1, 205; 2, 465, 466), "the sages of the law have qualified the rigour of the word according to reason"; they "have ever been guided by the intent of the legislature, which they have always taken according to the necessity of the matter, and according to that which is consonant to reason and good discretion"; they have "restrained the generality of the letter of the law by equity," and "equity, which in Latin is called *equitas*, enlarges or diminishes the letter according to its discretion" and "seems to be a necessary ingredient in the exposition of all laws." The Elizabethan common lawyers are under the strong influence of the renaissance: but the equity which they apply in the interpretation of statutes is the equity they have derived from the age of Azo and Bracton and of the early year books.

The wide royal powers of discretion possessed by the Edwardian justices enable them to do more than seek for intent. These powers permit them, in Mr Plucknett's words, "to take liberties with the new statute-law" in ways which, in later times, we associate only with the king's council. In *Bonham's Case* (8 Rep. 118) Coke cites precedents of the fourteenth century in support of his theory that "in many cases the common law will controul acts of parliament, and sometimes adjudge them to be utterly void." Whether or not this doctrine is true of the early fourteenth century we must not pause to enquire: to attempt an answer would lead us into the thicket of a vast and complicated controversial literature. Mr Plucknett's monograph and other recent researches point, however, to the need of a re-examination of Coke's doctrine in the light of European legal and political theories of the middle age. English as well as Continental jurists and judges were under the influence of doctrines which ascribed to the *ius divinum* and the *ius naturale* the quality of immutability and rendered the man-made positive law opposed to them null and void. Bracton writes under the influence of these doctrines; and the early common lawyers treat the common law itself as the embodiment of the *ius naturale* in the guise of "reason." Apart from these wider problems, however, there is no doubt that the justices of the early fourteenth century do actually "controul acts of parliament" in several ways. Mr Plucknett draws attention to cases where the justices refuse to apply statutes and where they make "exceptions out of the statute"; and these cases shew us that the early common law courts are actually exercising that dispensing power of the king which Henry III, through the *non obstante* clause, had borrowed from the papal *curia*. The controlling of statutes by the justices is also apparent from a study of other features of the relation between statute and prerogative; but Mr Plucknett doubts whether there was "much opportunity in early times for a serious conflict between statutes and the prerogative, which were in fact merely two aspects of the king's power." "We have a later warrant from the king, and that is as high as the statute," declares STAUNTON, J., in the case of *Scoland* v. *Grandison*, Y.B. 6 & 7 Edw. II (Eyre of Kent), I, 175 (Selden Society Year Book Series). ORMESBY, J., adds: "When the king commands, one must suppose that it is by common counsel, and besides, no one may counterplead the king's deed." "Droit le roy," "la lei de la Corone d'Engleterre," the "special" law of the royal prerogative in contrast with the general or common law, is a living body of law and practices in the fourteenth century; it is law which the king's justices enforce, on occasion, even when it conflicts with statute law.

IX

The enlightenment which one derives from Mr Plucknett's study inspires the hope that other scholars will trace, on similar lines, the later history of English judicial interpretation down to our own times. In their broadest scope such investigations would embrace the interpretation of enacted and unenacted laws by all the English courts. In such studies comparisons would be invaluable. Of special instructiveness would be a comparison of the interpretative methods and principles of the common law courts with those of the council, the chancery, and the admiralty—courts which derive a considerable part of their procedural and substantive law from the civil and canonical jurisprudence. The comparative study of the history of interpretation would permit us to observe the working of the judicial function, as the main creative force in English legal evolution, during the middle ages at least, in one of its most characteristic aspects. It would cause differences and contrasts, influences and borrowings, similarities and likenesses, to stand out in bold relief. It would explain to us how diversity in the modes and principles of interpreting and applying laws during the epoch of royal supremacy is finally transformed into a uniformity of modes and principles in the age of the legal sovereignty of parliament. Only by tracing the slow progress of interpretation in successive periods and in different courts can we understand the significance of Blackstone's statement that "there is not a single rule of interpreting laws, whether equitably or strictly, that is not equally used by the judges in the courts both of law and equity." Modern uniform canons of interpreting laws are embodied in modern cases and in the Interpretation Act. These canons themselves are in need of interpretation. History alone explains their meaning and scope in the light of origins and evolution.

H. D. H.

3. vi. 1922

AUTHOR'S PREFACE

THE following monograph is based on a detailed study of the Year Books of the first half of the 14th century, the limits of the period being defined and justified in the preliminary chapter "The Problem and the Evidence." Nearly all the previous modern work on the subject has been written from the point of view of American constitutional problems, and it is therefore strictly limited by this object[1]. Moreover, it has had the disadvantage of covering the long period from Henry I to the Revolution of 1688, and therefore has been based upon the evidence as presented and interpreted by Lord Coke in his Reports, especially in *Dr Bonham's Case*[2], rather than upon a detailed survey of all the evidence available. The result has been a judgment of the middle ages based solely upon the evidence of the very few cases to which Lord Coke had drawn attention.

The disadvantages of this method are obvious, and consequently it seemed worth while to attempt (for the first time, it is believed) to put the matter on a scientifically historical basis. This has necessitated two measures. First, not only the famous cases, but also the masses of hitherto unquoted reports preserved in the Year Books have been carefully scrutinised in order to discover what was the every day method of the courts in interpreting statutes. This is a safer guide than the few cases (generally exceptional, and misunderstood) which have been used to build an imposing edifice of theory in praise of the Common Law as the moderator of statutes. The result has been the discovery of much new material which has never before been used to illustrate this subject, while at the same time several other topics have incidentally been put in a new light—such, for example, as the connection between the beginnings of strict interpretation and the restriction of early judicial discretion.

[1] McIlwain, *The High Court of Parliament and its Supremacy*; Roscoe Pound, *Common Law and Legislation* (*Harvard Law Review*, XXI. 383–407).

[2] 8 Rep. 114.

Secondly, the intensive culture of one period has been made a necessity by the forbidding bulk of the Year Books. To work through them all, together with the early reporters, as far as the Revolution would be a magnificent piece of work, which would certainly reveal a fascinating history of legal and political theory culminating in the sovereignty of Parliament. Nevertheless, that long period is most emphatically not a unity. It consists of many portions, each having its own characteristics, and one of them is that covered by this study, namely from 20 Edw. I to 20 Edw. III. This section is compact, yet long enough to show historical movement and development in a significant direction.

The present study first took shape as a dissertation presented to the Special Board for Law of Cambridge University in candidature for the degree of LL.B. by research, and it was only after being considerably enlarged and much revised that it assumed its present form. The work has been under the constant supervision of Professor H. D. Hazeltine, whose learned criticism and friendly encouragement have laid upon the author a deep debt of gratitude which it is as great a pleasure as a duty to acknowledge. The work has also had the advantage of being read in manuscript by Professor A. F. Pollard of University College, London, and in proof by Professor C. H. McIlwain of Harvard University, while upon various questions the author has had the privilege of consulting Mr Buckland, Regius Professor of Civil Law, Mr Hollond, University Reader in English Law, and Dr Winfield, Fellow and Law Lecturer of St John's College, Cambridge. Finally the author desires to express his gratitude to the Governing Body of Emmanuel College whose generosity in exhibitions and studentships has made this research possible.

T. F. T. P.

HARVARD UNIVERSITY,
CAMBRIDGE,
MASSACHUSETTS.
March, 1922.

CONTENTS

TABLE OF STATUTES

TABLE OF YEAR BOOK CASES

SOURCES

Year Books.

- 20 & 21 Edw. I (ed. Horwood), Rolls Series.
- 21 & 22 Edw. I ,, ,,
- 30 & 31 Edw. I ,, ,,
- 32 & 33 Edw. I ,, ,,
- 33 & 35 Edw. I ,, ,,
- 1 & 2 Edw. II (ed. Maitland), Selden Society.
- 2 & 3 Edw. II ,, ,,
- 3 Edw. II ,, ,,
- 3 & 4 Edw. II (ed. Maitland and Turner), Selden Society.
- 4 Edw. II (ed. Turner), Selden Society.
- 5 Edw. II (ed. Bolland; 2 vols.), Selden Society.
- 6 Edw. II (ed. Vinogradoff, Ehrlich, and Lwöw), Selden Society.
- 6 & 7 Edw. II (ed. Bolland), Selden Society.
- 6 & 7 Edw. II Eyre of Kent (ed. Maitland, Vernon Harcourt and Bolland; 3 vols.), Selden Society.
- 8 Edw. II (ed. Bolland), Selden Society.
- 11 & 12 Edw. III (ed. Horwood), Rolls Series.
- 12 & 13 Edw. III (ed. Pike), ,,
- 13 & 14 Edw. III ,, ,,
- 14 Edw. III ,, ,,
- 14 & 15 Edw. III ,, ,,
- 15 Edw. III ,, ,,
- 16 Edw. III ,, (2 vols.) ,,
- 17 Edw. III ,, ,,
- 17 & 18 Edw. III ,, ,,
- 18 Edw. III ,, ,,
- 18 & 19 Edw. III ,, ,,
- 19 Edw. III ,, ,,
- 20 Edw. III ,, (2 vols.) ,,
- Various reigns (ed. Maynard).

Statutes of the Realm (Record Commission).

Rotuli Parliamentorum. 6 vols. Folio.

Registrum Brevium tam Originalium quam Judicialium. Folio, 1687.

FitzHerbert: New Natura Brevium (References to the foliation of the 1598 edition).

Commentaries and Treatises.

- Coke: Institutes of the Laws of England, Part II. Folio, 1642.
- Barrington: Observations upon the Statutes, chiefly the more Ancient. 2nd ed. 4to, 1766.
- Hatton: Treatise concerning Statutes. 1677.
- Dwarris: A General Treatise upon Statutes. 2 vols. 1831.
- Maxwell: The Interpretation of Statutes. 6th ed. 1920.
- McIlwain: High Court of Parliament and its Supremacy. New Haven, 1910.
- ,, Magna Carta and the Common Law (Magna Carta Commemoration Essays, 1917).
- Pound: Common Law and Legislation (Harvard Law Review, XXI. 383–407).

LIST OF INCIPITS

(See p. 11, n. 6)

Title	*Statute*	*Authority*
Cum Hugh	1 Edw. III, st. 1, c. 1	*Reg. Br. Orig.* f. 122
Cum quis	Westm. II, c. 40	Y.B. 30 & 31 Edw. I, 247
De averiis carucorum	Stats. Realm, i. 197	Y.B. 17 Edw. III, 2
De custodiis	Marlb. c. 7	Y.B. 16 Edw. III, i. 94
De finibus non vacuandis	27 Edw. I, c. 1	Y.B. 32 & 33 Edw. I, 314
De his quae recordata sunt	Westm. II, c. 45	Y.B. 20 Edw. III, i. 438
De ovibus[1]	Marlb. c. 21	Y.B. 4 Edw. II, 111
De pueris masculis sive femellis	Westm. II, c. 35	Y B. 5 Edw. II, ii. 94, 96
De quo antecessor	Westm. II, c. 16	Y.B. 6 Edw. II, 181
De Romemede	Magna Carta	*Magna Carta Essays*, 136[2]
De sectis	Marlb. c. 9	Y.B. 3 & 4 Edw. II, 61
Hue and Cry	Winton	*Reg. Br. Orig.* App. 12
Quia emptores	18 Edw. I.	Y.BB. *passim*
Quia fynes	27 Edw. I, st. 1, c. 1	Y.B. 30 & 31 Edw. I, 247
Quia multi per malitiam	Westm. II, c. 12	*Reg. Br. Orig.* f. 134
Quod unicum essoniam	Marlb. c. 13	Y.B. 15 Edw. III, 93 (37)
Si quis a latere veniens	20 Edw. I, c. 3	Y.B. 32 & 33 Edw. I, 407

[1] Thus in the heading; the text has the slightly more correct "*des bestes*."
[2] Styled "Provisio de Ronnemede" in Cambr. Univ. Libr., MS. Gg. i. 12

INTRODUCTION

THE PROBLEM AND THE EVIDENCE

ONE of the best known generalisations of the legal histories is to the effect that the reign of Edward I remained unparalleled until the 19th century as a period of constructive legislation. In both periods vast masses of enacted law were thrust upon the courts, and the judges were confronted with the task of interpreting and administering it as best they could. Here, however, the resemblance ends, for the judges of the 19th century were much more adequately equipped for their work than BEREFORD and STAUNTON and their fellows could possibly have been. They had the accumulated wisdom of five hundred years' experience available in reports, abridgements and commentaries; their predecessors had been applying statutes for centuries, and lawyers had the technical training necessary to create a science of interpretation.

§ 1. *The Forms of Legislation*

Above all, they had the inestimable advantage of knowing the exact meaning of several highly important words—"Parliament," "Statute," "Proclamation," "Court," "Sovereignty," and the like. Contrast this with the state of legal knowledge in the reigns of Edward I and Edward II. Who could then say what a statute was, or be certain that any particular document was a statute? Who could say, even, what the actual words of any acknowledged statute really were? And what was the precise significance of *carta*, *assisa*, *constitutio*, *provisio*, *ordinatio*, *statutum*, *isetnysse*[1], all of which come before the courts for interpretation? If they were all equally statutes, why so many different titles? If not, where do they differ?

§ 2. *The Nature of the Legislature*

Then again, what of those new devices, parliaments? Recurring periods of discontent, followed by threats of serious trouble, had several times produced crises which the Crown had

[1] Pollock and Maitland, *History of English Law*, I. 176.

successfully met by summoning meetings of notables—who grumbled, and dispersed. The result was generally a tax, sometimes a promise or even a measure of reform. Indeed, there were two especially remarkable years, 1275 and 1285, when the larger part of the law of England was drastically overhauled at the parliaments then held, but it would have been difficult to regard a tactical device employed by the king when in military or financial extremity as an acknowledged source of English law. Still less could one have said that parliament or anyone else was sovereign, for sovereignty at this time was more a theological than a constitutional conception, and was confronted with insuperable theoretical difficulties when applied to earthly monarchies.

If the theoretical aspect of parliament was unexplored, the practical questions of its nature and composition were only less obscure. A contemporary[1] described it in the well-known words, "The king has his court in his council in his parliaments," but no one can pretend that this explanation is very clear, more particularly to the 20th century mind. Indeed the modern investigator must make a sustained effort in order to enter into a realm of thought where what he would regard as the essentials of his legal training and equipment were practically non-existent. Only when he has done this can he watch with sympathy and admiration the long struggle of the early judges with masses of statute law, appreciating their difficulties, and marking the beginnings of a technique of interpretation as the court gradually devised the rudiments of a science.

§ 3. *The Year Books and their Contents*

Such, then, is the problem; the evidence available for its solution may now be briefly described. It is to be found in the magnificent series of Year Books which are now beginning to receive the attention they have long deserved[2]. Splendid as they are, certain difficulties in their use must be recognised. In the first place, they are largely concerned with extremely technical

[1] *Fleta*, lib. II. cap. 2, sect. 1; below, p. 20.

[2] For an admirable introduction to the questions related to these unique monuments of English Law, see Mr Bolland's *The Year Books*.

portions of the law which they often discuss so briefly as to be obscure, especially to a reader who is not prepared to devote some time to the study of the older abridgements where lengthy titles are devoted to such topics as aid-prayer, voucher and the counterpleas of voucher, view, receipt, age, and the almost hopeless tangle of process. Not only is the matter highly technical, but the language is very difficult to translate with certainty, and even the text is in many cases doubtful. Occasionally the very multiplication of manuscripts collated will make the value of a report difficult to ascertain, for in at least one case the manuscripts give exactly contrary decisions[1]. Another source of trouble is the frequency with which cases were left undecided—often after protracted proceedings had taken place. A report will suddenly break off after a point of law has been argued at considerable length; the record, if it has been identified, will note one adjournment after another, perhaps extending over several terms or even years, and then a blank space on the roll will indicate that the case was discontinued before judgment was given. The arguments will often be found of the greatest interest and importance, and one cannot help a feeling of disappointment at the curt "et sic adjornantur" which cuts short many a clever discussion, leaving the contested points as uncertain as before. But although the lawyer may express his dissatisfaction at no decision being pronounced after so much careful argument, yet the historian will accept the fact as evidence of a policy deliberately adopted by the courts and, it would seem, with good reason. The sudden and rapid development of the law in the later 13th and early 14th centuries gave occasion for very many questions of great technical interest, and often of considerable difficulty. There were circumstances under which a clever pleader would bring up such puzzling points, for the simple reason that he had no better matter to advance. Judges, however, were men of plain common sense, and not infrequently put an abrupt end to such attempts to "embarrass the court"[2], whereupon the

[1] *Wellington* v. *Brockwell*, Y.B. 6 & 7 Edw. II (*Eyre of Kent*), II. 151–2, 156, 158.

[2] Cf. *Anon.*, Y.B. 4 Edw. II, 169 where BEREFORD, C.J. was "enraged" with *Hengham* for "embarrassing the court." The editor, Mr Turner, uses "embarrass" to represent the original "rioter" which sounds even more strong,

ingenious pleader would immediately offer to take issue on some simple matter of fact. In some cases, however, the discussion of knotty problems was unavoidable; yet even then the court would not allow itself to be forced to a decision, but would rather adjourn the case term after term until one party or the other defaulted or until an agreement was reached out of court[1]. Indeed, considering the growing complexity of the law, and the serious consequences which rashness might involve, one can hardly blame the judges for distrusting their skill in deciding such matters[2]. Nevertheless, the arguments themselves are of enormous value, for they show how the most learned men of those days approached these questions, and what views they believed would be favourably considered by the court.

§ 4. *The Manner of Pleading*

A further element of uncertainty in the use of the Year Books is due to the very informal method of pleading in vogue during the period. Maitland has already described how a pleader would try first one defence, then another, cautiously feeling his way through masses of uncertain law and doubtful facts, until he had "licked his plea into shape"; the result was that considerable discussion might be followed only by the abandonment of the position if for any reason it appeared untenable. Such a reason might be a plain statement from the Bench that "if you demur there, you will lose the land," but it might be that the pleader only conjectured that the court was against him, and so the report says that "he dared not demur there," while it is not unknown for an advocate to abandon a particular course merely in response to a wink from the judge[3]. None of these judicial

and, taken in conjunction with the fragments of dialogue there reported, suggests that disputes might become violent. For the case of an advocate who drew his dagger against his opponent's advocate, and a murderous attack in the presence of the King, Chancellor, Great Seal, and Council, see Y.B. 20 Edw. III, ii, xlviii. (For the technical use, "presence," not being actual personal presence, see Baldwin, *Cases in Council*, XXI.) SHARESHULLE, J. in the interesting case of *Ros* v. *Graa* confessed that *Hilary* and he had once pleaded a certain difficult question "because we had no other matter." Y.B. 15 Edw. III, 390.

[1] See, for example, the very difficult case of *Aunger* v. *Aunger* and Mr Bolland's note upon it in Y.B. 6 & 7 Edw. II, lvii, 203–210.

[2] See, for example, *Lymesy* v. *Abbot of Westminster*, *ibid.* xxxvii, 31–45.

[3] *Anon.*, Y.B. 4 Edw. II, 132 *p*.

intimations is a formal judgment, yet historically they are good as evidence that the court was not inclined to favour that particular line of argument.

§ 5. *The Year Books as Evidence*

The Year Books have even been proved inaccurate in matters of genealogy and other like details which were not essential to the purpose of the compiler, while clear traces of "editing" are also to be found—particularly in the simplification of facts and the elimination of one question in order to display another more clearly. Without entering into the controversy of Year Book origins in general, it is perfectly plain that whoever was their author, his object was to teach (or to learn) law, as distinct from genealogy and family history, and thus he may be presumed to have taken what steps he could in order to make his book reasonably accurate from the point of view of legal doctrine. It is equally plain that the Year Books are not the work of mere beginners—they show too much command of technique for that, and in any case the redactors who "wrote up" the dialogue must have been men of considerable learning and experience in the courts. Although many questions must remain obscure, yet there is every reason to believe that the Year Books represent approximately what went on in court, and that even if they are unreliable in details of fact, yet the law they contain is what experienced practitioners regarded as good. For our own purpose they are assuredly historical evidence of what was the best professional opinion on the matter of statutes and their interpretation.

§ 6. *Editions of the Year Books*

These remarks, however, cannot be applied to the edition associated with the name of Sergeant Maynard; the exposure of this black letter edition of the years of Edward II by Maitland[1], and of Edward III by Pike[2] is conclusive as to the inadequacy of the folios as a basis of detailed historical research. Attention has therefore been confined to the re-edited volumes of the Master of the Rolls and the Selden Society, which afford a large

[1] Y.B. 1 & 2 Edw. II, xxi–xxxiii.

[2] Y.B. 18 & 19 Edw. III, xxviii.

amount of information in a much more accurate and intelligible form.

One more explanation is necessary, and that relates to the translations of statutes and Year Books given by their respective editors. Careful examination of them has produced the conviction that these translations, though useful as approximations for general purposes, cannot be made the basis for detailed research. The more one reads the Year Books, the more one is impressed by the linguistic difficulties which faced the early translators, Horwood, Maitland and Pike, who had no assistance from previous workers in the field of Law-French. Maitland heroically compiled his own grammar[1] and Pike undertook the equally necessary task of making a lexicon[2], but much still remains to be done in this field. Consequently, wherever a statute or Year Book is quoted in the succeeding pages in English, the translation is that of the present writer. Where it differs materially from the published version, the reasons will be discussed in a footnote.

§ 7. *The Arrangement of this Study*

The work that lies before us, then, is to make an examination of the Year Books the basis of a history of statutes and their interpretation during a period roughly described as the first half of the 14th century. The subject will naturally fall into two divisions; in the first part must be discussed the origin, form and nature of the statutes themselves, together with an account of certain legal notions which can be regarded as the technical equipment of the judges, and which played an important part in determining the court's attitude towards statutes. In the second part will be grouped a number of concrete examples illustrative of the court's methods, in which a few general lines of development will be traced.

[1] Y.B. 1 & 2 Edw. II, xxxiii–lxxxix.
[2] Y.B. 20 Edw. III, i, xvi.

PART I

LEGISLATION AND LEGAL THOUGHT IN THE EARLY FOURTEENTH CENTURY

THE SCOPE OF THE DISCUSSION

BEFORE proceeding to the discussion of specific examples of the interpretation of statutes, an investigation should be made of certain preliminary questions upon the answer to which will depend largely the point of view adopted in the more detailed study. The place of legislation in mediaeval law during our period must be estimated and its methods and forms described, while its records, together with the questions they raise both as to text and translation, will also call for comment. Something must be said of the differences, if any, between statutes and ordinances, of the legislative power and its relation to the other functions of government, of the incomplete differentiation of Courts, Council, and Parliament and the imperfect specialisation of their functions during the period, all of which must be considered as throwing light upon the subject of this essay. An investigation must also be made of the legal notions of contemporaries, many of them hardly definite enough to be called theories, but nevertheless powerful factors in the situation. Thus the idea of common law, and of the law of nature or of reason, and the influence of canon and civil law are all of considerable significance for our purpose. All these questions, moreover, must be approached from the point of view of the royal judge and the pleader. The one was a hard-worked and under-paid official, the other a busy professional man intent on winning cases and learning the practical wisdom of the courts. Neither class was in any sense of an academical turn of mind, and theories as such seem to have played little part in their thinking. Yet with such men one often finds that an unexpressed, half-conscious notion or prejudice is extremely influential, and, indeed, it is mainly to such factors as this that one must look for an explanation of the attitude of court and pleaders towards the statutes in our period.

CHAPTER I

ORIGINS AND EARLY FORMS OF WRITTEN LAW

THE forms of written law in our early legal history are very diverse, but must not be regarded as necessarily co-extensive with the forms of legislation. Conversely, all legislation must not be presumed to have been originally written, for the instructions given to the judges at various times[1], especially on setting out for the eyre, and unrecorded decisions of the council may have had an effect on the history of law which it is now impossible to estimate[2]. More can be said with certainty of the Edwardian period, and consequently attention will now be directed towards a brief analysis of the form and nature of the documents collectively described as "Ancient Statutes." A detailed study, however, would be too long to attempt here, and so only those points will now be considered which bear on the subject of Interpretation or which are particularly prominent in the reports of our period.

§ 1. *The Varied Forms of Statutes*

In the first place, it is remarkable that contemporary diplomatic contained no settled form appropriated to legal enactments. *Magna Carta* is in a form typical of crown grants of land and seignory[3], and the Provisions of Merton[4] are also characterised by the word "concessum," although in other respects they are in the form of administrative letters close. The diplomatic of the Statute of Marlborough[5] would seem to have been less familiar to "the Lord Henry" than to "the Lord Ottobon" (who was present at its making), while it is significant that the con-

[1] Pollock and Maitland, *Hist. Engl. Law*, I. 136.

[2] Many valuable references are collected, *ibid.* I. 180, n. 4.

[3] "Sciatis quod...concessimus et hac presenti carta confirmavimus...has libertates subscriptas tenendas in perpetuum" (preamble). "Pro hac autem concessione et donatione..." (final clause). *Magna Carta* is called a statute in Y.B. 3 Edw. II, 90; Y.B. 11 & 12 Edw. III, 62, 66.

[4] *Stats. Realm*, I. 4; cf. below, p. 13.

[5] "Anno gratiae M° C° CLx° septimo, regni autem domini Henrici regis filii regis Johannis quinquagesimo secundo in Octabis Sancti Martini providente ipso domino rege...."

veyancer's "concessum" is here replaced by the legislator's "provisum et statutum et concorditer ordinatum." Westminster the First has the suggestive beginning "Ces Sunt les Establissmenz...." The Statute of Mortmain, on the other hand, is simply a writ to the Justices of the Court of Common Pleas. It is only from Westminster II onwards that we find anything that can be described as a statute form, although even then lesser enactments are still to be found as letters patent, writs close, and even in less definite shapes.

§ 2. *Varied Forms the Result of Varied Origins*

These variations seem to be the direct result of what was then the novelty of enacted law, which as yet had not become a regular product of the routine of government. This conclusion can be confirmed by an examination of the circumstances under which some of the most famous of our early statutes were passed. Several will be seen to have resulted from what would be described to-day as "direct action." The barons in arms dictated *Magna Carta*, and a military crisis eighty-two years later put it on the statute roll; the Provisions of Westminster originated in what Stubbs called a "provisional government" and it was only as part of the pacification following the Barons' War that they became incorporated in the Statute of Marlborough. The "New Ordinances" of 5 Edw. II were likewise the product of a revolutionary movement. One statute—that of Bigamists, c. 5—is an interpretation of a papal constitution[1]. Others have a significant connection with the royal prerogative and its exercise in Prohibitions[2], and so a number of actions, notably Waste[3], *Contra Formam Feoffamenti*[4], and Champerty[5], are described in the appropriate writs as offences "against the king's prohibition." In the case of Waste instances have been found dating

[1] Cap. un. *De Bigamis*, in VI. 1. 12. See below, p. 37.

[2] On the general topic of prohibitions at common law, see Hazeltine, *Early English Equity* (*Essays in Legal History*, 270–284).

[3] See the Note from the Record in *Gravesend* v. *Chaumbre*, Y.B. 3 Edw. II, 76 *a*; the later rules governing this recital are in Fitzh. *Nat. Brev.* 55.

[4] *Reg. Br. Orig.* f. 176.

[5] For champerty see Winfield, *History of Conspiracy and Abuse of Legal Procedure*, 141–150, and *History of Maintenance and Champerty* (*Law Quarterly Review*, xxxv. 50); compare *Reg. Br. Orig.* f. 183 with *R.* v. *Anon.*, Y.B. 11 & 12 Edw. III, 539–40, 634.

from before the statute[1], which is thus seen to act as a general prohibition making available for all the stringent prerogative procedure formerly only obtainable as a royal favour[2], for as SHARDELOWE, J. explained, "What is done against the prohibition of the king and his statute, is done contrary to the peace, some people say[3]." The *Contra Formam Feoffamenti* is described as a "prohibition framed upon the statute"[4], while a writ of Champerty calls upon the defendants to show why they had acted "against the king's prohibition"—meaning the statute[5]. It also seems that prohibitions were issued forbidding parties to employ citations from Rome before the statutes 27 Edw. III, st. 1. c. 1 and 38 Edw. III, st. 2. cc. 1–2[6].

Still another source of enactment was the already existing law, which was declared and at times strengthened. The writ *Cui in Vita* formally given by Westminster II, c. 3 in 1285[7] occurs in a register dated 1227[8], and Formedon in the Descender occurs before the Statute *De Donis*[9]; the land of a man who went to France and fought against the king escheated—before the Statute of Treasons[10], and the executors of a testator's

[1] Pollock and Maitland, II. 9; Statute of Marlborough, c. 23.

[2] By Westminster II, c. 14 the prohibition process was changed to summons owing to popular misunderstanding of its nature.

[3] *Anon.*, Y.B. 17 Edw. III, 4.

[4] A note in Y.B. 21 & 22 Edw. I, 397; Y.B. 2 & 3 Edw. II, xiii, n. 4; Statute of Marlborough, c. 9.

[5] Westminster I, c. 25; *R.* v. *Anon.*, Y.B. 11 & 12 Edw. III, 540–2, 634; it is clear that there are here two reports of the same case. By comparing them it will be seen that "non-suit" (p. 635) is a blunder for "suit" and that "enteanz" is probably a corruption of "enquest."

[6] *R.* v. *Maners*, Y.B. 20 Edw. III, i, 524 of which no record has been found, however, to fix the date. Compare the writs *Ad Jura Regia* in *Reg. Br. Orig.* ff. 60 *b*–61, 64 *b*. *R.* v. *atte Cherche*, Y.B. 20 Edw. III, ii, 60 (dated from the record 1346) shows that obtaining provisors as well as citations in support of them was punishable before the statute. The case is also interesting as involving Adam of Murimuth and giving some facts that were not available to his editors and biographers, Sir E. Maunde Thompson and Bishop Stubbs.

[7] Not Westminster II, c. 40 as Maitland's second note to *Acclum* v. *Carpenter*, Y.B. 2 & 3 Edw. II, 150.

[8] Maitland, *Collected Papers*, II. 132.

[9] Maitland, *History of the Register of Writs* (*Anglo-American Legal Essays*, II. 586, n. 1); *Anon.*, Y.B. 6 Edw. II, 44; the statute can however be understood as implying that Formedon in the Descender is newly created by it, 2 *Inst.* 336. See below, p. 131, n. 1.

[10] *FitzJohn* v. *Esteneye and Lovel*, Y.B. 6 Edw. II, 40, in this case the statute (25 Edw. III, st. 5, c. 2) professes to be declaratory.

executors only failed to maintain an action of debt because the testator had willed otherwise, so that but for this they might have anticipated the statute by fourteen years[1].

§ 3. *Sealing, Language, and Modes of Reference*

Sealing as part of the authentication of statutes is occasionally mentioned in the Year Books. Thus BEREFORD, referring to the official Exposition of the Statute of Gloucester, says "ou sunt ceux explanations quil ne sunt pas desouth le seale le Roy"[2], while HILARY, J. condemned *Circumspecte Agatis* as not being a "sealed statute"[3]. On one occasion a party brought into court a copy of statute 14 Edw. III, st. 4. c. 2 under the great seal—whether an original or an exemplification, does not appear[4].

Even the language in which statutes should be couched was as yet unsettled, and sometimes one finds a sentence or two of French embedded in a long Latin text, of which the only likely reason suggested seems to be that French was used in these chapters in order to make their provisions perfectly clear to the general public[5].

The modes of reference employed in the 14th century throw some light on the way in which contemporary lawyers handled their material. Most frequently the reports give no explicit references whatever, saying merely "the statute," but when references are given the most frequent method seems to be citing the first words[6]. "The statute lately made at Westminster" is a common form of citation[7], but fails to distinguish between four (or more) documents answering to the description.

§ 4. *The Meaning of "Statute"*

Nor is it quite clear that we are correct in speaking of the first or second *Statute* of Westminster, for to contemporary lawyers

[1] *Anon.*, Y.B. 11 & 12 Edw. III, 186 (the reporter's query refers to Westminster II, c. 23); stat. 25 Edw. III, st. 5, c. 5.

[2] *Anon.*, Y.B. 8 Edw. II, 264–5 (*ed.* Maynard). See also below, p. 21.

[3] *Bishop of Winchester* v. *Archdeacon of Surrey*, Y.B. 19 Edw. III, 292.

[4] *R.* v. *Bishop of Coventry and Lichfield*, Y.B. 14 Edw. III, 138 (57), Note from the Record. Cf. *Rot. Parl.* II. 113 (7, 8).

[5] Westminster II, c. 34; Westminster II, c. 49; 2 *Inst.* 217, 484. Noteworthy observations on the subject of language are to be found in Barrington, 47 ff.

[6] An alphabetical list of such titles will be found on p. xliv.

[7] See for example, *Stats. Realm*, I. 130 where in c. 3 of 27 Edw. I it means Westminster I and in c. 4 it means Westminster II.

each such document was apparently a long series of separate units; thus we have one of these documents described as "Secunda Statuta Westmonasteriensia"[1], and indeed, the last chapter of Westminster II refers to the rest of the statute as "Omnia predicta statuta." Similarly, a pleader who mixed up chapter 3 with chapter 4 was corrected by his opponent who said that certain words were "not in that statute [c. 3] but another [c. 4]"[2]. Such passages as this suggest that the word "statute" means the provision made rather than the instrument embodying it[3]. In one case only do we find a contemporary reference to a statute by the number of its chapters[4], although by the end of the 14th century it was the usual custom for manuscripts to number the chapters of the longer statutes.

Without going further into the antiquities of legislation, enough has been said to show that our statutes, to an observer in the year 1300, would have appeared as novelties sprung from very different origins and exhibiting considerable diversity of form, and that it is unlikely that he would be able to form any very definite conclusion as to their exact legal nature and import.

§ 5. *Doubtful and Undated Statutes*

Such being the case, it is not surprising that there is an apocrypha between the Ancient Statutes and the New. The modern critic would enlarge it by using it as a depository for spurious and suspicious, as well as uncanonical documents, such as *De Tallagio non Concedendo*[5], *Circumspecte Agatis*[6], the Statutes of Essoins[7], *Prerogative Regis*[8], and others of the same nature which would have sorely puzzled a mediaeval lawyer if he had had any rigid theory as to the legal nature of statutes.

[1] *Plac. Abb.* 209 *b*.

[2] *Anon.*, Y.B. 33 & 35 Edw. I, 476.

[3] This is probably the explanation of passages in the *Court Baron* (Selden Soc.), 67, 71, where we read of "le statut de ceste ville," and "statutum curie."

[4] *Rex* v. *Bishop of Norwich*, Y.B. 16 Edw. III, i, 165, but the date of such a note as this cannot be fixed with certainty.

[5] Maitland, *Const. Hist.* 96.

[6] 2 *Inst.* 487; Prynne, *Records*, III. 336; Barrington, 120; Maitland, *Collected Papers*, II. 271.

[7] Y.B. 32 & 33 Edw. I, xxxiv, n. 3.

[8] Maitland, *Collected Papers*, II. 182–190; Henderson, *Engl. Hist. Rev.* V. 753; Maitland, *ibid.* VI. 367; *Wavere and wife* v. *atte Hurst and Haselholte*, Y.B. 20 Edw. III, II. 228.

CHAPTER II

TEXT AND TRANSLATION

IT would be proper to give here an account of the original sources from which the text of the statutes is derived, whether records or private exemplars, printed or manuscript. This unfortunately cannot be done, for much research in many libraries will be needed before the text of the early statutes is established on a scientific basis. No attempt yet made has been completely successful in doing this, with the result that the *Statutes of the Realm* edition is in many places unsatisfactory, and the undated statutes are still as far away as ever they were from being put into their proper years and categories.

§ 1. *The "Statutes of the Realm" Edition*

The edition by the Record Commission is undoubtedly a great advance upon previous editions, but nevertheless, it does not entirely meet the requirements of modern historical scholarship. In many cases it certainly does give the text of the statute, close, patent, or parliament rolls, and where these are not available collates several other manuscripts, Exchequer registers, and similar sources, but a collation of manuscripts is of little value unless their date is stated and their value estimated. Some examples will show the force of this criticism.

§ 2. *The Texts printed by the Commissioners*

In the *Introduction* the Editors profess to prefer official to unofficial manuscripts, but the Statute of Merton is printed from Claudius D. II (a private source of which no description is given) and readings from the close and patent rolls (official contemporary versions) are consigned to footnotes. Chapter 6 of this statute contains an interesting *varia lectio*.

The following is the Commissioners' printed text from Claudius D. II, the three words italicised being inserted by the manuscripts *Rot. Bodl.*, Harl. 493 A, and Cott. XVI:

De heredibus per parentes vel per alios vi abductis vel detentis, ita provisum est: quod quicumque laicus inde convictus fuerit quod puerum sic *detinuerit, abduxerit, vel* maritaverit, reddat perdenti valorem maritagii, etc.

It would be interesting to trace the history of these three words, which are not supported by the patent and close rolls, for when the statute was quoted in court in 1343 it was without the insertion[1], although they would have been very material to the case for it was being argued on one side that the damages could only be demanded when the infant was married, and on the other side it was urged that merely detaining the infant was sufficient ground for damages. We should therefore have expected the variant reading to be mentioned as it exactly covers the latter case. The report, however, says nothing of such a reading, whence it may be concluded with tolerable certainty that the insertion was not well known at this date—over a century since the making of the statute.

Another unexplained variant is the substitution of one hundred marks for one hundred pounds in *Magna Carta*, c. 2 of 1297 which thus differs from the issue of 1225 which it professes to reproduce by *Inspeximus*[2].

§ 3. *The Dates assigned by the Commissioners*

The Record edition also professes to be strictly chronological, and to have put all undated documents together[3]. But this promise was unfulfilled; a statute concerning sheriffs and their clerks is classed among the undated ones[4] but its preamble states that it was made on St Valentine's Day, 26 Edw., in a council where Walter Langton, the Treasurer, and a dozen other famous statesmen were present—the date being thereby fixed absolutely as 14th February, 26 Edw. I, 1298. Conversely, *Circumspecte Agatis* is put among the statutes of 13 Edw. I by the Commissioners, and the "Office of a Coroner" among those of 4 Edw. I although there is not a shred of internal evidence in either of the documents for these dates.

§ 4. *The Translation of the Statute of Winchester*

The translations in the *Statutes of the Realm* are very inadequate. In practically every case they are from Cay's version

[1] *Bassingbourne* v. *Archere*, Y.B. 17 & 18 Edw. III, 236.

[2] Bémont, *Chartres*, 47, n. 6.

[3] *Stats. Realm*, Introd. xxxi.

[4] *Stats. Realm*, I. 213.

of 1751 or else from even older versions still, the result being that the translation printed is not necessarily made from the text which accompanies it, and in a number of cases conceals variant readings. Moreover, when this translation is in error corrections by the Editors are made only occasionally, and then in footnotes in order not to disturb the work of the old translators, whose greatest merit in the Editors' eyes was their "having very much conformed to the Genius of the English Language, and not servilely fallen into Latin or French Expressions, or Forms of Speech"[1]. Without presuming to judge their style, we may remark that they certainly did not conform to the original text. For example: the Statute of Winchester says that town gates must be shut between sunset and sunrise,

> e qe nul home ne herberge en suburbe, ne en forein chief de la vile, si de jour noun, ne uncore de jour si le hoste ne voille pur luy respundre.

The translation renders this by "and that no man do lodge in Suburbs, nor in any place out of the Town, from nine of the Clock until Day without his Host will answer for him." The correct reading appears in a footnote. "Keynes" in chapter 5 are not "ashes," nor is a "park...pres del haut chemin" a "Park taken from the Highway."

§ 5. *The Translation of the Statute of Gloucester*, c. 2.

The Statute of Gloucester, c. 2, provided that

> If a child within age is kept out of his inheritance after the death of his *cousin*, *ael*, or *besael*, so that he has to buy a writ, and his adversary come into court and allege feoffment or say something whereby the Judges award inquest; whereas the inquest was delayed until the age, now the inquest shall pass as if he were of age.

Such a situation arose in a case[2] of *Nuper Obiit* brought by an infant, whom the tenant would have barred by the late father's quitclaim. In proffering the deed, the tenant argued that the infant could neither confess nor deny it until he was of age, and therefore prayed that the parole should demur until then (the tenant remaining in possession of the land the meanwhile). The infant objected to this course and referred to the Statute

[1] *Stats. Realm*, Introd. xlii.
[2] *Cauville* v. *Drax*, Y.B. 6 & 7 Edw. II (*Eyre of Kent*), III. 160.

of Gloucester which (in his opinion) allowed the court to proceed at once to take his confession or denial of the deed. At this point Staunton, J. intervened with the remark that the statute mentions only *Ael*, *Besael* and *Cosinage*, and says nothing of *Nuper Obiit* (which is of the nature of *Mort d'Ancestor*[1]). *Stonor* agreed with this, adding that there was no need to insert *Nuper Obiit* in the statute as there was in fact no such delay in that action even before the act. Now it is remarkable that although Staunton, J. and *Stonor* are right in saying that the text of the statute contains only *Ael*, *Besael* and *Cosinage*, yet all the old translations (including that printed in the *Statutes of the Realm*) agree in inserting before cousin the word "father," thus making the statute extend to *Mort d'Ancestor* and *Nuper Obiit*. There is no early manuscript authority for the word[2], but the later prints actually dared to emend their texts to make them agree with the traditional translation. Consequently Coke has some entertaining remarks[3]; he observes that ancient manuscripts do not contain the word, and that the Judges in 8 Edw. II evidently used a text which did not contain it[4], and that *Fleta* followed the same "error." He then proceeds to adopt the later printed form of the text, accusing the most ancient authorities of error[5].

§ 6. *The Translation of Westminster I, c. 37.*

Westminster I, c. 37 seems to have been mis-translated at a very early date. It says that

le jugement seit tiel q le pleintiff recovera sa seisine e ses damages, ausi bien des chateaus e del meoble avauntdit com del eel.

[1] F.N.B. 197.

[2] A brief examination of about twenty MSS in the University Library, Cambridge, shows that the only early authority for the word is Ee. II. 19 (which inserts it but afterwards deletes it) and Dd. IX. 38 which has the additional peculiarity of omitting *Cousin*, *Ael* and *Besael*. Both are 14th century MSS.

[3] 2 *Inst*. 290. He goes on to make a further emendation in a perfectly clear text by changing the first "enqueste" into "age"—thus introducing nonsense, notwithstanding that in this and the other point the Statute Roll was against him.

[4] *Anon*., Y.B. Hil. 8 Edw. III, 23, which however shows nothing of the sort, being virtually a case of *Ael*.

[5] For a further example of a similar nature relating to Westminster I see below, p. 36, n. 4.

The last word, *eel*, is rendered "Freehold" by the *Statutes of the Realm*, and in some early printed texts is corrupted into "soil." It should be read with a decision of 1314 when the judges would not allow an enquiry to be held as to chattels taken away in a disseisin, but only as to such chattels as were *attached to the soil*, for they said that the defendant might have recovery by a writ of trespass for the other chattels—"which seemed contrary to the statute" adds the reporter[1]. It is obvious that either "eel" had become "soil" by this date, or else that the distinction between "chattels" and "chattels attached to the soil" was the cause of the corruption of the text of the statute. It is not easy to decide between these alternative explanations although the remark of the commentator suggests that the text of the statute as he knew it was not yet brought into line with the case reported[2]. In any case the real meaning of the statute is that the demandant shall have damages "as well of the chattels and moveables aforesaid, as of the rest" for, as Mr Bolland points out[3], *eel* stands for the Latin *aliud*, and the statute is therefore drawn as widely as language will allow, although this mis-translation narrows it considerably.

§ 7. *The Translation of* De Ponendis in Assisis

French is admittedly difficult, but Latin is almost as often wrongly rendered. By the Statute *De Ponendis in Assisis* sheriffs and bailiffs of liberties are forbidden to put "in aliquibus recognitionibus...aliquem de ballivis suis extra comitatus suos proprios faciendis," i.e. "to put any man of their bailiwicks upon inquests to be held out of their own counties." The *Statutes of the Realm* renders "aliquem de ballivis suis" by "any of their bailiffs"—which seriously misrepresents the statute and confuses "balliva," a bailiwick, with "ballivus," a bailiff.

§ 8. *The Translation of Westminster II, c.* 4

The most remarkable blunder, however, is in Westminster II, c. 4. The following is the text, with the *correct* rendering beside it:

[1] *Sturry* v. *Cobham*, Y.B. 6 & 7 Edw. II (*Eyre of Kent*), III. 71: cf. 74.

[2] If the decision was the origin, then it seems that the object of the court was to read the statute so as to interfere as little as possible with existing trespass law.

[3] Y.B. 6 & 7 Edw. II (*Eyre of Kent*), III. p. xlix.; Godefroy, *s.v.* "EL"; Y.B. 20 & 21 Edw. I, 369, *l.* 7.

In casu quando vir implacitatus de tenemento reddit tenementum petitum suo adversario de plano post mortem viri Justiciarii adjudicant mulieri dotem suam si per breve queratur; set in casu quando vir amittit tenementum petitum per defaltam, si mulier post mortem viri sui petat dotem, compertum est quod per aliquos Justiciarios adjudicata fuerit dos mulieri petenti non obstante defalta quam vir suus fecit, aliis Justiciariis in contraria oppinione existentibus et contrarium judicantibus: ut de cetero amputetur huiusmodi ambiguitas, etc.

When a husband impleaded of a tenement renders the tenement demanded to his adversary, clearly, after the husband's death, the judges award her dower to the widow if it is sought by writ; but when the man loses the tenement demanded by default, if the widow after his death seeks dower it is found that dower is adjudged to her by some judges notwithstanding the default of her husband, although other judges are of the contrary opinion and adjudge the opposite: in order henceforth to remove this uncertainty, etc.

It is strange that "de plano" should cause any difficulty, but it misled some old translator, whose influence in turn fell upon the Commissioners causing them, moreover, to place a comma after "plano" instead of after "adversario" thus making it refer to "reddit" instead of to "adjudicant." The result was that instead of "clearly," "plainly" (contrasting with the "ambiguitas" a few lines later) we find that a new meaning for "de plano" had been invented and that it was translated "by covin," i.e. "fraudulently"—almost the exact opposite of its natural sense. The mediaeval use of the word may be seen from the two following extracts:

Numquam consenserunt nec consenciunt, set de plano eis contradicunt[1].

Concordatum est...quod Rex de plano resumat rem.

The last is from the statute 4 Edw. I, c. 4 where "covinously" would presumably not be the king's description of his own action.

But this is not all. A pleader in court quoted the statute[2], and speaking in French said that the statute meant that when the

[1] Bémont, *Chartres*, 74. On the continent "de plano" became a technical term. (A long disquisition on its meaning will be found in the gloss on the phrase in the Feudal *Extravagantes*.) Similarly, our own ecclesiastical courts could proceed "summarie et de plano, sine strepitu et figura iudicii" (*Vetus Liber Archidiaconi Eliensis*, ed. Feltoe and Minns, 192).

[2] *Anon.*, Y.B. 30 & 31 Edw. I, 155.

husband surrendered the tenement, "qe le Justice de pleyn deyvent juger a la feme son dower." He is following the statute and rendering "de plano" by "de pleyn." But in addition he makes it clear that "de pleyn" applies to the Justice, although (by misplacing a comma) the *Statutes of the Realm* make it refer to the husband. The editor of the Year Book noticed this, but finding no solution, rendered "de pleyn" by "covin" and misplaced it to agree with the *Statutes of the Realm* version[1]. No better example could be desired of the danger of following the Commissioners' translations or the punctuation of their texts.

[1] Compare 2 Dwarris, 835, who has adopted the same punctuation as the Commissioners, but has cautiously left "de plano" untranslated.

CHAPTER III

THE LEGISLATURE AND ITS PLACE

§ 1. *Parliament*

THERE is no need to enter into a full description here of the English constitution in the early 14th century, for the subject has been very fully treated by Maitland in his *Preface* to the *Memoranda de Parliamento* in the Rolls Series[1]. In that brilliant essay, working out the suggestions of L. O. Pike in the Prefaces to the Year Books of 12 & 13 Edw. III and 13 & 14 Edw. III, he showed the real meaning and importance of Fleta's well-known words: "The king has his court in his council in his parliaments, in the presence of the earls, barons, magnates, and other learned men, where judicial doubts are determined, where new remedies are established as new wrongs arise, and where justice is done to everyone according to his deserts"[2]. That parliament at this time meant an event rather than an institution, that pleas were held "at"[3] rather than "by" or "in" it, that it was a "parliament of the council," and that it was a "court"[4]—all this is familiar matter to the constitutional historian. The essential unity of council, courts, and parliament is no peculiarity of the earliest times, but can be traced even into the 15th century[5], and is typical of our mediaeval polity[6].

§ 2. *Extra-Parliamentary Legislation*

This being so, the functions of legislature, judicature, and administration must not be regarded as apportioned to different organs, for none had so completely separate an existence, as to

[1] Since the above was written there has appeared a full and authoritative treatment of the whole subject in Professor A. F. Pollard's *Evolution of Parliament*.

[2] *Fleta*, lib. II. cap. 2, sect. 1.

[3] "Placita...ad Parliamentum," *Rot. Parl.* I. 15, 46, etc.

[4] McIlwain, *High Court of Parliament*, ch. 3.

[5] Plucknett, "Place of the Council in the Fifteenth Century" (*Trans. Royal Hist. Soc.* 4th Ser. I. 171–5).

[6] See especially Baldwin, "Select Cases before the King's Council" (*Selden Soc.*), xv–xxxv.

be capable of performing highly specialised duties. Legislation, for example, was by no means the monopoly of parliament, although it had something like a claim to be consulted on matters of fundamental constitutional importance[1]. One statute is made by the Council, Judges of both Benches, and the Barons of the Exchequer sitting in the Exchequer[2], another by the Council with the advice of the Judges and the consent of the King at ("ad") a parliament[3], while HENGHAM tells us that he and his companions made the Statute of Westminster II[4].

§ 3. *Non-Judicial Interpretation*

The power of making authoritative interpretations was also exercised in various ways and by variously constituted bodies. The Council expounded Westminster II, c. 18[5], the King and most of the nobles explained *Magna Carta*, c. 35[6] while the King and Judges made the *Expositio* attached to the Statute of Gloucester[7], of which statute, moreover, one chapter was actually "corrected" by the King in Council[8]. In its early stages it seems to have been the practice if not the theory of English law that the maker of a statute should also be its interpreter if need be. Only gradually was this power abandoned to the courts of law, which by this time had separated from the legislature. Nor did the legislature ever completely resign its claims to interpret, as occasional examples of explanatory and declaratory acts bear witness. It may be conjectured that our English law may have received its early bias in this direction from the canonists who held that only the maker of a statute could authoritatively explain it where it was ambiguous or obscure, on the principle that "unde jus prodit, interpretatio quoque procedat"[9]. The canonists in their turn derived the doctrine from the civilians[10].

1 Lapsley, *Engl. Hist. Rev.* XXVIII. 118–124.

2 *Stats. of the Realm*, I. 213.

3 *Ibid.* 142, cf. 216 (latter part of *Stat. de Conspiratoribus*).

4 *Ibid.* 171; *Anon.* v. *Thomas the Notary*, Y.B. 32 & 33 Edw. I, 429; *Aumeye* v. *Anon.*, Y.B. 33 & 35 Edw. I, 82; *Bygot* v. *Ferrers*, *ibid.* 585.

5 *Bardolf* v. *FitzHumphrey*, Y.B. 30 & 31 Edw. I, 441.

6 *Stats. Realm*, I. 118.

7 *Ibid.* 50.

8 This seems the meaning of the ungrammatical heading, *ibid.* 52.

9 31, X. 5, 39.

10 "Eius est interpretari cuius est condere" is the comment of Bartholomaeus de Saliceto (c. 1363) upon 12, C. I. 13. Compare Lord Ellesmere's remark on *Tregor* v. *Vaughan*, mentioned below, p. 70.

§ 4. *Judicial Legislation and Administration.*

Judicial interpretation, moreover, was frankly acknowledged to be virtually legislation. When discussing an avowry by the Statute of Marlborough, for example, BEREFORD, C.J. declared, "By a decision on this avowry we shall make a law throughout the land"[1]. Indeed, open, frank law-making is by no means difficult to find among the speeches of the Judges in our early Year Books. "Consider this henceforth as a general rule," said HENGHAM[2], as he defined the scope of a Writ of Deceit, while still more striking is the following[3]:

HENGHAM (to all the clerks in the Bench), "Take care henceforth that none of you enter *Petit Cape*, when a party has denied his summons, and thereupon waged his law, but has defaulted on the day when he ought to have come to wage his law; but [instead, enter] seisin of the land."

And this was done judicially a short time after in this term.

In short, HENGHAM first propounds a general rule of far-reaching importance, privately to the clerks in the Court, and then proceeds later in the term to apply it. Nor must it be thought that a point of process such as this was regarded as an unimportant detail, for at the end of our period it was said that process could only be altered by statute[4].

Decisions as well as rules were also clearly understood by the profession as being virtually legislation, as a pleader said to a Judge, "The Judgment you shall now make in this matter will serve hereafter in every *Quare Non Admisit* in England"[5].

Indeed, the lawyers of Edward I's time took no especial pains to distinguish adjudication from legislation. If the two functions could be conveniently performed together and by the same routine, then they were, and no theory of the separation of powers was in existence to force a distinction. For example, there is on the parliament roll[6] of 1292 the record of certain litigation between

[1] *Venour* v. *Blund*, Y.B. 3 & 4 Edw. II, 161; see below, p. 30.

[2] *Anon.*, Y.B. 33 & 35 Edw. I, 6. [3] *Anon. ibid.* 16. [4] See below, p. 126.

[5] *Prior of Lewes* v. *Bishop of Ely*, Y.B. 32 & 33 Edw. I, 32. It has been estimated that two-thirds of the modern English civil law is judge-made, Jenks, "English Civil Law," *Harvard Law Review*, XXX. 19.

[6] *Rot. Parl.* I. 79. The reference to Westminster II is in error for the Statute of Gloucester, c. 5.

William Butler and Walter Hapeton. Their case was difficult, and in accordance with the procedure described in Fleta it was discussed "in pleno parliamento," whereupon the king "de communi consilio suo" ordained a remedy. This was something more than the judgment in the case of *Butler* v. *Hapeton*, for it explicitly professed to amend the Statute of Westminster II and to concede a new right of action. When men first began to entertain theories about the precise nature of statutes, this document caused some difficulty. Thus in *Whitaker and Whitaker* v. *Anon.*[1], *Toudeby* informed the court that "there was a statute that said that one should answer for waste done in the time of the [plaintiff's] ancestor, and he cited the case of William Butler." In short, Butler's case is on the way to being regarded as a statute—not without challenge, however, for *Scrope* also made a contribution to the discussion by alleging "that that statute is no statute for it was never sealed"[2]. *Toudeby* retorted with a piece of information which seems to have since been lost: "You will find in the rolls of Sir Gilbert Roubery that the king commanded that it be firmly kept, and if you direct a writ to Sir Gilbert he will certify you to that effect." Whatever the tenor of the King's command to Sir Gilbert, contemporaries regarded it as superfluous, for the parliament roll text was the only one to get into circulation. But this contains an apostil which clearly shows that contemporaries fully recognised its legislative effect, while two centuries later the early printers boldly entitled it the "Statutum de Vasto."

Administration, likewise, was not the exclusive province of the council for it was not infrequently treated in Parliament, and the Judges had an important share of it while on Eyre[3].

§ 5. *The Relations of Courts, Councils, and Parliaments*

The judiciary affords the most striking example of the way in which a function might be shared by the various organs. The case of *Staunton* v. *Staunton and wife*[4] is well worth tracing through its various stages, not one of which caused any change in venue. It began as Formedon in the Common Pleas where

[1] Y.B. 7 Edw. II, 231 (ed. Maynard). [2] For sealing, see above, p. 11.
[3] See especially *Eyre of Kent* (introduction).
[4] Y.B. 13 & 14 Edw. III, xxxvii–xliv.

after lengthy proceedings a difficult question of law occasioned (as was alleged) a mistake in the record. The demandant therefore petitioned the king in council in parliament and put the question before them, which they decided, and ordered the Common Pleas to proceed thereupon; after a further delay the Common Pleas considered the question whether it was good law for parliament to have decided the case in the absence of one of the parties, but on consulting with the Chief Justice of the King's Bench failed to reach a decision upon the point, and more delay followed. The demandant again petitioned the council, and then the prelates, earls, barons and others in full parliament sent the Clerk of Parliament to go in person to the Common Pleas and tell the Judges to give judgment before the bench rose, or else to take the rolls into parliament. The latter course was followed, and the Chancellor, Treasurer, Judges, Barons of the Exchequer and the King's Council in parliament assembled, read the record and agreed that the demandant should recover. Judgment was then given in the Common Pleas. A writ of error now removed the whole case into the King's Bench which was as slow as the court below. The plaintiffs in error now in their turn petitioned to the council, who ordered the judges of both Benches to consult. Delays continued; more petitions by both parties were addressed to the council recalling that the matter had already been heard "in two parliaments and in full parliaments."[1] After further proceedings before the king in Chancery[2] the plaintiffs in error were non-suited and the original demandant had execution.

There are many other illustrations of this; for example,

[1] The same petition first describes these proceedings as "en deux pleyns parlement [*sic*] et par graunt deliberacion de touz les sages de la ley," and afterwards as "en les ditz deux parlementz et en pleyn [*sic*] parlementz et par commune avys de touz les sages" (Public Record Office, Coram Rege Roll, Hil. 15 Edw. III, rot. 41, sched.). Even making allowance for the scribe's indifference to the concords, it still seems clear that "en pleyn parlementz" is meant to be in apposition to "les ditz deux parlementz." Consequently, Mr Pike's translation "in two parliaments and in full parliaments" fails to represent the original accurately, for it suggests a distinction between parliaments and full parliaments which did not exist (Pollard, *Evolution of Parliament*, 33, 57–8). The petitioner's meaning seems to be that the case was heard "in two parliaments—and they, full parliaments—and by common advice," etc.

[2] Y.B. 14 & 15 Edw. III, 288–300.

STONORE, J. once told a party[1] that he "had spoken with the council on this mischief" and therefore advised them to go to the Chancery, while SCOT, J. decided a criminal case "with the assent of the whole council"[2]. The case of the Town of Coventry was considered by "all the council of England"[3], and on another occasion the council "adjudged that the king should have" a certain warship[4].

§ 6. *The Legal Results of the Fusion of Powers*

Our period is remarkable for this fusion of powers, which frustrates all attempts to make the mediaeval constitution look like a system. These facts must be borne in mind when we come to the examination in detail of the relations between the courts and the legislature (whether council, or parliament, or council in parliament), for they will explain the absence of that feeling that a statute is something imposed upon a court from without, which is so typical of modern conditions. At the same time the great familiarity with which the statutes were treated will also be seen to have its justification in the fusion of powers and institutions which we have attempted to describe.

1 *Clavering* v. *Roke and others*, Y.B. 17 & 18 Edw. III, 13.
2 *R.* v. *Turnbole*, Y.B. 17 Edw. III, 210.
3 Y.B. 20 Edw. III, II. 107, 113.
4 *R.* v. *Earl of Warwick*, *ibid.* 140 (65).

CHAPTER IV

STATUTES AND THE COMMON LAW

THE nature of statutes and their relation to the common law is a question of extreme difficulty upon which it is unwise to present anything more definite than an opinion. Some details of the practical working will appear later; here we are only concerned with the underlying theory. The fullest treatment of the topic is that by Professor McIlwain[1], whose conclusions are as follows.

§ 1. *Was Common Law Fundamental Law?*

There was a body of unwritten custom which the old writers regarded as binding "law" although it would not easily fit in with the Roman jurisprudence which formed the conventional preface to our mediaeval law books. This was "Common Law" and Professor McIlwain is of the opinion that it was also "fundamental law"[2]; his authorities for this proposition need examination. One of them is the eccentric *Mirror of Justices* whose author opined that the Statute of Marlborough was bad since "no special ordinance ought to exceed common law"[3]. This statement will need no further discussion after reading Maitland's preface to this curiosity of legal literature. The second is the oath of the judges not to pervert law in deference to Royal letters—which proves nothing. The third[4] is a petition whereby certain persons unnamed hoped to get considerable windfalls in the way of escheats by impugning the statute which gave the lands of the disendowed Templars to the Hospitallers, their reason being that the Despensers "procured" it, that the judges did not agree to it, and that it was "against law and reason." Like all acts of disendowment and redistribution the statute had roused much ill-feeling, and lords who had hoped for escheats doubtless said the transfer was "unlawful," i.e. contrary to their idea of what law should be—similar remarks are to be heard even to-day. This petition, moreover, is from parties who were

[1] *Magna Carta Essays*, 122–179.
[2] *Ibid.* 128–130.
[3] *Mirror*, 184.
[4] *Rot. Parl.* II. 41–2 (52).

taking a "sporting chance" of getting some of the spoil (not of restoring it to the Templars, be it noted) and, above all, no one took any notice of their theory of the unconstitutional nature of the statute. Indeed, they themselves did not say that it was invalid but prayed that it might be repealed—clear evidence that the statute and not the common law was "supreme." In the fourth place is the famous incident of 1341 when Edward III had to make considerable concessions to parliament by a statute in return for money[1]. Knowing how incensed the king was at his temporary defeat, some officials and a few judges attempted to save their faces by protesting that they would not enforce the statute if it was against the law of the realm which they had sworn to maintain. The protest may have been, but probably was not, sincere; but their reason does not appear to us to be so "significant" as Professor McIlwain implies, for the remonstrants seem to place emphasis on their oaths to maintain the law, rather than any fundamental character of the law itself. Finally[2], for the year 1347 there is a petition on the parliament roll against a judgment made in parliament, which is declared to be "contre le leis de Roialme et les Usages approvez." This is constantly being alleged and simply means that the judgment was erroneous; there is nothing to suggest that the petitioner meant that common law was fundamental law. It is therefore submitted that these examples (some of which Professor McIlwain confesses "undoubtedly arise out of factional and even revolutionary struggles") afford no support for the thesis of a supreme, fundamental law.

Outside our period it is true we find that in confirming *Magna Carta* in 1368 words were used which at first sight suggest that this document was meant to be regarded thenceforward as fundamental, for it was declared that all acts contrary to it were void. But investigation makes it difficult to believe that this was the true meaning of the confirmation. Although *Magna Carta* was thus confirmed in general terms, considerable portions of it had long been repealed by previous enactments. Were these repeals still valid after 1368? The lawyers showed no doubts whatever and regarded the repeals as still operative[3]. It is in

[1] *Rot. Parl.* II. 131 *a*, 942.
[2] *Rot. Parl.* II. 173 (65).
[3] 42 Edw. III, c. 11; Jenkins, *Centuries*, 2.

fact as difficult to find a fundamental written law as it is to maintain that the unwritten common law was fundamental.

§ 2. *The Nature of Statutes*

In strong contrast to the common law our Year Books constantly put the "special" or "new" law of the statutes, and we must now investigate the theoretical relations between the two. Professor McIlwain's conclusions[1] are threefold:

(1) That enactments of law are in the nature of affirmations of common law—strengthening, interpreting, and freeing it from abuses.

(2) That enactments of law must have the consent of those affected by them.

(3) That if a statute affirms common law it becomes like it permanent and supreme.

We cannot discuss each of these important topics here in detail, but a few remarks may be made on the main arguments. For example the affirmation of common law as an element in enactment could be put on a much more firm foundation than the *Mirror* if the law previous to the statutes were examined; we have already given some indication[2] of the results that might be expected. It is curious to note how certain passages of the *Mirror* actually prove the opposite of what Professor McIlwain uses them to support. For example, he claims that the essence of a statute is the affirmance of common law by removing abuses[3], but quotes the words of the *Mirror* that Westminster II, cc. 1 & 3 "are no statutes but merely revoke the errors of negligent judges," and again, "this is no statute, but the revocation of an error"[4]. It is therefore the *Mirror's* opinion that if an enactment removes errors, it is not a statute. It may well be questioned whether the affirmance referred to is a juristic notion at all; we suggest that it was rather a political and administrative precaution. Instead of it being the essence of a statute to affirm and be affirmed, it was an unfortunate necessity in face of the fact that law-breakers abounded. The significance of this is shown by the growth in the 15th century of the practice of each parliament

[1] *Magna Carta and the Common Law*, 140–7.
[2] *Supra*, p. 10.
[3] *Magna Carta Essays*, 141.
[4] *Ibid.* 148.

solemnly affirming the whole body of statute law[1] for the express reason that "the law and statutes are not kept," in a period, moreover, when law was least obeyed[2]. As in many other provinces so here, the great difficulty of mediaeval statesmen was not theoretical, but practical—the purely physical difficulty of getting law of any sort efficiently enforced and generally respected in the absence of a standing army or a permanent police force. Another statement that is hard to accept is that "mere interpretation[3] in the 14th century belonged to the council"[4]. In Part II of this essay it will be shown how much interpretation was done outside the council.

The second of Professor McIlwain's conclusions being a matter of a purely political and constitutional character need not detain us; the third will form the subject of our next chapter.

§ 3. *Statutes as seen in the Year Books*

What, then, are we to say on the subject of fundamental law? Merely negative results such as these are unsatisfactory, and one indeed must form some conclusion on the attitude of contemporaries to their own legislation, if the period is to be understood aright. The suggestion here put forward is that an examination should be made of all the best sources for the legal history of the first half of the 14th century with a view to finding what opinions were held in the courts upon this matter. Our authorities will therefore be, not the erratic author of the *Mirror*, nor even the occasional outbursts of interested jurisprudence produced by times of revolutionary excitement, but the Year Books where we may read the every-day expressions used in the courts, "in time of peace" as their records say, by the men who after all had the most to do with statutes, in making, and criticising and applying them. Many details will be given later in Part II, c. XI; here, only general principles will be discussed.

[1] *Magna Carta Essays*, 142, 151; but why affirm fundamental law? Surely it is above affirmance or repeal.

[2] For the chronic lawlessness of the age, see works such as Plummer's *Fortescue*; cf. also the Salt Society's *Staffordshire Members of Parliament* where it seems that the local tyrant was frequently M.P. A solemn affirmance by such men would at least exact lip-service to the law and be of some moral value.

[3] Presumably interpretation of statutes, but the author's meaning is not entirely free from ambiguity.

[4] *Magna Carta Essays*, 151, n. 6.

In the first place, there is no trace in the Year Books of the first three Edwards of anyone thinking that statutes were essentially affirmations of common law; that they actually were so in a few cases was undenied[1], but that they always ought to be was never suggested. On the contrary, we find two epithets applied to statutes, which unmistakably imply the reverse. In the first place, "special law" is surely something extraordinary, outside of the usual law, and radically different from it; the constant occurrence of the term throughout our Year Books shows how striking was the contrast felt to be between common law and the "special law" which was then newly appearing. To hold that this statute law merely affirmed the common law, is to divest the word "special" of all its meaning. Secondly, they almost as frequently contrasted "novel law" with "ancient law." Not only were statutes "special," exceptional law, they were novelties as well[2].

§ 4. *The "Making" of Law*

It is sometimes suggested that the Middle Ages did not recognise the possibility of "making law"[3], but there is evidence which makes qualification of this view necessary. The frequent mention of this "novel ley" is itself inconsistent with the theory, and we have already mentioned BEREFORD's statement that his judgment in a certain case would "make a law throughout the land"[4]. This, it is important to observe, was by no means a new discovery upon his part, for Bracton had said precisely the same thing in words well worth quoting:

> Si autem aliqua nova et inconsueta emerserint et quae prius usitata non fuerint in regno, si tamen similia evenerint, per simile iudicentur, cum bona sit occasio a similibus procedere ad similia. Si autem talia nunquam prius evenerint, et obscurum et difficile sit eorum iudicium, tunc ponantur indicia in respectum usque ad magnam curiam, ut ibi per consilium curiae terminentur[5].

[1] *Billing* v. *Eton*, Y.B. 2 & 3 Edw. II, 38 (*v.l.* from MS "X"), and compare, above, p. 10.

[2] References to "special" and "novel" law occur in the Year Books *passim*; a few typical references are collected in *Magna Carta Essays*, 134, n. 1.

[3] McIlwain, *High Court of Parliament*, 46–51, 249–300.

[4] Above, p. 22.

[5] Bracton, f. 16.

Maitland's comment upon this is as follows:

Thus in a quite unprecedented case the court may have to declare for law that, as Bracton almost admits, has not as yet been law[1].

Again we have the words of *Inge* that "as one canon defeats many laws (*leges*), so the statute defeats many things that were at common law"[2]—this is obviously legislation, not affirmation; *Pole*, a prominent pleader in Edward III's reign, was able to contrast "common law" with "the law now in force"[3], while only one generation after our period closes, we have the following clear statement as the climax towards which things had long been moving: "The law of the land is made in Parliament by the King and the lords...and the commonalty of the realm"[4].

The only conclusion that seems warranted by the evidence is that legislation took place, and that contemporaries were conscious of it; they frankly faced the fact that special law—"novel law"—was being "made" and that it "defeated" the common law. But nothing resembling a theory of law and legislation is to be found. Fourteenth century England was content to see the fact and leave the theory alone.

[1] Pollock and Maitland, I. 183, n. I.
[2] *Venour* v. *Blund*, Y.B. 3 & 4 Edw. II, 162.
[3] *Staunton* v. *Staunton and wife*, Y.B. 13 & 14 Edw. III, 24.
[4] *Rot. Parl.* III. 234.

CHAPTER V

STATUTES AND ORDINANCES

THE controversy over the difference between statutes and ordinances is now in its third century and shows no sign of flagging.

§ 1. *The Distinction drawn by Sir Edward Coke*

Sir Edward Coke sought to distinguish between Statutes and Ordinances on the ground that the latter had not received the "threefold assent" of Crown, Lords, and Commons[1]. His doctrine was immediately challenged by William Prynne, who, in 1648, published his "*Irenarches Redivivus*...with a full Refutation of Sir Edward Cooks assertion and the commonly received Erronious opinion of a Difference between Ordinances and Acts of Parliament in former Ages: here clearly manifested to be then but one and the same in all respects...." There can be no doubt after reading Prynne's pamphlet that he has succeeded in his attempt

to refute the commonly received errour of these times, and of some pretended Grandees of the Law...for which there is not any one single pregnant convincing president extant to my knowledge in any Parliament Rolls or existing Acts: which errour has been principally propagated by Sir Edw. Cooks venerable authority and assertion,... whose misallegations and mistakes are too frequently embraced for Oracles of truth for want of due examination[2].

§ 2. *The Distinction drawn by Professor McIlwain*

Coming to more modern times, Professor McIlwain's contribution to the discussion is first, that "by Edward III's time some distinction existed between statutes and ordinances. The former were more permanent than the latter and more difficult to change"[3]; and secondly, "the real difference is that a statute in its original meaning is an affirmance of law....Like the law it authoritatively interprets, a statute in affirmance of common law is permanent also"[4]. "Ordinances are temporary provisions

[1] 4 *Inst.* 25.
[2] Prynne, *Irenarches Redivivus*, 42–3.
[3] McIlwain, *High Court of Parliament*, 313.
[4] *Magna Carta Essays*, 145.

which are not considered to affect the permanent law unless they are re-enacted in the form of a statute"[1].

§ 3. *The Identity of Statutes, Ordinances, and Provisions*

As far as our period is concerned (and we speak of nothing outside it[2]) there is no contrast expressed or distinction visible between statutes and ordinances. Neither of these words was as yet a technical term, and neither had any special meaning. Nor has Professor McIlwain quoted adequate evidence in support of his view. Some of his citations certainly show that some things were statutes and others were not, but there is no example of the others being called by contrast, "ordinances"[3]. In one case he cites an "ordinance" that the staple be fixed "perpetuelment" —which his theory would only allow of a statute[4].

It must be remembered that mediaeval "style" often meant using three words where one would do; hence we find enactments regularly beginning "provisum, ordinatum, et statutum est." No one surely would suggest that such a document had passed through three legal processes corresponding to these three terms. A statute was something established, and an ordinance was something ordained, and during our period the words were used interchangeably. The Statute of Gloucester describes itself as "statutes, ordinances and purveyances"; that of Marlborough as "provisions, ordinances and statutes." An enactment enforcing food rations upon the nation calls itself "istud statutum" although as it did not affect the law of the land it should only be an ordinance by Professor McIlwain's definition[5]. On the other hand, a document making an important definition of the offence of conspiracy, copies of which were sent to all the judges, only styles itself an "ordinance and final definition"[6]. There are moreover numerous phrases in the Year Books which show that no distinction was implied:

[1] *Magna Carta Essays*, 146.

[2] Shortly after our period there is a trace of some distinction between ordinances and statutes, but it was only made possible by the marked advance towards the differentiation of great council and parliament which took place in the latter portion of Edward III's reign. See *Rot. Parl.* II. 253, 257; Stats. 27 Edw. III, st. 2 and 28 Edw. III, c. 13; Dwarris, *Statutes*, I. 11; Baldwin, *King's Council*, 106.

[3] *Magna Carta Essays*, 161–2 citing *Rot. Parl.* II. 11 (3); 10 Edw. III, st. 2; *Rot. Parl.* II. 113 (7, 8), 133 (61).

[4] *Magna Carta Essays*, 163.

[5] *Stats. Realm*, I. 279, foot. (10 Edw. III, st. 3).

[6] *Ibid.* 145 (33 Edw. I).

"It was ordained by statute...by which ordinance"[1].

"By which statute it was ordained..."[2].

"By common ordinance" (meaning Westminster II, c. 30)[3].

Thorpe, J.—"When all the lords are assembled they can make an ordinance and it shall be held for a statute, and for this reason the King has commanded us to hold this [38 Edw. III, stat. 2] for a statute"[4].

Towards the close of our period comes the important discovery of Miss Bertha Putnam who has made a detailed study of the working of the Ordinance of Labourers of June 1349 and the Statute of Labourers of 1351[5]. The cases in the central courts which she has examined prove "that the ordinance, not the statute, was the essential document, and that during the long period before it was made a statute[6] it had all the force of statute law"[7].

As an indication of the meaning of "ordinance," we may recall that the claimants at Norham "submitted themselves to the ordinance of the King"[8]; private parties could do the same[9], while the adjustment of the rights of patron and vicar by the ordinary was properly styled an ordinance[10]. There is every reason to believe that "ordinance" and "statute" referred not to different instruments, but to the same act—namely, the "providing, ordaining, and establishing" of law. To put legal distinctions between the words is to attribute to the mediaeval constitution a subtlety and refinement which is altogether foreign to contemporary statecraft, and fails to take count of the love of synonyms which characterised the age.

1 *Talbot* v. *Wilynton*, Y.B. 14 & 15 Edw. III, 234.

2 *Anon.*, Y.B. 20 Edw. III, I. 99.

3 *Anon.*, Y.B. 32 & 33 Edw. I, 321.

4 *R.* v. *Bp of Chichester*, Y.B. 39 Edw. III, 7; cf. *Articuli Super Cartas* which are called a statute in *Strode* v. *Prior of Lodres*, Y.B. 4 Edw. II, 142 and in Stat. 5 Edw. III, c. 2, but are called ordinances in *Beauflour* v. *Godesfelde*, Y.B. 18 & 19 Edw. III, 568. Similarly, the Statute of Northampton of 2 Edw. III is styled an ordinance in *Rot. Parl.* II. 131 (39), although frequently also called a statute in the cases discussed below, pp. 79, 143. 38 Edw. III, st. 2 is described as "this statute" in c. 1 and "these present ordinances" in c. 4. See also, in general, Clifford, *History of Private Bill Legislation*, I. 332.

5 25 Edw. III, st. II.

6 By 2 Ric. II, st. 1, c. 8.

7 Putnam, *The Enforcement of the Statutes of Labourers*, 179.

8 *Breuse* v. *Mowbray*, Y.B. 16 Edw. III, I. 295.

9 *Ibid.* Y.B. 20 Edw. III, I. 57.

10 *Prioress of Holywell* v. *Anon.*, Y.B. 19 Edw. III, 358; *Prior of Coventry* v. *Vicar of Holy Trinity, Coventry*, Y.B. 20 Edw. III, I. 66.

CHAPTER VI

LEGAL THOUGHT

As we have already suggested, there was little legal theorising among those who pleaded or adjudged in our courts. Consequently the only general principles available in time of difficulty were so vague and incomplete that one could not justly give this chapter the more pretentious title of Jurisprudence.

§ 1. *The Law of Reason and of Nature*

Of the notions then current the first to be considered will be that of "reason" and the "law of reason." Whether the word meant anything at all definite must be judged from these—the only—examples of its occurrence in the period under survey. *Mowbray* in arguing declared that "law ought to be in accordance with reason and to take away mischief unless the contrary practice has been in use as law"[1]. The context (an intricate discussion of Joinder in Aid) shows that "reason" here will not bear a much more definite meaning than "legal symmetry," or "consistency with general principles" and that in any case it is of less authority than custom. Again, to obey a prerogative writ which contravened a statute by requiring the court to delay an assize was "against law and reason" in the opinion of HILARY, J.[2] but he seems to use the phrase in the colloquial sense of "unreasonable" rather than as a term of law. Similarly, STONORE, J. used a sentence which is only slightly more definite:

By conscience and the law of God it would be against reason (if the plaintiff speaks truth) that by such a fine, which is void, he should be disinherited. On the other hand it is a strong measure, by the law of the land, to take an averment against the fine[3].

Here it is difficult to distinguish "reason" from "conscience."

[1] *Tornerghe* v. *Abbot of Furness*, Y.B. 15 Edw. III, 126. Compare BEREFORD's speech in *Sampson* v. *Grene*, quoted below, p. 130.

[2] *Anon.* v. *Seneloun*, Y.B. 20 Edw. III, I. 493; Stat. 2 Edw. III, c. 8.

[3] *Uppecote* v. *Uppecote and others*, Y.B. 13 & 14 Edw. III, 97. It may be remembered that no decision was reached in this difficult case.

Reason and the law of reason were therefore very vaguely conceived—for these are the most definite illustrations to be found in our books. *Herle* indeed once argued that "In the beginning every man in the world was free, and the law is so favourable to liberty that he who is once found free in a court of record shall be free for ever..."[1], but we may doubt whether this effect ought not to be attributed rather to the doctrine of record than to an *a priori* doctrine of liberty in the beginning. It is in this connection, moreover, that we meet the only references to natural law by common lawyers who are not obviously transplanting foreign jurisprudence. They are both to be found in the *Mirror of Justices*, which tells us in one place that "all men should be free according to the law of nature," and in another place that "if you take what is mine and I at once take it back, I do no sin, for I am warranted in this by natural law"[2]. Edward I made a reference, probably unique, to *Jus Feodale* in claiming the lordship of Wales, but of this we hear nothing more[3].

§ 2. *Canon Law*

A few words may be said of the relations of common law and canon law. In those cases where the jurisdiction was undoubtedly the Church's the State was deferential; thus Edward I explained that forasmuch as it would be "great charity to do right to all men at all times when it is needed to take possessory assizes (by the assent of the Prelates) in Advent, Septuagesima and Lent.... The King prays this of the Bishops"[4]. But if the jurisdiction

[1] *Thorne* v. *Peche*, Y.B. 3 Edw. II, 94, cf. *Prior of St Denis* v. *John*, Y.B. 20 Edw. III, II. 468 (80).

[2] *Mirror*, 77, 66. The later lawyers identified this "Law of Reason" with the "Law of Nature," Pollock, "History of the Law of Nature" (*Journal of the Society of Comparative Legislation* (1900), 432). For the degree of importance to be attached to these and other borrowings by English lawyers from foreign theorists, see Pollock, "Has the Common Law received the Fiction Theory of Corporations?" (*Festschrift Otto Gierke*, 105–6).

[3] Barrington, 93. Its principal sources are the Lombardic *Libri Feodales* which are appended to old copies of the *Corpus Juris Civilis*. They have played an important part in Scots Law and were the subject of a commentary by Sir Thomas Craig.

[4] Westminster I, c. 51. This seems to be the sense, but the translation in the *Statutes of the Realm* interpolates "it is provided." The chapter provides nothing and merely prays the Bishops to allow the taking of the assizes. It is not stated whether they did so or not.

was disputed, the contest was vigorous and compromise out of the question. In a case of provisors, SCOT, C.J., K.B. said,

> The bishop is bound by the law of Holy Church, and is also bound to execute the king's commands. Therefore suppose the one law to be contrariant to the other, shall we therefore leave our judgments unexecuted, or would it be right that the bishop should be excused from executing the king's commands? (*quasi diceret non*)....I saw the Archbishop of Canterbury in a worse plight than this bishop is in, had not the king pardoned him;

and then BASSET, J. told a story of how Edward I had held the temporalities of the Archbishopric of York for the rest of the primate's life for his contempt in not ousting a man from a prebend into which he had been provided by the pope[1]. The canon law is sometimes quoted in court by way of illustration—that a statute defeats common law just as a canon defeats "leges," has already been noticed—or its maxims are taken over, thus from the Sext we get "volenti non fit injuria" and "nemo obligatur ad impossible"[2].

An extremely interesting illustration of the relations of statute to canon law is the following. Gregory X in the Council of Lyons enacted that bigamists should be deprived of all clerical privilege, and should be relinquished to the coercion of the lay courts[3]. The question arose whether this constitution applied to clerks who were bigamists before the constitution, or only to those who committed the offence after its publication. The general principle of the Canon Law is that statutes should not be retrospective[4], but the English statute *De Bigamis*, c. 5 interpreted the statute as applying to all bigamists, whether before or after the Statute.

§ 3. *Civil Law*

Civil law is occasionally quoted[5]—and mis-applied in the process[6]—while INGE, J. once put to *Denham* the puzzling question "What do you answer to the Imperial Law (upon which the law of the land is founded) which says that the inheritance

[1] *R.* v. *Bishop of Lincoln*, Y.B. 19 Edw. III, 168.

[2] *Hotot* v. *Rychemund*, Y.B. 3 & 4 Edw. II, 200. See Roscoe Pound, *The Maxims of Equity*, 34 *Harv. Law Rev.*, at p. 828.

[3] c. un. in VI. 1. 12. [4] c. 2, X. 1. 2. [5] Y.B. 3 Edw. II, xviii.

[6] *Anon.* v. *Page*, Y.B. 6 & 7 Edw. II (*Eyre of Kent*), II. 54 n.

ought to descend to the most worthy, because the possession of the brother makes the sister heir?"[1]

[1] *Audele* v. *Deyncourt*, Y.B. 6 & 7 Edw. II, 70. "Imperial Law" almost certainly means civil law, and so the reference may be to a passage in the Code, 6. 58. 3 (*De Legitimis Heredibus*). Even more to the point is the gloss by Accursius, as follows:

"Bertha habuit duos fratres: decessit unus relictis filiis, et decessit alter sine herede. Quaeritus quis debeat praeferri in successione istius fratris qui decessit sine herede—utrum Bertha soror, an filii alterius fratris qui sunt nepotes Berthae? Respondeo quod Bertha, cum sit in secundo gradu, at fratris defuncti nepotes sunt in tercio, et soror praefertur nepotibus."

This is analogous to the position in the Year Book, but the Code does not formulate the maxim "Possessio fratris facit sororem heredem." Coming as it does from the Bench, the remark may be merely a display of out-of-the-way learning, and not meant to be taken too seriously. If the text we have suggested be the true source of INGE'S statement, then *Denham* (either by ignorance or by policy) missed the opportunity for a crushing retort, for this passage in the Code was repealed by the Authentic "Cessante" (Nov. CXVIII.). By saying that the law of the land is founded upon the imperial law, INGE may of course simply mean that civil law could be used as a supplementary system. Even so, his example drawn from an abrogated portion of the Code does not suggest a very deep knowledge of the Roman Law. An additional complication in the Year Book case is due to the fact that the dispute lay between the uncle (not nephew) and the half-sister (not sister of the whole blood). There is, however, a passage in Azo, *Summa*, col. 721, § 6, which fits our case almost exactly; it runs: "Post fratres ex utroque parente et eorum filios, admittuntur ex uno latere fratres sororesue, cum quibus et filii eorum, si qui ex eis iam decesserint. Hi autem fratrum filii, cum pares sint defuncti fratribus, preferuntur proculdubio eiusdem patruis, et aliis similibus."

PART II

EXAMPLES OF INTERPRETATION

ARRANGEMENT AND GROUPING

THE second part now brings us to the more detailed portion of the discussion. It is not at all easy to arrange the subject in the logical and systematic manner expected of a modern commentator owing to the peculiar nature of the material. The formal side of judicial interpretation was so little developed that the courts themselves had no ordered ideas on the subject and were apt to regard each case purely on its merits without reference to any other case—still less to any general canon of interpretation—and trust implicitly to the light of nature and the inspiration of the moment. Very soon, of course, certain cases and decisions began to repeat themselves, and by the time the judges had become aware of the fact there had already been laid the foundations of a custom, though many years would have to pass before one could expect to find it a workmanlike structure. It is these *nuclei*, therefore, which will be described in the following pages, for the natural grouping of the material is more sound historically than an attempt to arrange mediaeval facts under the heads of modern legal science.

CHAPTER I

GENERAL WORDS AND LITERAL CONSTRUCTION

In the first place may be treated all those cases where the wording and grammatical structure of the statute are discussed as affording a basis for interpretation.

§ 1. *General Words*

The modern books contain much learning about "general words" and it is interesting to trace its beginnings in our period.

Briefly stated, the present law upon the subject is this. Where in a statute a general term follows other terms *eiusdem generis*, which are more specific, then the meaning of the general term is limited by the more specific words[1]. To take an interesting modern example. Section 43 of the Customs Consolidation Act, 1876, enacts that "The importation of arms, ammunition, gunpowder, or any other goods may be prohibited by Proclamation or Order in Council." In 1919 the Attorney-General claimed that the words "or any other goods" authorised the Crown to prohibit the import of goods of every sort and description—and in the present case, of pyrogallic acid. Sankey, J. held that this was not the case, and that the "other goods" must be taken as being goods of a like nature to "arms, ammunition and gunpowder." He held, moreover, that pyrogallic acid, though important in warfare as a photographic material, was not of the same *genus* as arms, ammunition and gunpowder[2].

It is possible to trace this important rule in 1338, when *Stouford*, arguing in a case of replevin[3], cleverly anticipated the modern doctrine. The second chapter of Westminster II makes a number of reforms in the law of distress. It begins by giving a remedy to lords whose tenants, after being distrained for arrears of customs and services, disclaim their tenure in courts that bear no record, thus depriving the lord of the service,

[1] Maxwell, *Interpretation of Statutes*, 583.
[2] *Attorney-General* v. *Brown*, 36 *The Times* L.R. 165.
[3] *Anon.*, Y.B. 12 & 13 Edw. III, 51; below, Appendix, p. 176.

although not divesting themselves of the tenure. The next clause fixes a date of limitation for the avowry of a distress upon a long-continued seisin—the word "distress" being in this case unqualified. Then follow various regulations of the action of replevin, concluding with the provision that whereas some people bring replevin and after being ordered to return the distress, again replevy it, and keep on repeating this process endlessly by defaulting when the lord comes into court to avow, therefore it is provided that when the return of the distress is awarded a second time the court shall adjudge it irreplevisable. Such a case as the last had arisen and the plaintiff having defaulted, the lord prayed that the court should adjudge the return irreplevisable, as the statute directed. *Stouford*, for the tenant, opposed this, "for the court was not apprised as to whether the distress was for arrear of service or not; and if not, then the case is at common law, for the statute only speaks of distress for arrear of service 'quia statutum est generale in fine'." *Stouford's* meaning seems to be that although the statute is general, yet the general words are in the end and must therefore be limited by the particular words at the beginning of the statute. No discussion of *Stouford's* argument is reported, for judgment went against him on another point.

The above case is unique as far as our period is concerned; the phrase "general terms" is occasionally to be found, but is used so rarely that it is clear that *Stouford* was far ahead of his contemporaries[1].

In another case of replevin[2], the verdict of the inquest was that the lord had levied a distress outside of his fee. HILARY, J.

[1] *Abbot of Woburn* v. *Braybroke*, Y.B. 13 & 14 Edw. III, 256–272, for example. Westminster II, c. 45 sets up the procedure by *scire facias* for the execution of matters contained in fines and records, the chapter ending with the provision that "nevertheless what has been said before [in c. 9] shall be observed concerning a mesne who is bound by cognisance or a judgment to acquittance." The case in question seems to be an attempt to use *scire facias* against a mesne, and when it was said that *scire facias* was not available, but that the process of c. 9 must be used, an annotator has remarked "*Quere*. The statute is in general terms." The query must be that of a person who was unaware of the last sentence in the chapter just quoted. See also *Wilby* v. *Vottone*, Y.B. 32 & 33 Edw. I, 450 (discussed below, p. 58).

[2] *Tryvet* v. *Audele*, Y.B. 18 & 19 Edw. III, 320. Further discussed below, p. 129.

was of opinion that the lord would therefore have to pay ransom to the king (by Statute of Marlborough, cc. 1 & 2). *Pole*, for the lord, disputed this, saying that ransom was only due when a special writ based on that statute was brought, and that the penalty of the statute could not be imposed in an action of replevin. STONORE, J. observed that "the statute speaks generally," but *Pole* maintained that his view was that most commonly held. There is no reported decision.

The very first printed Year Book contains a case[1] which shows that problems had already arisen in the interpretation of statutes according to their grammatical structure. A statute[2] had given recovery for lands lost under certain circumstances by default, but in an action of this nature it was said that the default in question had taken place before the statute. To this *Huntingdon* replied that although it was true that the default was before the statute, yet the statute says nothing of before or after but speaks generally (*indistincte*)[3]. This point was not discussed, however, for his opponent, *Howard*, quoted the words of the statute "...de cetero huiusmodi defalta non sit prejudicialis..." in support of his contention that it only applied to defaults after the statute. Then BEREWYKE, J. discovered a further difficulty. He thought that the statute could not bear *Howard's* interpretation unless it said "de cetero huiusmodi defalta facienda." This so complicated the matter that they were adjourned to await judgment, but none is reported. In the same reign we find a discussion as to whether the Statute of Westminster II, c. 3 which says "tenant" also includes a tenant by warranty. *Denham* argued that the statute spoke "generally" and the court accepted the wider interpretation[4].

The relation of general words to the rights of the Crown was discussed in a *Quare Impedit* brought in 1340 by the King against the Bishop of Coventry and Lichfield, upon a cause of action arising in his father's reign and therefore at least fourteen years

[1] *Anon.* v. *Mortimer*, Y.B. 20 & 21 Edw. I, 452–4. The action was *Quod ei Deforciat*, not Formedon, as the margin of the MS incorrectly states.

[2] Westminster II, c. 4.

[3] Cf. *Anon.*, Y.B. 6 & 7 Edw. II (*Eyre of Kent*), II. 2 for "indistincte" used in this sense.

[4] *Balsham* v. *atte Street*, Y.B. 5 Edw. II, II. 46.

old[1]. *Thorpe* defended by referring to the newly-made statute in which the king granted that he would not henceforth be answered in *Quare Impedit*, unless he had presented within three years of the vacancy by which his right accrued[2]. To this our friend *Stouford* replied in this wise:

You clearly see how of common right, time does not run against the king, unless it be by statute. Now this statute cannot foreclose the king from a presentation made before the statute unless by express words making mention thereof, and since the king took this writ on[3] a presentation [" dun presentement "] before the statute, from which the statute does not oust him (for it is to be understood of time since it was made) we demand judgment.

But *Thorpe* now tried his skill in using *Stouford's* weapon and demanded judgment "since the statute is general, saying that the king shall not from henceforth be answered in such a case." In judgment, SHARESHULLE, J. neatly combined both arguments and awarded the king a writ to the bishop "because the king is not ousted by express words from an action taken before the statute, nor from a presentation made before it, but the statute speaks generally, referring only to an action accrued and taken since the statute"[4].

§ 2. *Words of Prohibition*

Some other matters connected with the wording of statutes may be treated here, for they show to a remarkable degree how uncertain lawyers were upon points that now seem very simple. Thus, Westminster II, c. 27 which says that an inquest shall not be delayed for an essoin, drew from *Inge*[5] a speech to the effect that "the statute speaks in negative words 'non differatur' and an affirmation does not follow therefrom that the inquest is to be taken.... To say that something is not to be done is not to say

[1] Y.B. 14 Edw. III, 138–40.

[2] 14 Edw. III, st. 4, c. 2.

[3] The king's original writ would be based on the supposition that the presentation was attempted, but the defendant had impeded its acceptance by the ordinary. Pike's translation "*for* a presentation" gives the inaccurate impression that the presentation would not take place until after the judgment, and thus robs *Stouford's* words of their point that the statute forecloses the king from such presentations in the future but says nothing to invalidate one made (although perhaps unsuccessfully) before the statute.

[4] For a similar judgment, see *R.* v. *Bishop of Bath and Wells*, Y.B. 14 Edw. III, 122.

[5] *Lymesy* v. *Abbot of Westminster*, Y.B. 6 & 7 Edw. II, 34–44.

that the opposite is to be done." An essoin had been quashed in accordance with the statute, but the court had proposed to defer the inquest pending a bailiff's wager of law on a side-issue —hence the attempt to use the statute to get the inquest taken at once. This long and interesting case was not decided, for the defendant died "and all came to naught" as the reporter sadly remarked.

§ 3. *The Preamble*

As yet there was no distinction between the preamble and any other portion of a statute—doubtless owing to the formlessness of our early legislation. Thus a party[1] brought *Quare Incumbravit* in such a way as to use it to recover an advowson. Exception was taken to this on the grounds that the action should have been *Quare non Admisit*, since "the statute says that there are only three writs for recovering an advowson[2], and inasmuch as his remedy for being deforced is made certain and limited by the statute, therefore he cannot have any other writ than the one specified in the statute." It will be noticed that the words quoted are part of a long preamble introduced by "Whereas..." setting forth the motive of the statute. The point was not discussed, it seems, for the debate turned to a dispute concerning the nature of a *Quare Incumbravit*—upon which both sides appeared rather uncertain.

§ 4. *Reference to other Statutes*

Another point that puzzled many was the meaning of the words "sicut in aliis statutis continentur" which occur in the Statute of Westminster II, c. 11. After full consideration, BEREFORD, J.[3] deduced from these words that "the statute of Westminster had relation to the statute of Marlborough [c. 23]" and therefore interpreted the two together. Sometimes the court was more cautious, however; for example, the Statute of Marlborough, c. 9, benefits tenants "enfeoffed by charter for service certain, such as (*veluti*) for the free service of so many shillings

[1] *Prior of Budleigh* v. *Bishop of Worcester*, Y.B. 30 & 31 Edw. I, 272; Westminster II, c. 5.

[2] That is, Right of Advowson, *Darrein Presentment*, and *Quare Impedit*.

[3] *Anon.*, Y.B. 4 Edw. II, 3–4, the argument is variously attributed in the manuscripts.

a year payable as for all service." Does this extend to a feoffee whose charter expressed free alms? The court took refuge in the famous chapter 24 of Westminster II on writs *in consimili casu*, the opinion of all the judges being that the "veluti" in the statute would make the statute "in like case" applicable[1].

§ 5. *The Meaning of "Heirs" in Westminster II, c.* 3

A curious example of the earlier attempts at interpretation is to be found in a discussion[2] on Westminster II, c. 3 which allows (or was believed to allow) "the heir" of a tenant in tail to intervene in litigation if the tenant is about to surrender his lands collusively. Much argument took place, before the receipt was eventually allowed, as to whether anyone could be described as "heir" before his ancestor's death. This point is really dependent upon another important question of interpretation which was also involved in this case and may be conveniently considered here. The editor has appended to it the following note:

> The Statute of Westminster II does not, however, include the case of tenancy in fee tail amongst those in which the heir may be received to defend his right, though the *Statutum de Defensione Juris*, 20 Edw. I, enacting that persons received under the Statute of Westminster II to defend their right shall give security, seems to suppose that it does.

We have here the result of a confusion of very ancient date. The word "heir" in this connection may mean two things—the heir in the entail or the heir in the reversion, or, as the Year Books sometimes put it, "the heir in the tail" and the "heir in the descent" or "right." Bearing this caution in mind, let us now examine the Statute of Westminster II, c. 3. After laying down rules for the pleading of the action *Cui in Vita*, the statute next provides that if a husband's default imperils lands which are the right of his wife, she may be received before judgment to defend them. The statute continues as follows:

[1] *Attemulle* v. *Saunderville*, Y.B. 6 & 7 Edw. II, 12. (The connection of Report V with the others is doubtful.) So also *Thorpe* argued—with how much success is not apparent—that a reversioner whose receipt is allowed by statute "simili modo" (Westminster II, c. 3) has the same advantage as a feme coverte, *Anon.*, Y.B. 18 & 19 Edw. III, 26.

[2] *Anon.*, Y.B. 5 Edw. II, I. 160–2, the editor has not noticed that this case has been reported before in Y.B. 1 & 2 Edw. II, 70. Moreover, *A* must have brought "her" not "his" writ of dower. BEREFORD's speech in Y.B. 5 Edw. II, I. 161, seems a reminiscence of *Anon.* v. *Picot* which we shall discuss shortly.

Likewise, if a tenant in dower, by the courtesy, or otherwise for term of life, or by gift where reversion is reserved, make default or will render, let the heirs or those to whom the reversion belongs be admitted to their answer, etc.

Two things must be noticed, first, that the word "heirs" can only bear one meaning here—that of "heirs in the right." The object of the whole chapter is to safeguard the holder of the reversion from being robbed of his right by the collusion of his (or his ancestor's) lessees and others holding lesser estates. For obvious reasons it had long been customary to speak of an "heir" rather than a "reversioner" after a doweress, since he was most frequently her own son. Hence the statute says "heirs" and "reversioners," but these cannot be reasonably interpreted as "heirs in the tail or reversioners." Secondly, the case of a tenancy in fee tail is not omitted as the editor says, for he is none other than "the tenant by the gift where reversion is reversed." Westminster II, therefore, as we read it, does allow receipt upon the default of a tenant in tail[1], but it is the receipt of the reversioner, not of the issue in tail. The very objection that was made of the impossibility of a man being heir during the life-time of the ancestor should have convinced the court that "heir" in the statute meant heir in the right and not issue in tail—which is indeed no heir, but only heir presumptive. This being, we believe, the true meaning of the statute, it at once appears that there is no difficulty in the *Statutum de Defensione Juris* which merely substitutes the words "per feodum talliatum" for "per donum."

In spite of all this, however, there arose a custom at an early date of regarding "heirs" as meaning "heirs in the tail." Its first appearance is in 1307[2] when, notwithstanding the counter-plea that the statute means heirs of the reversion, the court adjudged that the receipt be allowed. The next instance is the present case[3] when receipt was again allowed, after which nothing more appears until 1346 when the receipt of the issue in tail was refused[4]. The matter is further complicated by the fact that the

1 There is nothing to warrant Coke's restriction of the statute to tenants in tail after the possibility of issue extinct. 2 *Inst.* 345.

2 *Anon.* v. *Picot*, Y.B. 33 & 35 Edw. I, 496.

3 *Anon.*, Y.B. 5 Edw. II, I. 160–2; above, p. 45.

4 *Anon.* v. *Casse*, Y.B. 20 Edw. III, I. 136.

decisions we have quoted were regarded by contemporaries as based on a special case. The circumstances were as follows: A gift was made to *A* and *B* his wife and the heirs of their bodies. After *A*'s death *B* is impleaded and is about to lose by default. The heir of the bodies of *A* and *B* was regarded as having a particularly strong claim to being received to defend his right, according to STAUNTON, J. in *Anon.* v *Picot*, the early theory being that after *A*'s death *B* is a tenant for life, the fee residing in the issue. This strange notion only becomes intelligible in the light of the ancient learning about conditional fees and the then orthodox meaning of "issue" as issue in the first degree only[1]. With the advent of the modern sense of "issue" this view was abandoned, while at the same time second and better thoughts prevailed as to the position of *B* after *A*'s death. When we get to *Anon.* v. *Casse* in 1346 the receipt was refused on the grounds that *B* was not a tenant for life but tenant in tail[2].

The history of aid-prayer of the issue in tail follows a similar course but as it was based only upon analogy of the statute, and not upon its direct provisions, it does not need detailed discussion here. It will suffice to say that receipt is the stranger's remedy when the tenant refused to pray him in aid. When the tenant, therefore, made a *bona fide* defence and prayed aid, the same points of law were raised as if he neglected to do so and the stranger came and prayed to be received.

The case of *Chamberlain* v. *Ashwood*[3] contains some very illuminating discussion on the point we have been considering. The tenant claimed to have been enfeoffed to him and the heirs of his body, and since he asserted that such an heir existed, he therefore prayed aid of him as of one in whom the fee resided. *Spigurnel*, for the demandant, did not deny this doctrine, but counterpleaded the aid-prayer on other grounds (i.e. that the tenant should first vouch his feoffor). *Miggeley*, however, expanded the tenant's argument by saying that the tenant could not render the tenements without him in whom the fee reposed, and therefore should have aid of him when impleaded, while

[1] See below, page 51.
[2] *Anon.* v. *Casse*, Y.B. 20 Edw. III, I. 136.
[3] Y.B. 6 & 7 Edw. II (*Eyre of Kent*), III. 44.

Toudeby, also for the tenant, expressed in very clear terms the doctrine under our notice: "In the case where tenements are given in fee tail," he said, "and the grantee has issue, the fee is severed from the freehold, the fee is in the issue, and only the freehold is in the father." This expression is all the more remarkable since BRABAZON, J., a very famous judge, assented to it, so long as the issue prayed in aid was truly issue in tail (a fact which he seemed to regard as unproved in this case). At this point, unfortunately, the discussion breaks off, the tenant having recourse to the less interesting, although doubtless more reliable defence of estoppel by record.

CHAPTER II

THE INTENTION OF THE LEGISLATURE

IT was only gradually that the courts made a practice of examining the intention of a statute in order to find a clue to its interpretation, and only then as a result of a curious process of development which may be divided into three stages.

§ 1. *Intention known to the Judges as members of the Legislature*

The first of these lasts until the early years of Edward II's reign and represents the period during which the judiciary had no difficulty whatever in discussing the intention of the legislature since the judges themselves bore the principal share in law-making[1]. Examples already quoted may be supplemented with further details here: thus, in many quarters there was doubt as to whether Westminster II, c. 3 would allow the receipt of a wife to defend her right when her husband was about to surrender it, unless the writ against the husband mentioned her also[2]. HENGHAM, J. settled the matter at once by declaring the intention of the legislature—of which he was a member—"We agreed in Parliament that the wife if not named in the writ,

[1] See above, p. 21. For the work of the Judges in drafting post-Restoration Statutes see Sir Courtenay Ilbert's *Legislative Methods and Forms*, 78.

[2] The case was particularly difficult when the husband answered to a writ brought against him alone in respect of his wife's heritage and surrendered it collusively (*Neville* v. *Neville*, Y.B. 1 & 2 Edw. II, 78). In one case the wife was apparently received although not named in the writ (*Woodward* v. *Anon.*, Y.B. 33 & 35 Edw. I, 3–4). The chapter begins with the provision that where a husband has lost his wife's right by default, she may recover after his death by *Cui in Vita*, and forces the tenant to plead it according to the title alleged in the first writ "against the husband and wife," and if he cannot show such a title, the wife may recover: "Hoc observato" that if the husband absents himself and will not defend the wife's right or will surrender it, she may be received. The statute is clumsily worded, for the chapter opens with the assumption of the husband's death, but at the end of the very same sentence implies that he is alive. See 2 *Inst.* 342 where the later doctrine of discontinuance is employed to give the wife a recovery in such cases by *Novel Disseisin*. The injustice was not finally remedied until 32 Hen. VIII, c. 28 which allowed the wife to re-enter.

should not be received"[1]; and again, "Do not gloss the statute for we know better than you; we made it"[2]. It is noteworthy that when HENGHAM's inside knowledge of the legislature's intention is no longer available, the court is put to an examination of the wording of Westminster II, c. 3 and only after some difficulty reached the same conclusion—that the wife was only receivable if named in the writ[3]. So also when BRABAZON, C.J. was doubtful about the nature of *Scire Facias* as given by the Statute of Westminster II, c. 45 he said, "We will advise with our companions who were at the making of the statute"[4].

§ 2. *Intention known to the Judges through professional traditions*

This brings us to the second stage. The great HENGHAM had gone, but the court still relies on his teaching, although at second hand. In other words, there is now a tradition which preserves the intention of the legislator.

This can be illustrated from several cases based upon the statute *De Donis*, the application of which was attended by so many difficulties that its effect was for many years imperfectly

[1] *Anon.* v. *Thomas the Notary*, Y.B. 32 & 33 Edw. I, 429. The report continues with a discussion whether the University of Oxford could be received by attorney instead of "in person."

HENGHAM, J. "We agreed in parliament that they ought to be received by attorney, and we have here [seynz] a warrant, etc."

Wilby. "We pray *oyer* of that warrant."

HENGHAM, J. "You shall not have it." The attorney was received.

Mr Pike suggests that the Statute of Westminster II, c. 10 is the "warrant" in question, but neither that nor any other statute has much bearing on the case. There is evidence, however, in *Neville* v. *Neville*, Y.B. 1 & 2 Edw. II, 78, that the word "warrant" could be used to mean a statute. Westminster II, c. 10 only allows appearances by attorney in Eyre when the party is impleaded elsewhere, and cannot appear in two different counties at once, but there is nothing to suggest that the present case was in an Eyre. *Wilby's* demand that the warrant be read and HENGHAM's refusal, show that the warrant was not a public statute but more probably an agreement reached privately among the Judges in parliament during a discussion (whether formal or informal) of the matter in question. It is not unknown for parliament to have given a long hearing to one party in a case during the absence of the other (cf. above, p. 24). It is characteristic that the making of a public general statute and the secret arrangement of a private cause are so much alike that HENGHAM can describe them both in the words "we agreed in parliament."

[2] *Aumeye* v. *Anon.*, Y.B. 33 & 35 Edw. I, 82; Westminster II, c. 2.

[3] *Neville* v. *Neville*, Y.B. 1 & 2 Edw. II, 78, cf. *Bruce* v. *Horton*, Y.B. 6 & 7 Edw. II (*Eyre of Kent*), III. 199.

[4] *Bygot* v. *Ferrers*, Y.B. 33 & 35 Edw. I, 585; cf. below, p. 161.

understood. This may be seen from the interesting case of Formedon in the Reverter brought by Isabel *Ros* against William *Graa*[1]. The tenant pleaded in bar a deed with warranty by one T. an ancestor of Isabel, giving him the land. Isabel said that the deed should not bar her claim, for T. was a tenant in tail and could not alienate, by the statute. After much discussion a pleader remarked to SHARESHULLE, J. that "according to what you say, he in the descent would be barred[2] by the warranty of the tenant in tail"; whereupon SHARESHULLE replied,

> Perhaps so, for *Hilary* and I pleaded that before SCROPE, J. in the Eyre of Northampton because we had nothing better to say...and we were adjourned here before HERLE, J., and he said that the strongest argument he knew against us was that HENGHAM who made ["fist"] the statute read it another way[3].

Another remarkable case based upon the same statute illustrates most clearly the casual methods by which legislation was carried out, and the correspondingly wide discretion which was exercised of necessity by the courts in the early 14th century. The statute *De Donis* enacts that lands given upon "condition," i.e. entailed, cannot be alienated by the donee to the disinheritance of his issue or of the reversioner (in the event of the donee having no surviving issue nor heir of the body of such issue). As may be seen from the statute, the word "issue" at this date signified only heir of the body in the first degree and did not extend beyond the first generation[4]. The statute there-

[1] Y.B. 15 Edw. III, 388–394.

[2] If a tenant could show title by a deed with warranty of the demandant's ancestor, whose heir is the demandant, then the demandant is barred and can recover nothing; in other words, one cannot demand tenements which one is bound to warrant.

[3] No record or reported decision. The situation might arise in some such way as the following: a man grants land in tail male to his only son with reversion to himself and his heirs; the son enters, has issue a son and a daughter, and alienates to a stranger with warranty. On the death of the father, the son, and the male issue of the latter, we will suppose only the daughter to represent the line. The entail is therefore at an end, and the land must revert to the donor's heir—in this case his grand-daughter. She therefore brings Formedon in the Reverter against the stranger who attempts to bar her by her father's deed and warranty. The report does not make the descent clear, and has partially suppressed a forfeiture at some stage.

[4] Cf. *Pavely* v. *Pouer*, Y.B. 18 & 19 Edw. III, 142 where "the issue died without issue," and *Anon.* v. *Thomas the Notary*, where a gift was made "ad vitam Thomae et uxoris suae et liberorum primi exitus sui."

fore prevents the donee disinheriting his own "issue," but does not prevent the "issue" alienating. This point was raised in 5 Edw. II, in a case of Formedon in the Descender[1], and it was claimed that therefore the writ should abate. BEREFORD, C.J. did not deny that this was the literal meaning of the statute, but made the following remarkable speech:

He that made the statute meant to bind the issue in fee tail as well as the feoffees until the tail had reached the fourth degree, and it was only through negligence that he omitted to insert express words to that effect in the statute; therefore we shall not abate this writ.

In other words, BEREFORD is using some tradition or other private information as to the intention of the author of *De Donis* —which had been made a quarter of a century before—to set aside the plain statement of the act and to bind the issue's issue (of whom the statute says nothing) although only to the fourth degree (a limitation likewise entirely absent from the act), the explanation being that the illustrious HENGHAM who drafted the act forgot to insert these details[2]. This act has been called one of the pillars of English real property law, and if such extraordinary carelessness attended its erection we can hardly blame BEREFORD for carrying out this drastic piece of underpinning. BEREFORD's statement concerning the fourth degree becomes all the more significant when it is remembered that the rule he states may be suspected of Roman origin, coming, it would seem, from the 159th Novel of Justinian[3].

[1] *Belyng* v. *Anon.*, Y.B. 5 Edw. II, I. 176–7.

[2] To Mr Bolland's remarks on limitations to the fourth degree (*ibid. Introd.* xxv), may be added the anonymous case in Y.B. 30 & 31 Edw. I, 104, where it is said that "attracted" relationship (by the Statute of Gloucester, c. 6) can only take place within the fourth degree. For limitations to the fourth degree in feudal law see *Feud. de success. feudi*, § *hoc quoque observatur*. From the gloss *usque ad septimum* it appears that the rule was obsolete in the time of Jac. Columbus who was a contemporary of Azo and Lanfranc, it would seem (Savigny, *Gesch. d. Röm. Rechts*, v. 85). See also *eod. qui Feu. dare poss.* § *hoc quoque sciend. est*, where it is stated that the text of some manuscripts has been emended in consequence (*gl. gradum*). BEREFORD repeated his statement about the fourth degree in another anonymous case in Y.B. 5 Edw. II, II. 225. The point was still unsettled in *Bastard* v. *Somer*, Y.B. 4 Edw. III, No. 4 (Maynard's ed.) and even as late as 1344–5 there was still dispute as to how many generations were restrained from alienating by the statute (*Helton* v. *Brampton and others*, Y.B. 18 & 19 Edw. III, 198).

[3] In the old books this is Auth. Coll. ix. tit. viii. See Buckland, *Equity in Roman Law*, 90–1.

This was not the only occasion, however, upon which BEREFORD was ready to apply a heroic remedy. The Statute of Gloucester, c. 7, deals with the case where a woman alienates her dower, and gives the heir or reversioner his recovery during her life and without any obligation to fulfil the warranty, if any[1]. BEREFORD had already applied chapter 24 of Westminster II to this chapter 7, thus creating the writ of Entry *in Consimili Casu*, to recover alienations by tenants for life—a decision of the greatest importance[2]. Now a case arose in 11 Edw. II where a man sought to recover his ancestor's lands, held in tail, which had been alienated by his father with warranty. It would be useless to bring Formedon in the Descender, as he would be barred by his father's warranty, but if only he could get a writ in the nature of *in Consimili Casu* he could recover in spite of the warranty. He therefore invented what we may call a writ of Formedon in the Descender *in Consimili Casu*. The tenant immediately objected that the Statute of Gloucester says nothing of Formedon. But the intrepid Chief Justice came to the rescue. The Statute of Gloucester was now some forty years old, but BEREFORD was able to declare that

> the intention of him that made the statute was that the claimant should be aided [in the cases of hardship it deals with] by any writ.... Every case cannot be specifically provided for and a statute can only mention the hardest cases; it must be inferred that less hard cases are also covered by it[3].

There is nothing whatever in the statute to suggest that the cases it mentions are only intended as typical examples or that it expects the Judges to fill in others, so it must be presumed that BEREFORD is acting upon tradition[4].

3. *Intention Inferred from the Statute itself*

Tradition, however, was not to be had for many of the problems that arose, and consequently the courts had to take

[1] Thus differing from c. 3 which binds the heir to fulfil the warranty if his father has alienated lands held in curtesy.

[2] *Devereux* v. *Tuchet*, Y.B. 3 Edw. II, 16–19; *Stirkeland* v. *Brunolfshead*, *ibid.* 106–9.

[3] *Mauleverer* v. *Favelthorp*, Y.B. 11 Edw. II, 348 (Maynard's ed.) and Y.B. 6 & 7 Edw. II, xxiii, n. 2.

[4] For the influence of tradition upon interpretation, see below, p. 79.

the third step and infer the intention of the legislator solely from internal evidence in the statute. The practice had become more frequent by the 11th year of Edward III although we do find a single instance in 5 Edw. II where *Herle* asserted that Westminster II, c. 3 was made to shorten delays and that the proposal he was arguing against would create more delay[1]. In 11 & 12 Edw. III it was argued that a statute was made for the advantage of the plaintiff and therefore his writ should not be abated—which would be to his disadvantage; then in the important *Ascham's Case* SHARDELOWE, J. said that the intention of the first statute of 14 Edw. III, c. 17 was to enable ecclesiastical dignitaries who had no chapters or colleges to use the writ of *Utrum*, and adjudged that the statute applied to hospitals[2]. The Statute of Marlborough, c. 12 enacted that there should be specially short adjournments in cases of *Quare Impedit* in order that the judgment might be given upon litigation between the rival patrons of a vacant living before the bishop acquired his right to collate, which would happen if the living were vacant more than six months. *Stouford* argued that this ought not to apply to a *Quare Incumbravit*, which is brought after the bishop has admitted a presentee (in spite of the prohibition *Ne Admittas*[3]) and so the intention of the statute is no longer applicable. WILLOUGHBY, J. agreed with him and granted a common day[4].

In another case a man and wife brought (in right of the wife) a writ of Entry *in Consimili Casu*[5] to recover lands which a lessor had alienated in fee. The tenant objected that the husband was under age; to this the demandant replied that even so, his wife was of age, and the statute gave "immediate recovery" after the fraudulent alienation. Then the tenant tried to turn the words to his own advantage: as the statute gives "immediate recovery," he argued, it must be inferred that the statute intended the action to be brought immediately after the alienation but this

[1] *Plumberewe and Foghtlestone* v. *Montfort*, Y.B. 5 Edw. II, I. 210. *Herle* was unsuccessful.

[2] Y.B. 14 & 15 Edw. III, 42; *Reg. Br. Orig.* f. 33. SHARDELOWE himself had adjudged the opposite only the term before in *Anon.* v. *Master of St Mark's Hospital, Bristol*, Y.B. 14 Edw. III, 210–8.

[3] F.N.B. 48 H.

[4] *Anon.* v. *Bishop of Exeter*, Y.B. 17 & 18 Edw. III, 624.

[5] *Sybeling and others* v. *Mussendene and others*, *ibid.* 444–6, Statute of Gloucester, c. 7.

writ (which is in the *per* and *cui*) confesses that the land has changed owners twice since then, so the action has been delayed too long for this writ to be available. Precedent, however, was against him, and SHARESHULLE, J. made him answer over[1]. Even in those cases where the statute states its motive, it does not seem to have been taken very seriously. Thus the statute 4 Edw. III, c. 9 annuls the election of coroners "who have no lands whereby to answer all men." The writ customarily used, however, alleges the quite different reason of "having no lands whereby to maintain their state in exercising the office." The intention of the statute was to secure men of substance who would be able to reimburse those who might have suffered wrongly through their official acts (and incidentally be good security for the king's dues) but the writ seems to assume that it was primarily men of leisure who were required[2].

The results reached in the present chapter may be briefly stated in conclusion. First, the intention of the legislature was a matter of personal knowledge to the Judges in the earliest period, for they bore the chief part in the work of legislation. But there inevitably came a time when the great Judges of Edward I's day were no longer living, and the new generation of Judges could only learn the intentions that produced his epoch-making statutes from the tradition preserved among themselves. This forms a second stage and may be roughly dated from the death of HENGHAM in 1311. The third stage is that in which the Court infers the intention of the law-maker from the statute without the aid of personal knowledge, or professional tradition, and is only reached gradually and as the result of constitutional changes of wide-spreading importance.

§ 4. *The Institutional Aspect of this Development*

The lateness of this development is largely due to the close union of powers which rendered it at first unnecessary, while even later the courts were so willing to refer disputed points to

[1] *R. Thorpe* had also argued that *Quare ei Deforciat* was a parallel case, the writ only lying against the first alienee, but SHARESHULLE corrected him here, saying that during that year there was a case where a stranger had to answer and vouch the recoveror, Statute of Westminster II, c. 4. See also below, p. 74.

[2] *Reg. Br. Orig*. f. 177 *b*; App. 16. In these writs "14th year" is an error for "4th year."

the council or parliament that they would not feel the need for extending their technical equipment. One cannot expect a very highly developed science of interpretation until the courts are conscious of their isolation; when no outside help is to be expected from the legislature or the executive, and when the Judges no longer take so much part in the functions of government other than judicature, then the courts will have to accept statutes as the commands of an authority external to themselves whose will is known to them only as expressed in the written word[1]. Then, too, will be felt the necessity of devising some means for making a document a satisfactory substitute for the verbal explanations of one man to another—in short, scientific drafting and scientific interpretation will have begun.

[1] The change from verbal to written orders has been recognised as marking the beginning of a new era in industrial organisation (see for example, Denning, *Scientific Factory Management*, 35), but its significance in constitutional history has not yet been noted. In the realm of law the change from verbal instructions to Judges which was typical of the age before Henry III, to the written legislation of the 14th and succeeding centuries, can hardly be over-estimated. It is the difference between primitive and modern modes of government.

CHAPTER III

"EXCEPTIONS OUT OF THE STATUTE"

THE present and the two succeeding chapters will illustrate the extent to which the courts were prepared to take liberties with the new statute-law. The material is ample and many of the cases afford striking contrasts with the modern relations between the judiciary and the legislature. Instances are significantly more numerous before the reign of Edward III than afterwards —a fact that becomes of considerable importance when regarded in the light of similar conclusions which will appear later[1]. For the present, attention will be confined to those cases where the court restricts the scope of a statute by excepting particular cases from its operation although the statute itself contains little or nothing to warrant such a procedure. These are described in the older books[2] as "Exceptions out of the Statute."

§ 1. *Exceptions made in the Reign of Edward I*

Lands lost by default in certain circumstances may be recovered by an action on the Statute of Westminster II, c. 3—but METINGHAM, J. denied this remedy where the surrender had been made in the country and not in a court that bears record, although there is nothing in the act to suggest such a distinction[3]. Ten years later a case arose where a possessory writ of Cosinage had abated after view had, and the demandant then had recourse to the droiturel writ of *Precipe in Capite*. The tenant again prayed the view and had it by judgment of BEREWYKE, J. although the demandant pleaded the Statute of Westminster II, c. 48, which says that when view has been had in one writ which has been abated, it shall not be had again in a second writ. The reporter conjectured that the reason for the decision was that the statute only applies to writs of Entry and the like but not to a writ of

[1] Below, pp. 90, 124–6.

[2] 2 *Inst.* 25.

[3] *Anon.*, Y.B. 21 & 22 Edw. I, 128. For the record of things *in pais*, see *Anon.*, Y.B. 20 & 21 Edw. I, 236.

Right[1]. A woman had appealed a man of murdering her husband but finally waived the appeal. Thereupon prosecution was made at the king's suit and the accused was found not guilty. He then prayed the benefit of Westminster II, c. 12 which gives an inquest to discover those who had abetted the woman in her false appeal in order to recover from them damages for the imprisonment (the original appellant being unable to pay). BRABAZON, J. however refused to enquire of the abettment on the ground that the woman had since died—a contingency quite unforeseen in the statute[2].

In an assize of *Utrum*[3] the tenant's defence was that he had recovered by judgment upon default against the demandant's predecessor in an action of *Cessavit*. To the demandant's objection that his predecessor was only guardian as it were and that the church is always under age, the tenant replied that "the statute speaks generally" in saying that after judgment in *Cessavit* the tenements shall be lost for ever, concluding with the remark that "The judgment is specified by the statute, and we do not think that you have power to undo[4] this judgment which is given by common counsel." HENGHAM, J. had no such scruples, however, and adjudged that "the statute is to be understood as speaking only of the writ brought against one who is capable of losing, but that is not the case here"; he therefore ordered them to plead the *Utrum* as if it were the *Cessavit*. In the next reign the same defence was made to a writ of Right, but this time in spite of *Denham's* efforts it was adjudged that loss by default in a *Cessavit* was a bar, since the statute said the tenements should be "forfeit (*encoru*) for ever"[5].

Another instance of great importance was a decision on Westminster I, c. 40 which gives a demandant power to counterplea a voucher to warranty by the "tenant" against whom he is claiming. HENGHAM, J. held that the voucher of a reversioner by a tenant for life is not affected by the statute "which is only

[1] *Aldan and others* v. *Engleys*, Y.B. 30 & 31 Edw. I, 235; the explanation is not easy to accept, for the statute expressly applies to Dower, which is in the nature of a writ of Right. (1 Roscoe, *Real Actions*, 39.)

[2] *Anon.*, Y.B. 32 & 33 Edw. I, 171.

[3] *Wilby* v. *Vottone*, Y.B. 32 & 33 Edw. I, 450; Statute of Gloucester, c. 4.

[4] Not "delay" as in the Editor's translation.

[5] *Greetham* v. *Lung*, Y.B. 8 Edw. II, 214. For *encoru* see below, p. 127, n. 1.

to be understood of voucher in fee simple"[1]. The statute makes no qualification of the estate by virtue of which the tenant vouches, but the "exception" may be justified by the general principle that tenants who only have "weak" estates cannot plead as "high up" as the statute implies, while the vouching of a reversioner by a tenant for life does not involve going out of the degree.

Westminster II, c. 40 removed a great hardship from women who used *Cui in Vita* to recover their heritage when alienated during their coverture. By the old law the alienee could vouch the husband's heir to warranty and then the action would demur until the heir was of age—usually a considerable period, the alienee retaining the lands in the meantime. The statute enacts that in such a case the widow shall receive seisin at once, and "let the purchaser (who ought not to have been ignorant that he was buying the right of another) tarry until the vouchee is of age." The question arises as to whether the statute only applies to the first purchaser who bought direct from the husband or whether it applies to all subsequent purchasers. In this case the decision was that it applied only to the first purchaser, in spite of a precedent quoted by the demandant from the Rolls of a case in his favour[2].

A creditor by statute merchant whose debtor dies cannot detain his lands during the minority of the heir—they must go to the guardian; but when the heir is of age the statute gives to his creditor all the debtor's lands "into whosesoever hands they have come by feoffment or otherwise." It appears, however, that the court allows a widow to retain her dower assigned to her by the debtor, notwithstanding the words of the statute[3]. It is typical of the age that such an important—and obvious—point as this was left unprovided for by the statute.

[1] *Anon.*, Y.B. 32 & 33 Edw. I, 189; STAUNTON, J. gave the same decision in *Taverner* v. *Anon.*, Y.B. 6 & 7 Edw. II (*Eyre of Kent*), II. 8.

[2] *Anon.*, Y.B. 33 & 35 Edw. I, 242. At various times the following "exceptions" have been made: the voucher of an infant by a tenant by warranty (*Anon.*, Y.B. 18 & 19 Edw. III, 488); lands alienated before the statute (*Anon.*, Y.B. 21 & 22 Edw. I, 476; *Rote* v. *Anon.*, Y.B. 32 & 33 Edw. I, 480); voucher of an infant by the heir of the first purchaser (*Bernewyne* v. *Alkeshille*, Y.B. 16 Edw. III, II. 46); voucher of infant by the first purchaser's assign (*Anon.*, Y.B. 6 & 7 Edw. II (*Eyre of Kent*), II. 149).

[3] *Anon.*, Y.B. 33 & 35 Edw. I, 293.

When the lands of infant tenants-in-chief fell into the wardship of the Crown they were frequently made over to a subject either by grant or gift of the king. In such a case, if the guardian were impleaded by the widow for her dower, or the heir vouched to warranty, he would, by the old law, say that "he cannot answer without consulting the king"—which meant indefinite delay. The statute *De Bigamis*, c. 3, therefore ordained that henceforth he should answer without the king. A case arose, however, where the wardship was held at the king's will by an annual rent. The heir having been vouched pleaded that he could not answer without the king, whereupon the demandant prayed that the case should not be delayed, but proceed at once according to the statute. It appeared to the court, however, that if this course were adopted and the tenant of the wardship had to surrender some land, his profit would be less, and yet he would still be liable to the crown for the rent. It was therefore held that in such a case the court ought not to proceed until the king had been consulted[1]. Much the same point arose thirty years later, and again the court allowed a guardian (this time the lessee of the wardship) to have aid of the king[2]. The statute has only twice been discussed in our reports and, as we have shown, it was in each case set aside by the court.

§ 2. *Exceptions made in the Reign of Edward II*

Coming to the reign of Edward II, we find that a lord attempted to distrain his tenant within his own fee; the tenant took to flight, driving his beasts away. The lord pursued the tenant and levied the distress at the place where he overtook him, which place was outside the lord's fee. In Replevin proceedings it was argued that this distress was illegal, for the Statute of Marlborough forbids lords to distrain outside their fees. The court held that this case was not within the statute, and allowed the lord to avow the distress[3].

A frequent exception to a writ was that of Joint-Feoffment, whereby the tenant declared that he had nothing in the lands in question save jointly with another person who was not named

[1] *Gatton* v. *Norwood*, Y.B. 6 & 7 Edw. II (*Eyre of Kent*), II. 76.
[2] *Basset* v. *du Le*, Y.B. 18 & 19 Edw. III, 104 (31).
[3] *Kirkman* v. *Lelly*, Y.B. 8 Edw. II, 88.

in the writ—the consequence being that the writ abated and a new one had to be obtained. Unfortunately it was easy to use the exception merely as a means of impeding justice, for although the tenant on receiving the writ might have been sole tenant, yet it was easy for him to convey the land to a friend, who would re-convey it to the tenant and another person (frequently his wife) jointly; thus by the time they came into court they could produce the charter of joint-feoffment and so abate the writ. As a remedy for this fraud it was enacted in 34 Edw. I that if the plaintiff was willing to aver by the country that on the day he bought the writ the tenant was "sole tenant, so that neither his wife, nor any other had anything in the said lands" then the tenant is compelled to take issue on this averment. An assize of *Novel Disseisin*[1] was brought by Bampton against two defendants of whom one was Ross. The discussion in court followed these lines:

R. I have nothing in the lands save jointly with my wife.
B. I will aver that she had nothing on the day of writ purchased.
R. Then you must offer the averment as the statute gives it, and say that I was sole tenant.
B. I cannot do that; it would abate my writ for there were other tenants and my writ mentions them with you.

The statute, in fact, will only work where there is only one tenant named in the writ. The court therefore received *B.*'s first averment and treated it as though it were the one given by the statute.

§ 3. *Exceptions made in the Reign of Edward III*

Not all the cases however needed such drastic treatment as the last, although the judges still thought fit to exercise their discretion upon them. The Statute of Marlborough, c. 4 clearly makes it a serious trespass to drive beasts distrained in one county into another county, but nevertheless STONORE, J. and the whole court agreed that the statute would not apply if the beasts were driven into another county as long as it was all

[1] *Bampton* v. *Bolham and Ross*, Y.B. 6 & 7 Edw. II (*Eyre of Kent*), III. 131; there are traces of more than two defendants, but the report has simplified the facts somewhat.

part of one liberty extending into the two shires[1]. This may be compared with another case where a statute enables a demandant to prevent the tenant from vouching to warranty by offering a certain averment, but SHARDELOWE, J. held that if the voucher had been allowed in a previous plea it could not afterwards be counterpleaded by offering the statutory averment[2]—which might mean that if an unskilful advocate allowed the voucher once he would have to allow it in all subsequent litigation. Even *Magna Carta* itself was not taken too seriously by the courts; thus, an assize might be taken outside of the proper county if the latter is in the liberty of a lord who possesses regalia, on the ground that he cannot do justice in his own case[3]. Similarly, the chapter saying that common pleas shall not follow the King, although regularly held to imply that the King's Bench cannot hold a plea of land[4], was not always obeyed. "In certain cases all pleas are pleadable in this court," said SHARESHULLE, Chief Baron of the Exchequer, while sitting in the King's Bench[5], and there is some evidence to illustrate his statement[6]. Nor was the court of Common Pleas always stationary, as *Magna Carta* was held to require, for we read of considerable inconveniences due to its visit to York[7]. Again, the Statute of Gloucester, c. 1 enacts that the demandant in the possessory assizes shall have damages when he recovers; but we find this general rule limited by the courts to those cases in which the recovery is by judgment upon the verdict of the inquest, or upon a point of law—thus

[1] *Fourneux* v. *Prior of Blythe*, Y.B. 14 Edw. III, 88. Cf. *Anon.*, Y.B. 33 & 35 Edw. I, 252 where the difficulty due to the manor extending into two counties was avoided by taking issue on the maliciousness of the driving.

[2] *Anon.*, Y.B. 14 Edw. III, 40; Westminster I, c. 40.

[3] *Anon.*, Fitz. *Assize*, 382; *Magna Carta*, c. 12; cf. *R.* v. *Prior of Pembroke*, Y.B. 15 Edw. III, 148.

[4] *Thorpe*, arguing, in *Nutil* v. *Kyllum*, Y.B. 14 & 15 Edw. III, 144; *Magna Carta*, c. 11.

[5] *R.* v. *Hovel*, Y.B. 19 Edw. III, 142.

[6] *Prior of Kenilworth* v. *Anon.*, Y.B. 16 Edw. III, II. 445; *Anon.*, Y.B. 19 Edw. III, 104. Although assizes of *Mort d'Ancestor* might not follow the King, they were nevertheless liable to follow the Judges in their tour round the country, this being permitted by *Magna Carta*, c. 12. Cf. *Montgomery* v. *Anon.*, Y.B. 20 & 21 Edw. I, 270, which began at Hereford and ended at Shrewsbury.

[7] Y.B. 11 & 12 Edw. III, xxviii; Y.B. 12 & 13 Edw. III, xxxv, lxiii n, 16 (10); Y.B. 6 & 7 Edw. II, xxiv; *Magna Carta*, c. 11).

excluding default[1]. Similarly, the same statute includes Entry *Sur Disseisin* among the actions it affects, but HILARY, J. seemed uncertain at first as to whether he should award a writ to inquire of damages when the defendant had departed in contempt of the Court[2]. This attitude is all the more remarkable as it provides a disseisor with an easy escape from the penalties of the statute.

Toward the end of our period a remarkable case occurred of voucher in a writ of Entry within the degrees. The Statute of Westminster I, c. 40 is clear: "In all manner of writs of entry which make mention of the degrees none shall vouch out of the line." In the present case the tenant defaulted twice so that a stranger (outside the degrees) was admitted by judgment to defend his right which was at the point of being lost by the default in his absence. Having been admitted, the stranger vouched to warranty another stranger who was also out of the line. The demandant immediately counterpleaded the voucher saying that the statute forbids absolutely voucher out of the degrees. To this it was replied that "The statute is to be understood of one who can abate the writ, but it does not apply to a stranger intervening." WILLOUGHBY, J. then told the demandant that the voucher would be allowed unless he said something else —in short, the words of the statute "none shall vouch, etc." are held only to apply to those who could abate the writ[3]. The discussion is briefly reported and no reason is given, but we may surmise that the exception out of the statute worked for justice since the admission of a stranger would show that the degrees mentioned by the demandant in the writ were false; it would therefore be unjust when the rightful owner intervenes, to prevent him vouching because his feoffor is not in the degrees which were wrongly laid in the writ—most probably on purpose to exclude him.

The next year an exception was made out of the Statute of Marlborough, c. 7 which gives a specially stringent process, i.e. Proclamation, against the deforciant of a wardship who, when

[1] *Anon.*, Y.B. 6 & 7 Edw. II (*Eyre of Kent*), II. 2.

[2] *Anon.*, Y.B. 16 Edw. III, I. 180. It would seem from the report (which is not very clear) that it was only one out of several defendants who left in contempt of the Court.

[3] *Gille* v. *Anon.*, Y.B. 18 & 19 Edw. III, 134.

impleaded, makes default after the issue of the grand distress. In this case there were two deforciants against whom the writ was brought. Process was continued as far as the grand distress, to which the sheriff returned that one had been distrained, but the other had no distrainable property. Both defaulted. The plaintiff therefore prayed the issue of proclamation according to the statute. This the court refused on the ground that the one who had nothing could not be held to have been distrained—this is obvious; and secondly, the one who had been distrained could not be proclaimed unless the other was—of which there is nothing in the statute. Again the statute had failed to make provision for a case that might easily have been foreseen[1].

It seems generally to have been assumed that statutes do not apply to the ancient demesne of the Crown. Thus Bereford, C.J. refused to hear a case on Westminster II, c. 2 where a lord would have forced his tenant to disclaim in the Court of Common Pleas, saying that the land was ancient demesne; it so happened that the lord suffered no wrong by this decision for a disclaimer in a court of ancient demesne was sufficiently of record to bar the tenant[2]. In another case we read that

> The defendant said that at common law a man might levy a distress as well on beasts of the plough as on other beasts; and the statute says naught of ancient demesne, and ancient demesne is not known to the common law, and the judges were of opinion that the writ did not run in ancient demesne[3].

[1] *Anon.* v. *Braybroke and another*, Y.B. 19 Edw. III, 122. For another report of the same case see below, p. 87, n. 4.

[2] *Barker* v. *Dudekyn*, Y.B. 3 & 4 Edw. II, 15–7; the operation of the statute has been illustrated above, p. 40.

[3] *Noreis* v. *Northcott*, Y.B. 5 Edw. II, II. 76–8; *Estatut del Eschekere* (*Stats. Realm*, I. 197 *b*). The peculiarity of ancient demesne lay more in the soil than in the tenants, for they are at Common Law for personal actions (Britton, II. 13). An interesting discussion of ancient demesne will be found in *Abbot of Burton* v. *Earl of Lancaster*, Y.B. 2 & 3 Edw. II, 59. One cannot have *Elegit* (under Westminster II, c. 18) of land in ancient demesne (*St Quentin* v. *Anon.*, Y.B. 20 Edw. III, II. 520 (99)), and the provisions of the Statute of Merchants can only be enforced against such lands in ancient demesne as are alienable without the lord's leave (*Pykerel* v. *de la Lee*, Y.B. 1 & 2 Edw. II, 92, 192). There is a short *Tractatus de Antiquo Dominico* printed in Y.B. 20 & 21 Edw. I, xix where it is attributed to Aunger of Ripon (a manuscript in the Salt Library, Stafford, ascribes the work to Ralf de Hengham). For the application of statutes to the palatinates see Crompton, *Jurisdiction of the Courts*, f. 158 *b*.

This remarkable freedom with which the courts treated statutes in the cases mentioned above must be compared with the complete absence of any technique of legislation: judges certainly bore their part in drafting statutes, and in many cases they showed ingenuity and resource, but it must be confessed that often they are clumsily drawn and would be unworkable in many cases but for the free use of judicial discretion.

CHAPTER IV

REFUSAL OF THE COURTS TO APPLY STATUTES

In the preceding chapter[1] we called attention to the fact that on each of the only two occasions when a certain statute was mentioned in our reports, the court declined to apply it, and other examples must now be considered of cases where the judges refused to apply the statute. Excepting a particular case out of a statute was doubtless a frequent necessity if it was to be applied in circumstances for which the legislature had made no provision, and it was only one step further for judges to except all cases out of a statute, so as to leave it inoperative.

§ 1. *The Statute of Gloucester*, *c.* 4, *and* Cessavit

Thus, although the Statute of Gloucester, c. 4 enabled a tenant in *Cessavit* to save his land from being adjudged to his lord by offering to pay the arrears of service and damages, nevertheless the court held that a tender of the arrears without the damages was sufficient for the purpose[2]. Moreover, as Westminster II, c. 21 amends this statute, it extends the lord's right of action to his heir after the lord's death. Bereford, C.J. however, refused to maintain an heir's action by the statute on the grounds that:

(1) The statute allows the tenant to save his land by tendering arrears, but an heir has no right to arrears due to his ancestor, since they should go to the ancestor's executors;
(2) As the heir has no right to receive the arrears which are the cause of action he can take nothing by his writ[3].

This technical difficulty had apparently escaped the notice of Hengham and the other judges who drafted the statute, but it was felt to be so great that Willoughby affirmed the judgment half a century later and it became the settled law on the matter[4].

[1] Above, page 60.
[2] *Anon.*, Y.B. 32 & 33 Edw. I, 462.
[3] *Copper* v. *Gederings*, Y.B. 3 Edw. II, 105.
[4] *Anon.*, Fitz. *Cessavit*, 42; F.N.B. 209 F; 8 Rep. 118; 2 *Inst.* 404 (cf. 460).

§ 2. *Writs* "Non Omittas"

When the owner of a franchise who had "return of writs" neglected to make prompt return to them, the course of justice was seriously delayed, for until the writs were served and returned nothing could be done, the sheriff having no right to enter the liberty to execute the writ himself. The Statute of Westminster II, c. 39 therefore enacted that in such a case where the sheriff reported that the bailiff of a liberty refused to execute a writ, there should issue a fresh writ commanding the sheriff not to desist ("*Non Omittas*") on account of any liberty from executing the writ himself, providing, moreover, when once in any plea a writ *Non Omittas* has been issued, that then all subsequent writs shall be in the form of *Non Omittas* as well[1]. The statute is perfectly clear, and was duly pleaded by *Burton* in 1314 in applying for a judicial writ with the clause *Non Omittas*. No argument is reported and no reason can be assigned for the decision of the court, which was a curt refusal to insert the clause. The fact that this judgment was given by Chief-Justice BEREFORD may be regarded as significant, however[2].

§ 3. *The "Bill of Exceptions"*

The Statute of Westminster II, c. 31 seems to have been particularly distasteful to the judges. It provided that if anyone put forward an exception which the judges refused to allow, he could write it down and present it to them and they must seal it. If a writ of error is subsequently brought upon that exception and it is found that the exception is not recorded, then the bill so sealed shall be sufficient warrant for the action as if it were the record, after the judges have confessed their seals. Litigants seem to have had considerable difficulty in getting bills sealed. Judges began by holding that if they enrol the exception they need not seal a bill, but this is not to be found in the statute, which on the contrary clearly anticipates that in some cases the exception may be found on the roll as well as in the bill, and provides rather a duplicate than an alternative record. Parties were often forced to have recourse to strongly worded writs from

[1] This provision does not yet seem to have received enough attention from the constitutional point of view.

[2] *Scut* v. *Scut*, Y.B. 8 Edw. II, 97.

the Chancery ordering judges to fulfil the statute[1], and on one occasion HENGHAM, J. was commanded to appear in person "devant le corps le Roy" to show why he refused to seal a bill[2]. Besides the offer to enrol the exception judges in one case offered the party "the testimony of the whole court"—as if that could be made a ground for proceedings in error[3], while even the court's promise to enrol an exception could not be relied upon, for in at least one case it was broken[4].

A most important consequence of the statute *De Donis* would have been that the wife of a tenant in tail who died without issue would not be entitled to dower, for the statute says that the whole gift shall immediately revert to the donor, but nevertheless she was allowed to recover her dower[5]. The Statute of Marlborough, c. 7 says that although a man lose a wardship by default after proclamation nevertheless his action is saved to him to recover it afterwards if he have any right to it, but HILARY, J. declared that "if a man lose by proclamation he shall not have an action for the same wardship"[6]. After this frank statement one need not be surprised to find that a statutory regulation of the law of essoins was liable to be quietly ignored[7].

§ 4. *Tregor's Case*

A case of much less historical value has succeeded in securing more attention than it deserves to the exclusion of those mentioned above owing to the prominence given to it by Coke. The Statute of Westminster II, c. 38 forbids sheriffs to put poor, infirm or non-resident persons on juries and petty assizes, since this practice caused much delay to litigants by making it difficult for them to get sufficient jurors, and therefore orders that officials convicted under the statute shall pay damages to the party aggrieved as well as fine to the King. The ninth chapter of the

[1] *Reg. Br. Orig.* f. 182; in Y.B. 12 & 13 Edw. III, ciii–civ, 47–9 (*Earl of Devon* v. *Lucy*) Pike remarks on the use of the Royal prerogative in these writs of *Mandamus* to secure the observance of a statute.

[2] *Anon.* v. *Parson of St Mary's, East Salenam*, Y.B. 33 & 35 Edw. I, 138.

[3] *Scoland* v. *Grandison*, Y.B. 6 & 7 Edw. II (*Eyre of Kent*), I. 175–6.

[4] *Stonore* v. *Abbot of Buckfastleigh*, Y.B. 20 Edw. III, I. 242.

[5] *Herle* arguing, in *Anon.* v. *Prior of Bridlington*, Y.B. 5 Edw. II, II. 82–4. This became the established law, Lit. s. 36; Digby, 166, n. 7 gives the later explanation.

[6] *Anon.*, Y.B. 16 Edw. III, I. 94.

[7] *Anon.*, Y.B. 19 Edw. III, 206 (38); Westminster II, c. 27.

Articuli super Cartas confirms this and increases the penalty to double damages and "grievous" fine. It will be observed that neither the statute nor the article makes any mention of the recovery of lands lost by the verdict of an insufficient jury. Thomas *Tregor*, however, brought a writ against *W. Vaughan*, Sheriff of Sussex, calling upon him to show why, in spite of the article, he had put insufficient, remote, and suspect men on an inquest in a plea of land, whereby the land was lost[1]. After some discussion resulting in the decision that the sheriff's offence was none the less an offence because the jury was by consent of the parties and was not challenged by either of them, the following debate is reported:

HERLE, J. "What do you want—double damages, or what?"

Parning. "That, Sir, remains for you to decide, but the statute is useless if we do not have our recovery."

HERLE, J. "There are some statutes made which even the maker would not wish put into effect, but this statute can be understood to mean that in the case where the demandant's suit is delayed by the sheriff's return, he can recover damages against him by a certain statute, and also in the case where the tenant has lost the land by the verdict of such an inquest and has brought attaint against them, thereby attainting them and recovering the land, he can then get damages against the sheriff, and etc."

HERLE's reading therefore is that the statute gives damages for delay, but he says nothing of giving recovery of the land save by the old action of attainting the dishonest jurors; his construction is therefore obviously well within the statute. Coke tried to make the case prove that "In many cases the common law will control acts of Parliament and sometimes adjudge them to be utterly void," but was unsuccessful, in spite of shamelessly misquoting the report. Still, an attempt has been made to revive Coke's doctrine by Professor McIlwain who in discussing this case shows that Coke has several times quoted HERLE's first sentence thus: "Some statutes are made *against law and right*, which those who made them *perceiving*, would not put them into execution." Coke's modern apologist explains the interpolations italicized by saying that Coke "clearly considered that HERLE's

[1] Y.B. Pasch. 8 Edw. III, 26.

words could mean only one thing, and that the addition of the words 'against law and right' in no way changed their original sense"[1], a confession, surely, that Coke clearly misunderstood them. But whatever the meaning of HERLE's first sentence, it is of little consequence, for as we have shown he immediately interpreted the statute in a perfectly reasonable manner and drew nothing startling or unexpected from his premise. Finally, there is nothing in the report about a "controlling common law" which adjudges statutes to be "utterly void." Even accepting Coke's version of HERLE's speech, the "controlling" is by the legislator, not by the courts as representing the Common Law. In fact, the fairest gloss that can be put upon HERLE's words is that of Lord Ellesmere whose comment was: "It is *magis congruum* that Acts of Parliament should be corrected by the same pen that drew them, than be dashed to pieces by the opinion of a few Judges"[2]. HERLE evidently had in mind some example of hasty legislation soon repented, and Lord Ellesmere was not unnaturally reminded of the ancient doctrine, noticed above[3], that statutes were best interpreted by their makers.

§ 5. *The Absence of Constitutional Theory*

The above are the only cases in our period at all suggestive of the theory that the courts could, upon occasion, disregard the plain words of a statute. Two points must be emphasised. First, the courts undoubtedly did disregard statutes when they thought fit, and secondly, they expressed no principle of jurisprudence or political theory which would serve as an explanation—still less as a reason—for their attitude. The evidence has been recited here with as little gloss as possible, and the absence of any discussion in the reports of the juridical and constitutional questions involved is really its most significant feature. Only one explanation is possible, and put quite simply it is this—that such questions as these were not asked during our period. If reasons of however great technicality made it desirable to neglect some words of a statute, then they were quietly set aside, but in doing so neither counsel nor judges enquired into the nature of statutes and legislation, the sovereignty of Parliament, the

[1] McIlwain, *High Court of Parliament*, 288.

[2] Quoted in 2 Dwarris, 643.

[3] Above, p. 21.

supremacy of the Common Law, the functions of the judicature, and all the other questions which the modern mind finds so absorbingly interesting. They made no fuss about it, either. No sensational judgment that a statute was "void," no thrilling vindication of the Common Law and *Magna Carta*, nothing of the judges' professional pride as Coke felt it, will be found in these cases. The reporters note them in just the same way as all the other cases, and with as little expression of surprise or question. It is needless to pretend that such a state of mind is easy to imagine, but on the other hand it is not impossible in these days when historians recognise the value and the necessity of thinking in unfamiliar dimensions. We shall be getting nearest the truth, it seems, when we remember that the 14th century was in urgent need of good law, firmly enforced, for then we shall understand that the judges' great preoccupation was to apply the best law they knew as courageously as they could, and that our modern difficulties, whether political or juridical, to them would have seemed, if not unintelligible, at least irrelevant and pedantic.

CHAPTER V

EXTENSION OF THE WORDS OF A STATUTE

The two preceding chapters have shown the activities of the courts in the direction of imposing limitations upon statutes which they believed were too widely drawn, but the converse operation was equally frequent and will form the subject of the present chapter which will provide several striking examples of virtual legislation by the judges.

§ 1. *Extension of Statutory Actions to the Heirs, Executors and Assigns of Principals*

Thus, a statute gives a special process when the action of Debt is brought against the debtor's executors, but the court twice adjudged that the statute would apply also to Detinue, a closely related action, it is true[1], but certainly outside the words of the statute.

A point of much difficulty at the time was the question whether an action could be brought by or against the successors, assigns, alienees or executors of parties who are affected by a statute, and the answers given were not always consistent or referable to any general principle. In one case[2] we even find it stated that the executors of a creditor by a statute merchant obtained execution of the bond although the Statute of Merchants contains no provision in favour of either heirs or executors. In another case[3] the discussion arose over the Statute of Westminster II, c. 16 which gives a preferential right to the wardship of an heir's body to that lord from whom the tenant holds by the earliest feoffment, the question being whether the wardship would also belong to one to whom such a lord had granted the tenant's services. *Herle* had argued that "the words of the statute must be taken in their

[1] 9 Edw. III, st. 1, c. 3; *Warde* v. *Executors of Wullesthorpe*, Y.B. 17 Edw. III, 142; *Anon.*, Y.B. 17 & 18 Edw. III, 516.

[2] *Anon.*, Y.B. 13 & 14 Edw. III, 328 (49), Fitz. *Executours*, 86. Both these reports imply that the date of the case is 14 Edw. III and there is no reason for doubting it. The action was formally given by 25 Edw. III, st. 5, c. 5.

[3] *Stapledon* v. *Stapledon*, Y.B. 1 & 2 Edw. II, 60.

certainty so that the wardship belongs to him of whom the ancestors of the tenant held by the more ancient feoffment"[1]—and clearly, the tenant's ancestors held nothing of the recent grantee of the services. But BEREFORD told him "that the statute is to be understood otherwise, that is to say, whether the estate has accrued by purchase or by ancestry." This decision enables the reporter to deduce the excellent rule that "purchase of the lordship does not change the priority, but purchase of the tenancy changes the seignory." This remained the law in Edward III's reign[2]. Similarly, where the Statute of Westminster II, c. 35 makes special provision for the continuation of the action of Ravishment of Wardship upon the death of either of the parties, the statute was also applied to other actions, such as Wardship[3].

A tenant being impleaded[4], said he was the assignee of a certain person, in virtue of which fact he then vouched two infants to warranty. The demandant, however, did not counterplead the estate of the vouchees by saying that neither they nor their ancestors had ever been so seised that they could have enfeoffed the tenant (all which is set forth in the statute), but instead, offered this same statutory counterplea in respect of the estate of the assignor, who, he alleged, had never been seised of

[1] This seems to be the sense, the text is "les paroulles del estatut si serrount mys en certain, issint qe celuy de qui auncestres le tenaunt tient par plus anncien feffement a lui appent la garde." Maitland renders "de qui auncestres" by "of whose ancestors" and makes "tenaunt" the subject of "tient." (Note that MS *P.* also does this with disastrous results.) But *Herle* clearly insists on a literal construction of the statute, and his remark only conveys this idea accurately when we translate "auncestres le tenaunt" by "the ancestors of the tenant" (the omission of "de" is frequent in French of this style and date) and make "auncestres"—for it must be done—the subject of "tient." Law-French had already begun to be less a language than a cypher for embodying legal learning, and its symbols must be understood in the light of good law rather than of good grammar. The law of the case leaves no doubt as to *Herle's* meaning. Moreover, there are the words of the statute, "ille dominus habeat maritagium de quo antecessor suus prius fuit feoffatus" and Maitland himself has explained in a footnote that "antecessor suus" means "antecessor tenentis"—which is exactly what *Herle* meant by "auncestres le tenaunt." (For French as a system of legal notation, see the quotations by Maitland from the *Lives of the Norths* in Y.B. 1 & 2 Edw. II, xxxiv, notes 1 and 2.)

[2] *Anon.*, Y.B. 12 & 13 Edw. III, 352.

[3] *Abbot of Croyland* v. *de Vere*, Y.B. 17 & 18 Edw. III, 482, where *R. Thorpe* argued the contrary but without success.

[4] *Anon.*, Y.B. 11 & 12 Edw. III, 374–6; Westminster I, c. 40.

the lands since the date of the gift upon which he based his claim. This was clearly outside of the statute, but nevertheless HILARY, J. drove the tenant to take issue upon the seisin of the assignor in spite of protests by the assignee that he had the estate of his assignor, which estate could not be counterpleaded. In short, where the statute compelled parties to take issue upon one fact, the court drove them to take issue upon a different fact. It will be seen from the report[1] that HILARY made no pretence that this was within the statute or even warranted by it. His point of view seems rather to have been that the statute had laid down a principle in one case which could be extended with advantage to a different case. He therefore had no scruple in depriving the tenant of his warranty and forcing him to accept a particular issue, without making even a formal appeal to the statute, relying solely upon his own discretion, and regarding the statute as the recommendations of an advisory body instead of the command of the sovereign legislature. Similarly, where the Statute of Marlborough, c. 9 speaks of ancestors, it seems generally understood that purchasers have as good an answer[2].

It was long a matter of debate whether the action of *Quod ei Deforciat* lay against one to whom the deforciant had alienated the tenement. A clever discussion in 1310 led to no decision, and in 11 Edw. III, HILARY, J. refused to maintain such a writ; doubts reappeared five years later, and it was not until 1344 that SHARESHULLE, J. declared that "within this year the writ has been seen maintained against a stranger who vouched the original deforciant"[3]. By chapter 4 of *Magna Carta* those to whom the wardship of a tenant in chief had been "committed" or "granted" were forbidden to do waste on pain of answering for it to the king: this was held sufficient warrant for giving the heir (not the king) an action of waste against one of the executors of a lessee of a wardship, BEREFORD regarding it as a "personal trespass"[4].

[1] See below, Appendix, p. 181,

[2] *Passeley*, arguing, in *Heslartone* v. *Saluayn*, Y.B. 6 Edw. II, 53.

[3] Westminster II, c. 4; *Walding* v. *Fairfax*, Y.B. 3 & 4 Edw. II, 104–110; *Anon.*, Y.B. 11 & 12 Edw. III, 128; *Vilers* v. *Wolvershey*, Y.B. 16 Edw. III, II. 518; *Sybeling and others* v. *Mussendene and others*, Y.B. 17 & 18 Edw. III, 446; 2 *Inst.* 352.

[4] *Durnel* v. *Beauchamp*, Y.B. 3 Edw. II, 89–91.

§ 2. *Extension of Specific Words to include others* Eiusdem Generis

The statute 14 Edw. III, st. 1, c. 17 gives the writ of *Utrum* for chantries, and in *Ascham's Case* this was held to include hospitals[1], while Westminster II, c. 5 which mentions "chapels, prebends, vicarages, hospitals, abbeys, priories, and other houses" was generally understood to apply to chantries also[2]. Where *Magna Carta*, c. 33 mentions abbeys, priories are also held to be included[3], and the Statute of Merton, c. 10 which allows the appointment of a general attorney for all suits in county, tithing, hundred, wapentake, and seignorial courts, was regarded as allowing a general attorney for pleas in eyre—a vastly more important matter[4].

§ 3. *Extension of Receipt by Westminster II, c.* 3

These, however, are by no means all or even the most important of the directions in which the court went in extending the application of statutes, for the principle as well as the detail was subject to such extension or restriction as the judges thought expedient—but more frequently, it will be observed, in the reign of Edward I than of his grandson. In the earliest published Year Book, for example, there is a striking instance to be found based on the Statute of Westminster II, c. 3 which provides that when a tenant in dower, curtesy, tail, or for life is impleaded and is about to suffer a collusive recovery, the reversioner may be received to defend his right. In this case the statute was held to authorise the receipt of a lessor who had only a life estate when his lessee for a term of years was impleaded and made default[5]. It will be recognised that this is more than the extension of a small detail, for the law of the time had fixed a great

[1] Y.B. 14 & 15 Edw. III, 42–50; it was also held in *Anon.*, Y.B. 17 & 18 Edw. III, 416, that the words "perpetual chantries" cover those annexed to chapels as well as those annexed to churches.

[2] *Reg. Br. Orig.* f. 31; cf. *Tenery* v. *Parson of Sawley and others*, Y.B. 17 Edw. III, 198.

[3] *Reg. Br. Orig.* f. 162 *b*; cf. f. 171 *b* for another writ "which is not in the statute...but can be maintained by it."

[4] *Reg. Br. Orig.* f. 266. Cf. Y.B. 6 & 7 Edw. II, xi–xvii. The doubt expressed in *Reg. Br. Orig.* f. 9, as to whether one may appear by attorney in Court Baron, seems settled in the affirmative by Westminster II, c. 10 provided that an Eyre is in progress.

[5] *Anon.*, Y.B. 20 & 21 Edw. I, 42.

gulf between the life tenant who had a freehold and the termor whose interest was only a chattel—a gulf which still exists. There are several other instances of this statute being treated as though it were more a statement of general policy than an enactment of a specified remedy for a particular wrong. For example, the statute also provides that if a husband is impleaded in respect of his wife's heritage, and makes default, thereby imperilling her right, the wife shall be "received to defend her right." Thus we have the assize of *Hothom* v. *Hothom*[1] in which the defendant made default and his wife prayed to be received. The receipt was counterpleaded on the grounds that first, no land or tenement was involved but only an advowson; and secondly, as no continuance was made against her, she was out of court; and thirdly, that the default alone would not lose the presentation, its effect being simply that the verdict of the assize would be taken at once without any further pleading. But in spite of these very cogent reasons the woman was received. Again, the statute strictly speaking only refers to the loss of the wife's right by the default of her husband, yet we find that the statute has been applied to cases where the right was not solely the wife's but purchased to her and her husband as joint-tenants[2].

Moreover, the statute strictly only allows the receipt of the wife if she was named in the writ with her husband, and HENGHAM once said that this was the interpretation settled by him at a parliament[3]. Certainly it was the one most frequently adopted[4], although one case is to be found where the benefit of the statute was extended to the wife even when she was not named in the writ[5]. This same statute, moreover, strictly applies only to cases where lands or tenements are in peril of being lost[6],

[1] Y.B. 11 & 12 Edw. III, 106.

[2] *Anon.* v. *Charer*, Y.B. 21 & 22 Edw. I, 344; once it was extended even to unmarried joint feoffees, *Anon.*, *ibid.* 610–2.

[3] *Anon.* v. *Thomas the Notary*, Y.B. 32 & 33 Edw. I, 429. *Mutford's* argument in *Anon.* v. *Charer*, Y.B. 21 & 22 Edw. I, 344, that the statute only operates when the husband is impleaded alone, must be regarded as a curiosity.

[4] *Neville* v. *Neville*, Y.B. 1 & 2 Edw. II, 77–8; *Stapleford* v. *Barbot*, Y.B. 3 & 4 Edw. II, 85.

[5] *Woodward* v. *Anon.*, Y.B. 33 & 35 Edw. I, 3–4; the wife had, however, been named in a previous writ in respect of the same matter.

[6] For example, the benefit of the statute could not be claimed in a *Quid Juris Clamat* for that action does not imperil land; *Stonore* v. *Cotesmor*, Y.B.

but instances of its application to other circumstances are occasionally to be met with, such as in an action of Waste[1] and an assize of *Darrein Presentment*[2], while towards the end of our period, the words "lands and tenements" of the statute are paraphrased (and expanded) as "realty, *seignory or rent*"[3].

§ 4. *Other Examples*

Examples can be found upon many different statutes. Thus, there is a case where a writ given by statute against such ravishers of wards as have no right to the wardship was upheld against one who had a right to it[4]. Westminster II, c. 48, which prevents a man having view in a second writ when he has had it in a previous action upon the same matter, was also extended to the case where in the first writ he had prayed the view, but did not have it, since he was essoined the next day and abated the writ[5]. Westminster II, c. 25 authorises the use of the assize of *Novel Disseisin* for the recovery of certain rents and profits, but was also held to warrant the use of *Mort d'Ancestor* as well for this purpose[6]; another statute which forbids the petty persecution of tenants by the abuse of process in seignorial courts was held by Howard, J. to apply *a multo fortiori* to a lord who abetted a false accusation in his court leet, which he holds not in his seignorial capacity but as the king's judge[7]. A termor was liable to be ejected from this term if the lessor had suffered a collusive recovery thereby conveying his rights to another, and therefore the Statute of Gloucester, c. 11 allowed the termor to intervene when he suspected that litigation was being used to defraud him of his term. A very important extension of this principle was to allow intervention in the peculiar and somewhat different case of a termor

16 Edw. III, ii. 58; cf. *Anon.* v. *Ufford and Latymer*, Y.B. 14 & 15 Edw. III, 314, where receipt was refused in respect of wardship which was there only a chattel interest.

[1] *Anon.*, Y.B. 33 & 35 Edw. I, 476.

[2] *Hothom* v. *Hothom and others*, Y.B. 11 & 12 Edw. III, 106.

[3] *Sigeston* v. *Anon.*, Y.B. 18 & 19 Edw. III, 98–100.

[4] Westminster II, c. 35; *Anon.*, Y.B. 21 & 22 Edw. I, 554.

[5] *Anon.*, Y.B. 21 & 22 Edw. I, 542.

[6] *Anon.* v. *Abbot of Westminster*, Y.B. 21 & 22 Edw. I, 324–30. In *Spigurnel's* second speech on p. 328, "forbidden" is an erroneous translation; the text and the context require "allowed."

[7] *Chelmsford* v. *Dalle*, Y.B. 30 & 31 Edw. I, 401; Westminster II, c. 36.

who had received the freehold by a deed of release and quit-claim[1]. In this particular case issue was taken upon the genuineness of the release, but the reporter points out the technical difficulty that might arise if the release were found to be a forgery, because the termor has then obviously no case for intervention under the extended interpretation of the statute, but it is difficult to say whether subsequently he could still claim to be received in virtue of his term (which apparently was not denied) in accordance with the plain words of the statute. Similarly, the statute "De Conjunctim Feoffatis"[2] only professes to touch the assizes of *Novel Disseisin*, *Mort d'Ancestor* and *Utrum* and other writs where tenements are demanded. The Court indeed refused to apply it to an action for a wardship, on the ground that a wardship is a chattel[3], yet process upon it was granted in an action of *Scire Facias* where land is virtually recovered, although strictly speaking it is not a "plea of land"[4]. Again, it was virtually decided that since Formedon in the Reverter is a possessory writ, it was subject to the limitations of date laid down by statute for other possessory writs[5].

A frequent hardship was the alienation by a husband of lands which belonged to his wife and in which he only had curtesy. The Statute of Gloucester, c. 3 provided for the case when the heir after his parents' deaths tried to recover such lands by a possessory assize—*Mort d'Ancestor*, *Ael*, *Besael* or *Cosinage*. The tenant would, of course, put forward the father's deed alienating the property with warranty, by which at Common Law the heir would be barred. To remedy this, the statute said that henceforth, if the heir had inherited nothing from his father (this being a particularly oppressive case) then he should not be barred by his father's deed from claiming his mother's inheritance. Now in 1314 an heir sought to recover his grandmother's inheritance by a writ of Entry *Dum Non Compos Mentis*. His father's deed with warranty being produced in bar, he argued that by the

[1] *Bishop* v. *Folyot*, Y.B. 2 & 3 Edw. II, 35–6.

[2] 34 Edw. I.

[3] *Anon.*, Y.B. 11 & 12 Edw. III, 404.

[4] *Passon* v. *Anon.*, Y.B. 11 & 12 Edw. III, 398.

[5] *Anon.*, Y.B. 1 & 2 Edw. II, 159; Westminster I, c. 39. BEREFORD, J. stated this as his view, and the parties demurred in judgment, but eventually the demandant was given leave to depart from his writ.

statute he could not be barred since he offered to aver that he had nothing by descent from his father. To this the tenant replied by urging that the statute applied only to possessory writs, and that the present case was vitually a writ of Right, also suggesting that the father was not tenant by the curtesy, and pointing out that they were not pleading in the particular writ which had been founded by the statute. Nevertheless, BEREFORD, C.J. ruled that although it was a writ of Right, yet the statute applied, and drove the parties to accept an averment as to whether the demandant had or had not assets by descent[1].

Almost equally serious is the extension of the operation of the statute 2 Edw. III, c. 17 which provides a writ of *Desceit* when *Scire Facias* is fraudulently sued in respect of land, to a case where not land but only a recognisance for £40 was involved[2].

But probably the most far-reaching extension made was that of the statute *De Donis* which was held at an early date to authorise Formedon in the Remainder, although the statute really gives no remedy whatever to remaindermen[3].

An interesting example is also afforded by the action of *Cessavit* which was given by various statutes at different times for the recovery by the lord of lands which the tenant had held for over two years without paying the due rent, suit of court, or other service. A lord brought the action[4] on a cesser of rent for two years and of suit of court for one year. The tenant tendered the arrears of rent but protested that the statute did not apply to the suit. SHARESHULLE, SHARDELOWE, JJ. and the whole court agreed in applying the statute to the one year's cesser of suit as well.

In certain instances custom seems to have played an important part in the extension of the operation of statutes. Thus it was customary to give damages under the Statute of Merchants, although the statute only specified "costs and expenses"[5]. At

[1] *Whittlesey and Sedgeford* v. *Laurence*, Y.B. 8 Edw. II, 135–6.
[2] *Melton* v. *Ryther*, Y.B. 16 Edw. III, II. 290–5 (record).
[3] F.N.B. 218; Pollock and Maitland, II. 24, 28. For a statement that Formedon in the Remainder actually existed before the statute, see below, p. 131, n. 1.
[4] *Prior of Plympton* v. *Anon.*, Y.B. 17 & 18 Edw. III, 234.
[5] *Anon.*, Y.B. 12 & 13 Edw. III, 354.

a later date HILARY, J. gave as a reason for following this judgment that "damages had been awarded hitherto by others more learned than we are"[1].

Professor Maitland called attention to what might have been a striking example of our thesis when he remarked that chapter 29 of the Statute of Marlborough, which authorised writs of Entry in the *Post*, only applied strictly to Entry *Sur Disseisin*, although it "seems to have been construed to give a general authority for writs in the *Post*"[2]. In the first place there is no mention of *Sur Disseisin* in the statute, and secondly, the only writs to which the statute may be strictly applied are those brought upon "alienations" (*not* disseisins) too remote to be brought within the degrees. In fact, the statute does authorise most writs of Entry in the *Post*, but it may be doubted whether it applies to those *Sur Disseisin*[3].

We may conclude with a series of cases which have more than a merely legal interest, for they throw some light on the tendency of London customs to spread to other parts of England. Chapters 11 and 12 of the Statute of Gloucester make a number of procedural reforms in the law of fraud and of voucher which however only apply to tenements in London. But we find these statutes applied to tenements in Chester[4], Hitchin[5], and to the manor of Dickleborough in Norfolk[6]. Fleta[7], without any apparent statutory authority, describes the law laid down in these chapters of the Statute of Gloucester as applying not only to London but also to other "privileged burghs." But even this will not explain the Norfolk manor; nor does much help come from the fact that certain boroughs had royal permission to adopt

[1] *Anon.* v. *Lacy*, Y.B. 16 Edw. III, I. 148; there is another instance in *Anon.*, Y.B. 16 Edw. III, II. 290, of damages being awarded although the Statute in question (Westminster II, c. 35) does not give them. (In the same year, however, the reverse had been adjudged; *Anon.*, Y.B. 16 Edw. III, I. 94.)

[2] Pollock and Maitland, II. 71, n. 1.

[3] Apparently at this time the only case where *Sur Disseisin* could be brought in the *Post* was when the tenant was an ecclesiastic who had obtained the lands by succession, the reason being that succession is not a degree, the latter term being confined to descent. See below, p. 107, n. 3.

[4] *Anon.*, Y.B. 14 & 15 Edw. III, 78 (31).

[5] *Bishop* v. *Folyot*, Y.B. 2 & 3 Edw. II, 35–6.

[6] *Segrave and Montague* v. *Broun*, Y.B. 19 Edw. III, 441.

[7] Lib. II. c. 55, sect. 8, cited (with wrong reference) in 2 *Inst.* 322, 325.

London customs and may thus have imported the peculiar procedure laid down in the statute, for it is fairly certain that Chester did not possess this privilege[1].

Here again the concluding remarks of our fourth chapter apply. The judges legislated on an ambitious scale, as may be seen from a study of the technical details of the cases mentioned above, but it was always done with a singular absence of any feeling that constitutional problems of great difficulty were involved. One thing is noticeable, however, and that is the tendency for such decisions to become much rarer in the reign of Edward III than in that of Edward I, and this fact must be considered later.

[1] Their long series of charters is printed in Morris, *Chester under the Plantagenets and Tudors*, from which it is clear that Chester possesses no extant evidence of its possession of London customs.

CHAPTER VI

STRICT INTERPRETATION

GREAT as was the liberty enjoyed by the courts in applying statutes, there were occasions when they expressed a determination to interpret the text strictly. At first such instances are only to be found scattered among the examples of expansion or restriction noticed above, and there is no apparent reason assigned for treating any one case in a different manner from any other case. As our period advances, however, the judges begin to show a decided preference for one policy, namely, that of strict interpretation, examples of which steadily become more numerous, while at the same time there is a marked diminution of cases of expansion and restriction.

§ 1. *The Earliest Examples*

When compared with the freedom of the interpretations already discussed, the following early case offers an interesting contrast. The Statute of Westminster II, c. 35 said that if the defendant in an action of ejectment from wardship died, the plaintiff could continue the process against his executors or heir. In this case (which appears in the earliest published Year Book) the defendants in such an action were a man and his wife. The man died and the plaintiff desired to continue the action against the wife, without purchasing a new writ, whereupon she objected that she was not his heir. The plaintiff argued that if the man and wife had both died, the same writ would undoubtedly have served against the heir, therefore a *multo fortiori* will it stand when only one is dead. Even this last ingenious argument was ineffectual, however, and the writ abated with the result that the whole action had to begin anew[1]. A well-known chapter of *Magna Carta* saves a lord from losing his court by the wrongful use of the writ *Precipe in Capite*, but when a tenant objected to a demandant's use of the writ, the court refused to act. SPIGURNEL, J. remarked that the exception could only be made after the

[1] *Anon.*, Y.B. 20 & 21 Edw. I, 310.

wager of battle, and BEREWYKE, J. added that such an exception was for the lord himself to make, and that if he omitted to do so, then the parties could not raise the matter[1].

The early attempts at establishing a writ of Entry *in Consimili Casu* were wrecked owing to the insistence of the judges upon taking the statutes in a sense unusually strict at that time, for when it was pointed out that the Statute of Gloucester, c. 7 speaks of reversion and that of Westminster II, c. 24 of "similar cases," they held that a remainder could not be regarded as "similar" to a reversion[2]. In the next reign Chief Justice BEREFORD put the difficulty very clearly: "If you rely on the statute," he said, "it must be by some words in the statute;... your writ says 'by the form of the statute,' but there is no statute in that form"[3]; and again, "no writ is maintainable out of the common law 'by the form of the statute' unless it is expressly worded in the statute"[4]. Even when Westminster II, c. 24 was quoted BEREFORD maintained that the cases were not similar. Yet when a settlement was finally reached at an important conference of judges and chancery clerks it was embodied in the change of only one word—the writ was to say "in *consimili casu*" instead of "in *casu proviso*." The whole incident shows a literalism and caution among the judges which contrasts strangely with many of their contemporary decisions recounted in the earlier chapters.

The Statute of Westminster II, c. 48 has the express intention of preventing tenants from having view unless it is necessary, yet at times the details of the statute were followed with surprising closeness although to the apparent detriment of the object of the enactment. The statute says that a view had in one writ which has abated will toll view in a second writ, but when cases arose where the first writ was not abated but only discontinued it was held that the statute did not apply[5]. Nor was it even allowed to extend to the case where view was had and the

[1] *Aldan and others* v. *Engleys*, Y.B. 30 & 31 Edw. I, 233–5; *Magna Carta*, c. 24.

[2] *St Michael* v. *Beauchamp*, Y.B. 33 & 35 Edw. I, 428.

[3] *Devereux* v. *Tuchet*, Y.B. 3 Edw. II, 16–19.

[4] *Stirkeland* v. *Brunolfshead*, Y.B. 3 Edw. II, 108.

[5] *Corbychoun* v. *Anon.*, Y.B. 33 & 35 Edw. I, 378; *Anon.*, Y.B. 11 & 12 Edw. III, 348; *Anon.*, Y.B. 13 & 14 Edw. III, 78.

parole had then demurred by reason of a protection, and the demandant, rather foolishly, bought a new writ instead of suing a re-summons upon the old one[1]. There is also an instance of an attempt to make a statutory averment with the substitution of "predecessor" where the statute said "ancestor" since the subject was a prior, but the Court refused to accept it[2].

As an example of strict adherence to the statute which involved some hardship we may take the following. Lords whose bailiffs refused to render proper accounts of their management of a manor did not find it at all easy to bring them to justice. The Common Law writ of Account was far from effective, since it depended upon process against the bailiff's land. But if the bailiff had no land the lord seems to have been helpless. To meet this case the Statute of Marlborough, c. 23 ordained a specially stringent process called *Monstravit de Compoto*[3] involving the arrest of the bailiff's body against those bailiffs who had no lands. In 1310 the *Monstravit* was brought[4], and the bailiff took exception to the writ, alleging that he had lands open to distress, and that therefore the writ did not lie. The lord objected that every lord might be defrauded in this way; the bailiff might owe two hundred pounds, and if he bought two acres of land and two pennyworth of rent the lord would be bound to use only distress, and so never bring him to account. Nevertheless, the Court forced the lord to accept the bailiff's averment that he had lands distrainable, after two interesting reasons had been put forward. First, BEREFORD, C.J. made the important statement that "we ought to maintain ancient writs where they can be upheld, rather than new ones"; and, secondly, *Scrope* made the suggestion that the Court should consult the King's interest, which was that the

[1] *Anon.*, Y.B. 33 & 35 Edw. I, 289.

[2] *Anon.*, Y.B. 3 Edw. II, 158; Westminster I, c. 40. Indeed, there seems to have been a marked tendency to insist upon averments being offered in the exact words of the statutes giving them; *Anon.*, Y.B. 6 & 7 Edw. II (*Eyre of Kent*), II. 72, 73, 75 (the editor's reference should be to Westminster I, c. 40, not to 20 Edw. I).

[3] The form of the writ is in F.N.B. 117 H. Later, the Statute of Westminster II, c. 11 gave outlawry against defaulting bailiffs, which was generally preferred to *Monstravit* (F.N.B. *u.s.*). Why outlawry was not sued in this case, does not appear.

[4] *Box* v. *Palmer*, Y.B. 3 Edw. II, 91–2; it was not a writ of Account as in Maitland's translation.

sheriff should have the distress of the land (the King having the issues), rather than that process should run against the person of the bailiff, whence the King derives no profit—but how much weight this had with the Court is not indicated[1].

When a lord avowed a distress for relief by alleging that he was seised of so much scutage at the hands of the tenant (thereby establishing the fact of military tenure), the latter produced a deed showing that he was enfeoffed at less scutage than the lord had avowed upon, and invoked the aid of the Statute of Marlborough, c. 9 which said that no man should be distrained against the form of his feoffment. It was held that the deed would not avail the tenant, for "relief" was not in the statute, which only spoke of "services"[2]. When either of the parties to an assize of *Novel Disseisin* died, the heir of the demandant could have a writ of Entry *Sur Disseisin* irrespective of his or the defendant's minority by virtue of the Statute of Westminster I, c. 47; but such a writ was adjourned by the Court when brought by an infant heir, against a lessee of a disseisor, although the infant's father had died during a plea previously[3].

A particularly striking attempt to obtain a very strict interpretation of the Statute of Gloucester, c. 3 was made by *Hengham* in 1311. The statute enables an heir to bring a writ *Sur Cui in Vita* upon the death of his father and mother to recover land formerly held by her but alienated by her husband. The writ was brought by the grandson of the woman, and *Hengham* argued that the writ was not warranted by the statute since he alleged the seisin of his grandmother but the statute only said mother. *Huntingdon* took the same line, and the report ends without deciding the point[4].

[1] His income was returned by the jury at six shillings a year.

[2] *Ryde* v. *Tregoz*, Y.B. 3 & 4 Edw. II, 95–100.

[3] *Anon.*, Y.B. 5 Edw. II, I. 107–8. It seems that the father's plea was against the alienee and not the original disseisor, although the report explicitly states that it was an assize. Either we must understand "assize" here to mean entry in the nature of an Assize (commonly called Entry *De Quibus*) or else, if he did bring assize, the alienation was made after his death and before his heir sued *Sur Disseisin*. In either case the statute strictly did not apply. See below, pp. 105–7.

[4] *Marum* v. *le Clerk*, Y.B. 4 Edw. II, 169. The Editor's Note from the Record does not seem to have any necessary connection with this case, and the identification must be regarded as doubtful. If they are indeed the same case,

§ 2. *The Beginnings of a Theory of Strict Interpretation*

It is in Edward II's reign that we find the first statements of a theory as to the relations between judge and statute. In a writ of Right the tenant had vouched a husband and wife, who, in turn, vouched over upon someone else. They did not sue out a summons against their warrantor, however, and were therefore in danger of having to recompense the tenant for his probable loss of the land. At this point the wife prayed to be received to defend her right which her husband was imperilling by refusing to sue out process against the warrantor. *Scrope* in arguing against her receipt at first suggested that the Statute of Westminster II, c. 3 is only to be understood as allowing the receipt of the demesne tenant and does not apply to tenants by warranty. He further added that

> we ought not to understand the statute otherwise than it says; but the statute says nothing save of the case where the tenant is about to lose by default, but the tenant here is not losing by default but by failure to prosecute a summons against a warrantor[1].

The Court, it is true, gave judgment against *Scrope's* point and the woman was admitted, but his argument is a sign of the new tendency in legal thought, and it is only one year later that we find it stated from the bench by BEREFORD, "the law that applies in this case is statute law, and we shall therefore accept no averment contrary to the statute which is our authority"[2]. The same tendency may be seen in *Spigurnel's* argument that the reversioner cannot claim receipt on the default of a tenant for life who is impleaded by a *Mort d'Ancestor*, since in the assize land is not lost by the default, the only effect of which is the award of the assize straightway. The land may be lost by the verdict of the assize but that is not the same thing as being lost by default. We have no information as to how this argument was received, but the fact that no decision was given at once seems

then *Hengham's* argument was unsuccessful, for issue was taken upon the deeds. (This was not RALF DE HENGHAM, who had just died, 18 May, 1311, but the less known *John de Hengham*, or *Hingham*, who was a pleader and not a Judge.)

[1] *Balsham* v. *atte Street*, Y.B. 5 Edw. II, II. 46.

[2] *Mauleverer* v. *Stapleton*, Y.B. 6 & 7 Edw. II, 148–50.

to suggest that the Court felt it worthy of consideration and may have adjourned the case for that reason[1].

§ 3. *Growing Strictness under Edward III*

Passing to the reign of Edward III, there is a noticeable tendency to read statutes more strictly. Thus the process by proclamation which the Statute of Westminster II, c. 35 gives in actions of Right, Wardship, and Ejectment of Wardship, was refused in Ravishment of Ward[2], while the proclamation itself can only be made in the original county, for even when it is returned by the sheriff that the defendant has distrainable lands in another county there can be no proclamation there[3]. The reason is stated in a later case on a similar statute to be that as the statute says "ibi denuncientur" it can only mean in the original county. Moreover, as the plaintiff has sued a *Testificatum est* in another county he has put himself outside the statute and is therefore at Common Law where there is no proclamation[4]. Such a result as this is clearly dependent upon the habit (now being formed) of keeping Statute Law rigidly separate from Common Law.

The Statute of Westminster II, c. 39 allows a litigant to offer an averment that the sheriff's return of the value of distrainable issues of persons summoned and defaulting is fraudulent, in that it understates them. Now in one case a party said "we will aver for the king that the bailiff of the liberty could have had £10 each" from certain jurors, but WILLOUGHBY, J. replied "that is not given by statute and not receivable," his reason being that the statute mentions the frauds of sheriffs but not of bailiffs of liberties[5]. It is noteworthy that the reporter adds that such an averment used to be received—whence we may conclude that the interpretation of this particular statute had lately become more strict. It has already been shown[6] how in *Ascham's Case* statute 1, chapter 17 of 14 Edw. III was extended from chantries to hospitals, but other points of difficulty arose

[1] *Anon.*, Y.B. 6 & 7 Edw. II (*Eyre of Kent*), III. 58. Receipt was allowed in the later law; 1 Roscoe, *Real Actions*, 69.

[2] *Anon.*, Y.B. 11 & 12 Edw. III, 464, 592.

[3] *Anon.*, Y.B. 12 & 13 Edw. III, 356.

[4] Marlborough, c. 7; *Anon.* v. *Gerard de Braybroke and another*, Y.B. 17 & 18 Edw. III, 392. For another report of the same case, see above, p. 64, n. 1.

[5] *Anon.*, Y.B. 14 Edw. III, 160 (65).

[6] Above, p. 75.

soon after. The prioress of a hospital brought her writ of *Utrum*, but the tenant objected that by Common Law *Utrum* lies only for a parson, and by statute for the warden of a hospital, but in the writ the demandant is not described by either title. The Year Book report ends with the prioress' counter-assertion, that the statute enures to the head of a hospital, whatever her style. From the record it appears that she was asked whether she was elected or donative, and as it appeared that she was elective, the writ was not held to be supported by the statute[1]. In this case it is the interpretation as settled in *Ascham's Case* that the court follows so strictly.

At the same date, too, the recently drawn distinction between executor and administrator was applied to the Statute of Westminster II, c. 23 thus debarring administrators from the action given by the statute to executors[2], which they had hitherto enjoyed, the result being a considerable restriction of the operation of the statute.

Statute 1, chapter 6 of 14 Edw. III gives relief where slight errors of spelling have been made, whereby at Common Law the process would have been discontinued. Thus where the original writ said "Haselhawe" and the process was continued as "Heselhawe" the defect was amended by the statute and the case proceeded, although all the rolls had the same error[3]. Where "Hugh le Spenser" is continued as "Hugh" the statute will not avail, however, since the omission is more than a letter or a syllable[4]. Further, if "Waghan" sues a fine into court, and "Uaghan" then sues *Scire Facias* upon it, he is out of the statute, as SHARESHULLE, J. explains:

> the statute only says that defects in process shall be amended, but does not say that mistakes in writs are to be thus amended; wherefore we cannot take the statute further than the words of it say,

consequently the writ was abated[5]. At Common Law the

[1] *Prioress of the Hospital of Long Stow* v. *Anon.*, Y.B. 16 Edw. III, II. 286.

[2] *Administrators of Wedergrave* v. *Prior of St John of Jerusalem*, Y.B. 18 & 19 Edw. III, 532, continued in Y.B. 19 Edw. III, 12. The action was again made available for administrators by the statute 31 Edw. III, st. 1, c. 11. See Y.B. 12 & 13 Edw. III, cxxi.

[3] *Heselhawe* v. *Bishop of Bath and Wells*, Y.B. 17 & 18 Edw. III, 538.

[4] *Le Spenser* v. *Earl of Huntingdon*, Y.B. 16 Edw. III, I. 198 (18).

[5] *Waghan* v. *Anon.*, Y.B. 20 Edw. III, II. 198.

executors of executors had certain actions[1], but WILLOUGHBY, J. said that "perhaps they should not have Account which a statute gives to executors but says nothing more"[2]. His doubt shows an interesting hesitation between the growing tendency to construe statutes strictly, and the old feeling that a statute did not abolish antecedent Common Law unless by express words.

There are a few cases where a series of decisions upon one point occurs and the growing strictness of the interpretations can be shown. Thus by a considerable stretch of the Statute of Westminster II, c. 3 a freeholder was received to defend his right when his lessee's default had imperilled it, but eleven years later this was reversed as not being in the statute[3]. Again, receipt had formerly been allowed although no land or tenement was in danger[4], but later decisions resolutely denied it in such cases[5]. This statute strictly read, moreover, only refers to the wife when the husband is about to lose her right by default, but in early cases it was applied equally to cases where the husband and wife were joint feoffees and both named in the writ[6]. In the next reign it was said that a wife jointly enfeoffed was not receivable by statute or Common Law, save where the feoffment was by fine "and then," said BEREFORD, "only because a fine bears record in itself, but it would be otherwise if she were enfeoffed by charter"[7]. The time at which the wife must make her prayer is defined by the statute as "before judgment"; this had been interpreted as any time before final judgment[8], even after the mise[9], but soon afterwards doubts arose[10], and later still a wife nearly lost her chance by coming the day after the default; fortunately for her HILARY, J. held that both days were technically one[11].

[1] *Pole* and *Sadelyngstanes* differed as to this in Y.B. 18 & 19 Edw. III, 534, cited above, p. 88, n. 2.

[2] *Anon.*, Y.B. 13 & 14 Edw. III, 174; Westminster II, c. 23.

[3] *Anon.*, Y.B. 20 & 21 Edw. I, 42; *Staneley* v. *Gokeshunt*, Y.B. 30 & 31 Edw. I, 410.

[4] *Hothom* v. *Hothom*, Y.B. 11 & 12 Edw. III, 106.

[5] *Anon.*, Y.B. 14 Edw. III, 106–8; *Anon.* v. *Ufford and Latymer*, Y.B. 14 & 15 Edw. III, 314.

[6] *Anon.* v. *Charer*, Y.B. 21 & 22 Edw. I, 344; or even to unmarried joint-feoffees, *Anon.*, *ibid.* 610.

[7] *Anon.*, Y.B. 3 & 4 Edw. II, 176.

[8] *Shineholt* v. *Maldus*, *ibid.* 143.

[9] *Abbot of St Evroul* v. *Vylers*, Y.B. 21 & 22 Edw. I, 196.

[10] *Anon.*, Y.B. 11 & 12 Edw. III, 336–8.

[11] *Anon.*, Y.B. 17 & 18 Edw. III, 426.

The Statute of Marlborough, c. 9 said that a man should not be distrained for services contrary to his feoffment, and in 1313 it was held by BEREFORD to apply equally to a release whereby the lord had surrendered a portion of the services[1]; this free but sensible interpretation, however, did not persist into the next reign for one of the reasons assigned by SHARESHULLE for ousting a tenant from the benefit of the statute was that he was pleading a release, while the statute only said feoffment[2]. The other reason was that the avowant was a stranger to the deed, but in the previous reign this again would not have ousted him[3]; thus, both points were now decided in a more strict and literal manner in Edward III's reign than in Edward II's.

§ 4. *The Latest Theory*

We have already noticed the beginnings in Edward II's reign of an attempt to state a policy in this connection, and it is in Edward III's reign that it is embodied in a short phrase. It first appears in 1342–3 in a speech by *Thorpe*[4]: "Privilegia statuti sunt stricti juris." The next year the words reappear in another speech by *Thorpe*[5], and finally get noted in the Year Book as a useful maxim[6], while in the last year of our period we find the principle acknowledged from the bench in SHARESHULLE's speech (already quoted)[7] which marks an important turning point in the history of interpretation: "Nous ne poms prendre lestatut plus avant qe les paroles en ycele ne parle."

[1] *Attemulle* v. *Saunderville*, Y.B. 6 & 7 Edw. II, 11.

[2] *Anon.*, Y.B. 11 & 12 Edw. III, 62–4. The editor's reference to *Magna Carta*, c. 10, is in error for Marlborough, c. 9.

[3] *Venour* v. *Blund*, Y.B. 3 & 4 Edw. II, 157–162.

[4] *Le Warde* v. *Wullesthorpe*, Y.B. 17 Edw. III, 142.

[5] *Sybeling and others* v. *Mussendene and others*, Y.B. 17 & 18 Edw. III, 446.

[6] *Anon.*, Y.B. 18 Edw. III, 131 (31).

[7] *Waghan* v. *Anon.*, Y.B. 20 Edw. III, II. 198; above, p. 88.

CHAPTER VII

CONFLICT OF STATUTES

WHEN there are two statements upon a subject of equal authority, but mutually inconsistent, the mediaeval mind was not a little exercised, and only slowly discovered a way out of the *impasse*. For example, two conflicting charters left the court no other course (in *Malberthorpe's* opinion) than to promote a compromise between the parties. True, he did not convince BEREFORD, but even that daring and original Chief Justice could think of nothing better than that "seeing that both parties have put forward charters of the king which are inconsistent, keep your days on the Quindene of St Michael, and in the meanwhile, sue to the king to get your charters interpreted." The council accordingly inspected the records of the case but found no way of overcoming the difficulty save that of ordering the judges to ignore both the charters, which they therefore did, and received an averment as to the point at issue instead of attempting to settle it from the charters[1]. Nor was English law exceptionally undeveloped in this learning when compared with other contemporary systems, for we find that the canonists had a similar difficulty—much argument having been occasioned, for example, by the conflict between one delegation and a later and different one in the same matter[2].

§ 1. Contra Formam Feoffamenti *and Replevin*

Conflict between two statutes was even more puzzling, and it will be the object of the present chapter to trace the various attempts that were made during our period to arrive at some solution. First place must be accorded to the discussions of the inter-relation of the Statutes of Marlborough, c. 9 and Westminster II, c. 2, not only because it was the earliest opportunity for attacking the question that the courts received, but also because we have particularly fine detailed reports of the debates occasioned by it.

[1] *Abbot of Battle* v. *atte Bregge and others*, Y.B. 5 Edw. II, II. 16–17, 23–24.
[2] c. 14, X. I. 3.

Marlborough, c. 9 enacts, *inter alia*:

In doing suits to the courts of magnates and other lords of courts, from henceforth this order shall be observed: i.e. that no one who is enfeoffed by charter be distrained in the future to do suit to the court of his lord unless by the form of his charter he is specially bound to do so; except those who (or whose ancestors) used to do the suit before the king's first crossing to Brittany thirty-nine and a half years ago [i.e. 1230].

Likewise none that is enfeoffed without deed from the Conquest or other ancient feoffment, shall be henceforth distrained to do such suit, unless he or his ancestors used to do the suit before the said date.

After further details, the statute establishes a process whereby the tenant can bring the lord into court and secure the benefit of the statute. This became known as the action *Contra Formam Feoffamenti*, and took the form of a "prohibition upon the statute." Conversely, the lord could by similar process exact his lawful dues in suit from the tenant, this being the action *De Secto Subtracto*.

Beside these statutory actions there was also the Common Law action of *Replegiari* (also called Replevin) which could be made the means of deciding a large number of miscellaneous questions of suit, service, customs, tenure and the like, thus covering the same field as the statutory writs; but it differed from them (as we shall see later) in being decidedly possessory in character so that a comparatively short recent seisin of an alleged due was sufficient title without going into questions of deeds or ancient seisin, the process upon it being moreover rapid and convenient. The statutory actions on the other hand "sounded in the right," the deciding factors being the terms of the feoffment, or the fairly long seisin required by the statute. The process (beginning with a prohibition) was long and solemn, while the old Common Law proprietary counterpart to the *Replegiari*—the action *Ne Injuste Vexes*—was even more cumbersome[1]. Hence there was a natural desire to make the speedy *Replegiari* serve the same purpose as the more stately proprietary writ. BEREFORD even said of such a course that "for twenty years

[1] "It is an abuse that the writ *Ne Vexes* is thus falling into decline." *Mirror of Justices*, 173.

past there has not come into England so good a law for poor folk"[1].

Now about eighteen years after the Statute of Marlborough came the Statute of Westminster II, c. 2 which reformed the action of *Replegiari* in so far as it related to customs and services (no mention is made of suit, be it noted) especially in the following particulars:

In order that the judges may be sure upon what recent seisin lords may avow a reasonable distress upon their tenants, it is agreed that henceforth a reasonable distress may be avowed on the seisin of the lord's ancestors or predecessors from the time from which the writ of *Novel Disseisin* runs [i.e. 1242].

The evident object of the enactment is to bring *Replegiari* into line with the other possessory actions by setting the same date of limitation to it as had been applied to the petty assizes by Westminster I, c. 39 (amending the Statute of Merton, c. 8). It will be observed that if the two statutes are strictly interpreted, there is no room for conflict; but the early 14th century mind easily got bewildered, especially since the new processes laid down by the Statute of Marlborough were not regarded as superseding the former Common Law but as being an alternative to it. Nor was this the only or even the greatest confusing factor, for it became the practice to use the forms of the writ of *Replegiari* although pleading it as if it were a *Contra Formam Feoffamenti*[2], and hence arose the crucial question—which of the two dates of limitation then applies?

The earliest mention[3] we have of the subject is in 1294 when it was stated that if a man is distrained to do suit of court against his feoffment, although he do it, he may yet bring the action of *Contra Formam Feoffamenti*. But if he has done the suit, he cannot discharge himself by *Replegiari*. This seems to us the only reasonable way of looking at the matter, for it strictly maintains the character of each writ, the one being much "in the right" and the other being "the tenderest and most possessional thing

[1] *Venour* v. *Blund*, Y.B. 3 & 4 Edw. II, 162.

[2] Similarly, where no deed was pleaded, *Replegiari* could be pleaded as high up in the right as a writ of Customs and Services; HOWARD, J. in *Atteholdehalle* v. *Bishop of Ely*, Y.B. 33 & 35 Edw. I, 344.

[3] *Anon.*, Y.B. 21 & 22 Edw. I, 397.

there is "[1], and avoids forcing a conflict between the two statutes by forbidding a tenant in *Replegiari* to attempt to discharge himself in the statutory manner by pleading a deed of feoffment. From this clear and logical statement, however, we must trace a steady declension, and the introduction of an ever-growing confusion.

§ 2. *Aumeye's Case*

The first step in the process is a case where, moreover, we can hear the words of HENGHAM, the author of the Statute of Westminster II, on the matter. *John of Aumeye*[2] brought *Replegiari* against a certain abbot to recover beasts taken in distress. The abbot avowed the distress on the grounds that John held of him by homage, fealty and suit of court. The questions of homage and fealty being settled, the discussion turned upon the suit of court, and John's advocate, *Toudeby*, pleaded the Statute of Marlborough by offering the averment that neither the abbot nor his predecessors had been seised of suit of court from Aumeye's holding before 1230[3]. The abbot quite properly replied that if he wanted to plead the Statute of Marlborough he should have brought a prohibition upon the statute (in other words, he should have used the action of *Contra Formam Feoffamenti*)[4]. But HENGHAM, J. who was on the Bench, fell into the attractive error of *Toudeby* and rehearsed the Statute of Marlborough, whereupon his deliberate confusion of the two actions met its inevitable fate at the hands of *Herle*, who appeared for the abbot. *Herle* took the only possible course; HENGHAM had said that the case fell under the Statute of Marlborough and that the averment should be "never seised before 1230," so *Herle* pleaded the later Statute of Westminster II, c. 2 which undoubtedly said that the averment should be "seised since 1242." *Toudeby's* colleague, *Malmesthorpe*, found this very difficult to answer and it looked very much as though they had fallen into their own pit; he did not think that the new statute contradicted

[1] *Herle* arguing in *Anon.*, Y.B. 3 & 4 Edw. II, 72.

[2] Y.B. 33 & 35 Edw. I, 79–82.

[3] As a matter of detail it will be noted that *Toudeby* is not pleading a deed, but the second of the paragraphs of the statute quoted above.

[4] Y.B. 2 & 3 Edw. II, xiii, n. 4; the prohibition was the usual preliminary to the statutory action, F.N.B. 163 C.

the other, but as to what it did do, he was rather vague; he supposed that the statute was made to prevent an undue strain being put on the memories of jurors. *Toudeby's* plea had roused HENGHAM'S interest, but now *Herle's* brilliant counter to it brought the judge to the other side, and he spoke words which have since become famous: "Do not gloss the statute; we understand it better than you do, for we made it, and one often sees that one statute defeats another." With this *dictum*, that the Statute of Marlborough was amended by that of Westminster II, the report concludes. The confusion was now complete. There was only one way in which the two statutes could conflict, and that was by destroying the possessory nature of a *Replegiari*, and pleading it "in the right" in accordance with the Statute of Marlborough. HENGHAM had allowed this to be done, and had so brought himself up against the discrepancy of the dates. He refused to turn back, but kept blindly on; the later statute must consequently be understood to have amended the earlier. The result was truly astonishing;—*Replegiari*, which is a possessory action, can be pleaded as if it were a droiturel one, and moreover, when it is so pleaded the issue is not on the deeds or an ancient seisin (as one would expect in pleading the right), but on a fairly short, recent seisin which was expressly limited for possessory writs!

"We know better than you, for we made it." What is one to say when one of the most famous of the 14th century judges anticipates our criticism with such an emphatic rebuke? At this distance of time it is all the more hazardous to dispute a point of mediaeval law, yet it must be confessed that as we read the statutes, it is impossible to believe that the author of Westminster II intended at the time of its enactment to amend Marlborough, c. 9 or that he thought that he was in any way covering the same ground as the older enactment. HENGHAM'S claim to a different motive as author of the statute was made twenty years after the passing of the act, but even this affords little help in face of the grave difficulties in accepting his statement. The most we can do is to leave the material before the reader, who may "gloss the statute" at his own discretion.

§ 3. *Mareys* v. *Cogan*

We have found it impossible to resist the conclusion that *Aumeye's Case* left the law in a very unsatisfactory state, and we must now observe how the situation developed in the next reign. *Hubert de Mareys* brought Replevin against *Thomas de Cogan*[1] in 1309, and Cogan avowed the distress for suit of court, alleging that he was seised of the suit at the hands of Mareys himself. *Willoughby* (for Mareys) did not answer this purely possessory avowry, but produced a deed in which suit of court was not specified. *Scrope* at once put Cogan's plea on the basis of Westminster II and offered the formal possessory averment:

> We say that our father and our grandfather were seised of this suit without interruption since the limit of the writ of *Novel Disseisin* (1242), and since we are here in a plea of possession where we aver our own seisin and that of our ancestors, we demand judgment whether our averment be not good.

and of course it is undeniable that he was right if the statute means anything at all. *Scrope's* appeal to Westminster II was followed by an offer of his opponent to aver in the form of the Statute of Marlborough, and again these two statutes were forced into conflict. Once again, however, the logical solution was suggested to the court, this time by *Denham*, who showed that if the plaintiff thought he was ill-treated he should have brought *Contra Formam Feoffamenti*, and *Passeley* supported him, saying that his client had done nothing more than continue the seisin of his ancestors, and had therefore done nothing wrong. At this point BEREFORD interrupted him to tell a tale of three gallows with the moral "Do not trust to what you say as to doing no wrong in continuing the estate of your ancestors, for if their estate be wrongful, so is yours." The whole of BEREFORD's speech shows that he was thinking of the right rather than of the possession; nevertheless, no decision was made and several adjournments followed[2]. Finally, it appears from the record that

[1] Y.B. 2 & 3 Edw. II, 116–118.

[2] The report gives *Denham* a speech after BEREFORD's tale, in which he discusses whether the Statute of Marlborough applies to strangers as well as to privies. This speech is almost certainly misplaced for that question did not arise in this case, as may be seen from the record.

the avowant had to accept issue on the averment of the Statute of Marlborough, or else answer the deed. *Mareys* v. *Cogan* therefore confirms the previous case of *Aumeye* on the one point that *Replegiari* must be pleaded according to the Statute of Marlborough if the tenant puts forward a deed, but reverses the decision on the second point by laying down that the limit of the Statute of Marlborough holds good in such a case and not that of Westminster II. The apparent conflict of the two statutes was not discussed as far as the reports show, the earlier having been followed without question, and the later one ignored.

§ 4. *Hauterive* v. *Painel*

Our next case, *Hauterive* v. *Painel* (1310)[1] makes one further contribution to the question. The facts are the same as in the last case; a lord avowed a distress for suit of court, alleging seisin since the date of limitation set to the assize of *Novel Disseisin* by the Statute of Westminster II, while the tenant would have him answer a deed or else aver a seisin before the limit set by the Statute of Marlborough. *Denham* repeated his arguments in the former case, and his colleague *Scrope* drew the distinction between the statutory *Contra Formam Feoffamenti* and the Common Law replevin on the familiar and sensible lines, urging that the limitation set by the Statute of Marlborough only applied to the statutory action which it established, and that replevin is governed only by the Statute of Westminster II. BEREFORD, however, would hear none of this, and brusquely ordered them to answer whether they were seised before the limit set by the Statute of Marlborough. To this *Geoffrey Scrope* replied: "If I were driven to answer to that, when our avowry is given by the Statute of Westminster II, it would follow that the earlier statute would defeat the later"[2]. HENRY SCROPE, J. seemed to incline once towards keeping the various actions separate[3], but at the end he re-stated the old confusion:

You desire to charge them because your avowry lies in the possession, but in every avowry both right and possession are involved.

[1] Y.B. 3 & 4 Edw. II, 56–64.

[2] *Ibid.* pp. 57-8. This is certainly the point of *Scrope's* remark, but Maitland's translation misses it, and instead makes *Scrope* express surprise that one statute should defeat another—he knew better than this.

[3] *Ibid.* p. 60.

You cannot be received unless your avowry goes to defeat their right and also their title put forward to destroy your avowry[1].

It is quite probable that right and possession might both be involved in *Replegiari* at times[2], but that does not alter the fact that it is primarily possessory and that only the *Ne Vexes* is truly droiturel. Consequently the two statutes made it necessary to be perfectly clear about the true nature of the respective writs; but as we have seen, the court persisted in treating a possessory writ as droiturel. To return. *Denham* nearly succeeded in passing off an averment based on the Statute of Westminster II, but BEREFORD eventually made him aver according to the Statute of Marlborough. The decision thus agrees exactly with that of *Mareys* v. *Cogan*, but the debate contains two new features: first, *Scrope* exposes the startling fact that virtually the court has been assuming that it is the earlier statute which is to be followed when two statutes are at variance; secondly, BEREFORD made the discovery that Westminster II speaks of customs and services only, and that Marlborough[3] speaks of suit only, but as far as we can judge from the reports failed to find a practical use for it[4].

§ 5. *Thorgrim* v. *Bishop of Hereford*

The next case to be considered, *Thorgrim* v. *Bishop of Hereford*[5], is practically contemporary with the preceding, but carries the matter much further; indeed there are traces of some useful thinking having taken place. For example, BEREFORD is found saying, "If the Bishop were seised for so long a time that a freehold accrued to him, and afterwards he was disturbed, would he not have the assize?—*quasi diceret sic*"—which is the exact opposite of the moral drawn from his parable of the three gallows[6]. Then again, when the tenant pleads the deed of feoffment, he says that the lord must confess his deed or else aver a seisin ever since 1242, i.e. by Westminster II[7]. This remarkable voluntary admission by the tenant that Westminster

[1] Y.B. 3 & 4 Edw. II, 63.

[2] See for example, *Malberthorpe's* speech, *ibid.* p. 57.

[3] That is to say the portion dealing with *Contra Formam Feoffamenti*.

[4] *Ibid.* pp. 59, 60.

[5] Y.B. 3 & 4 Edw. II, 64–71.

[6] *Ibid.* p. 65. The lord was under the impression that a seisin of any time since 1242 however short, was sufficient. (BEREFORD had decided against this in *Hauterive* v. *Painel*, *ibid.* p. 62.)

[7] Above, p. 93.

II has amended Marlborough removes the anomaly of interpretation pointed out by *Geoffrey Scrope* in the previous case, but only by reverting to the equally unsatisfactory position reached in *Aumeye's Case*. By escaping one horn of the dilemma, he was impaled on the other. No decision was reached as other difficulties arose, and eventually Thorgrim was non-suited.

§ 6. *The Later History of the Conflict*

An anonymous case[1] that follows immediately in the Year Book gives us the important decision that the Statute of Marlborough only applies to parties and privies to the deed; consequently when the parties to a replevin are strangers to a deed, the Statute of Marlborough cannot possibly apply, and the avowry for a seisin must run from the limit set by Westminster II (which is assumed to cover suit as well as "customs and services"). This later became the established law but there is a case (*Prior of St Mary's, Bishopsgate* v. *Habenhache*)[2] to the opposite effect, for both parties were strangers to the deed, and yet the avowry was maintained by an averment of seisin before 1230, according to the Statute of Marlborough.

Having pursued the history of *Replegiari* so far in this connection it may be of interest to enquire into its ultimate fate. This is not easy to ascertain, but a note in the *Registrum Brevium* states that in *Replegiari* an avowant must answer to his ancestor's deed if put forward by a tenant as evidence of what his services should be. Eventually, the custom became established, then, of pleading this possessory action in the right, and as time went on the difference in the dates of limitation set by the two conflicting statutes caused no inconvenience; the averment of such a long seisin as even the shorter of them would have become impracticable. Other forces were at work, too. The charter of feoffment occupied an increasingly important place in the law of the land, and litigants who had no deed were at a serious disadvantage in the Royal Courts. It is highly improbable that a feoffment of any considerable value would have been made without a charter after our period; consequently the parties who disputed their services would naturally plead in the right, and

[1] Y.B. 3 & 4 Edw. II, 71–2. [2] *Ibid.* 91–5.

the need would be felt of a convenient droiturel remedy. *Ne Vexes* was out of the question; *Contra Formam Feoffamenti* was only less solemn and costly. Moreover, we have reached the period when new actions are hardly ever born, although old ones may enter upon unexpected careers. Hence we find the possessory Replevin turning into a droiturel action. As for a possessory action in later times, there seems to have been little need of it. The preamble to the Statute of Marlborough clearly shows that the heyday of the lord with a possessory title was during the Barons' War. But those days were gone, and with the gradual settlement of the nation there was less and less call for the protection of possessory titles as such. *Replegiari* in its original possessory form, therefore, was not in great request; two characteristics only fitted it for survival. The first was that by its use one immediately regained the distress; the second was its convenient process. We therefore find the equally useful principle of *Contra Formam Feoffamenti* grafted on to the older form of action of Replevin. In the early stages of the change, much uncertainty arose; two statutes were forced into conflict, the ancient distinction between possessory and droiturel actions would not fit the altered circumstances, and legal theory generally suffered rather badly when it was applied in arguments in Court. Uncertainty is a cardinal sin in law, but once the victory of custom and precedent over theory was assured, it is clear that the transformed Replevin was a very serviceable action.

§ 7. *Examples of the Inter-relation of Statutes*

The following cases will afford further illustrations of the methods adopted by the Courts in determining the mutual relationships of statutes.

When a "tenant" vouches, the Statute of Westminster I, c. 40 gives the demandant a number of counterpleas, and it was provided by the statute that this should also extend to a tenant by warranty; but what if a man vouch who is only "admitted" under the later Statute of Westminster II, c. 3 to defend his right? The latest theory to be put forward is that he is not a "tenant" for the purpose of the statute and therefore the statutory counterpleas would not apply to him. When this question was raised in 1344 an interesting debate took place[1]. The demandant's first counterplea of the voucher by the admittee was that the admittee's ancestor was the first to abate upon the death of him on whose seisin he had counted. To this the admittee replied: this counterplea was given by the Statute of Westminster I, but admission to defend one's right was not allowed until ten years afterwards by the Statute of Westminster II. Therefore the counterplea given by the first statute cannot apply to us who are only tenant in virtue of the second statute. After further discussion, but not, it would seem, for this reason, the Court adjudged that the counterplea would not avail. Judging from the fulness with which it is reported, the writer of the Year Book was evidently most interested by the suggestion that a man admitted under the Statute of Westminster II to defend his right could not be a tenant for the purposes of the earlier Statute of Westminster I. His report would also tend to show that the Court was similarly impressed. The further pleadings, however, make it clear that the point, although much argued, was eventually lost, for we find the demandant trying a new counterplea of the voucher, the first having failed. This second counterplea, moreover, is based on the very same statute as the former, and since the admittee finally took issue upon it, it is clear that he conceded the point that the counterplea did apply to tenants by admission. Indeed, very serious difficulties would have arisen had it been otherwise, but the fact that the matter was contested and reported at some length clearly shows the nature of contemporary doubts upon the matter.

In a *Monstravit de Compoto de Tempore quo fuit Receptor* the defendant was attached by his body and objected to this process as not warranted by the Statute of Marlborough, c. 23 which only gives it against bailiffs and not receivers. But Bereford, C.J. read the Statute of Westminster II, c. 11 which referred to "servants, bailiffs, chamberlains and all manner of receivers" and said that it "had relation to the Statute of Marlborough for it said 'sicut in aliis statutis continetur'" and adjudged the writ good[2].

[1] *Anon.*, Y.B. 18 & 19 Edw. III, 258–260.
[2] *Anon.*, Y.B. 4 Edw. II, 3–4.

William Latimer brought trespass against *Robert Constable*[1] and others for ravishing and taking away Marjory, his wife, together with his goods and chattels against the Statute of Westminster II, c.34. To the writ it was excepted that the statute gives suit for the goods to the king, but the judges held that it does not therefore take it away from anyone else, and that the husband still has the suit which was given to him under the Statute of Westminster I, c. 13. They do not seem to have found any difficulty in the fact that Westminster I does not say anything about the carrying off of goods, but speaks only of the ravishment (for which a subject may sue within forty days, and the king after). Nevertheless, they thought the statutes covered common ground, and the case shows their method of dealing with the situation so produced.

§ 8. *Interpretation of Statutes* in pari materia

A few examples may be given of the way in which piecemeal legislation by different statutes was knit together into a coherent whole by the courts. The Statute of Gloucester, c. 4 enables a lord by the action of *Cessavit* to recover possession of land let at a substantial rent if the tenant has ceased to pay for two years, and has so neglected the land that there is nothing distrainable on it; and the Statute of Westminster II, c. 21 extends the action of *Cessavit* to a cesser of customs and services. The court construed the two statutes together, and held that a *cessavit* of customs and services was also conditional on there being no available distress[2]. *Magna Carta*, c. 4 forbids waste and exile of men in the lands of an infant by his guardian; the Statute of Gloucester, c. 5 gives an action of waste against tenants by the curtesy, for life, for years or in dower, and the Statute of Marlborough, c. 23 had forbidden the exile of men by termors; from these three *data* the Court deduced that a doweress should answer for exile of folk[3]—and this, it seems, without invoking the aid of the Statute of Westminster II, c. 24 "in consimili casu," which is mainly associated with the writ of Entry so named, the history of which has been recounted above.

[1] Y.B. 32 & 33 Edw. I, 316; this (not *Gyse* v. *Baudewyne*, Y.B. 3 & 4 Edw. II, xxxiii, 5) is the first reported action upon the statute.

[2] *Herle* arguing in *Dowdeswell* v. *Mustel*, Y.B. 6 & 7 Edw. II, 89.

[3] *Anon.*, Y.B. 2 & 3 Edw. II, 148–9.

CHAPTER VIII

IGNORANCE OF STATUTES AMONG CONTEMPORARY LAWYERS

THIS is surely the very last heading one would think of finding in a law-book. The maxim of the modern books that "Every man is presumed to be cognisant of the statute law of this Realm and to construe it aright"[1] has good mediaeval authority in the Year Books, where we read that

Every man is bound to know what is done in Parliament even although it has not been proclaimed in the country; as soon as Parliament has concluded any matter the law presumes that every person has cognisance of it, for Parliament represents the body of all the Realm[2].

Similar opinions are to be found in Canon[3] and Civil Law[4]. We are concerned, however, with the fact that professional lawyers —and judges, too—were guilty of serious errors in quoting and applying the statute law. The situation is difficult for us in these days to imagine; that legislation of vast importance should only be published in a few manuscript copies (mostly unofficial), and perhaps also by proclamation, would certainly account for widespread popular ignorance of its provisions; but the courts themselves seem to have been dependent on memory rather than on writing for their knowledge of statute law. Thus we find that the reporters take care to note when a judge has "looked at the statute" for this is evidently a special precaution reserved for difficult cases, the report of which would be particularly valuable.

§ 1. *The Texts used in Court*

It would be most interesting if one could say with certainty what copy of the statutes the court used—whether the statute roll[5], close roll, patent roll, or one of the semi-official registers

[1] Broom, *Maxims*, 217.

[2] *R.* v. *Bishop of Chichester*, Y.B. 39 Edw. III, 7.

[3] De reg. jur. in VI. reg. xiii; "Ignorantia facti, non juris, excusat."

[4] "Constitutiones principum nec ignorare quemquam nec dissimulare permittimus," Cod. 1. 18. 12.

[5] Even the Statute Roll was not infallible; for example it misses out an important passage from c. 5 of Westminster II, which has had to be supplied from the registers.

now preserved in the Exchequer, or whether they had a copy for their own use—but as to this there is no evidence. It would seem that the court had not always a text at hand, judging as well from what has just been said, as from such incidents as when a party brought into court a copy of the statute 14 Edw. III, st. 4, c. 2 sealed with the great seal[1], or when BEREFORD said to a party "Show us the statute" and when he had seen it, told them that they were not in the case provided for in it[2]. This impression is confirmed by the cases now about to be considered, the evidence all pointing to the same conclusion, namely, that reference by the court to an official copy of a statute was decidedly unusual, and that the court did not possess a copy of its own for ready reference. We have already had occasion to charge the legislature with clumsy and sometimes careless work, but this must not be considered alone, for it is closely connected with the equally serious failure of the courts to secure accurate knowledge of the details of the legislature's enactments. The negligences of the one and the ignorances of the other will go far to explain much that is obscure in the reports of our period.

If this was the state of the court's equipment, the pleaders would seem to have been even less favourably placed, and the importance of these factors becomes apparent in any attempt to reconstruct the conditions under which the first steps in the scientific interpretation of statutes were made.

Even the statutes themselves contain remarkable blunders. For example, Westminster II, c. 21 quotes the Statute of Gloucester, c. 4 as giving an action of *Cessavit* to a lessor "or his heir," but Gloucester says nothing of the lessor's heir and only gives the action to the lessor. Westminster II, c. 28 also cites the Statute of Gloucester as forbidding essoins for tenants after appearance in assizes, but this time the provision is not to be found in Gloucester at all, but in Westminster I, c. 42[3]. If the authors of Westminster II (HENGHAM and others) were so uncertain on the matter, we may not be surprised that KAVE, J.

[1] *R.* v. *Bishop of Coventry and Lichfield*, Y.B. 14 Edw. III, 138 (57), note from the Record. Above, p. 11.

[2] *Tauney* v. *St Omers*, Y.B. 32 & 33 Edw. I, 290.

[3] The provisions of the Statute of Gloucester, c. 5, are erroneously attributed to Westminster II by the Statute of Waste, and to Westminster I by Westminster II, c. 14.

received "by the statute of Gloucester" an averment that was really given by the Statute of Westminster II, c. 20[1]. HENGHAM himself quoted this as a statute: "quod vivente altero ipsorum vendor ou achator quia ignorare non debet quod jus emit alienum, locum habeat predictum breve." This consists mainly of Westminster II, c. 25 with a portion of c. 40 (which deals with a totally different subject) interjected[2].

§ 2. *Westminster I, c. 47, and* Sur Disseisin

It is little short of astonishing how wildly misquoted statutes were in a number of cases; a pleader hoped to use Westminster I, c. 40 for example (which gives several counterpleas of voucher) in order to oust a man from view—an entirely unrelated subject[3]. *Passeley* expounded Westminster I, c. 47 thus: "You do not come within the statute unless you say that the disseisee brought a writ of *Novel Disseisin* and died during the plea." The report continues: "The statute was read and agreed with what *Passeley* said." This is inexplicable seeing that the statute as we have it says: "Let the heir or heirs of the disseisee have their writ of Entry against the disseisors of whatever age they be, if perchance the disseisee die *before he has made his purchase* [of the writ]." The statute, in fact, supposes that the death occurred before the action was commenced, but the court believed it to apply only when proceedings had been begun before the death of the disseisee[4]. Although this was not the main point in dispute, yet it was sufficiently prominent in the arguments to make it probable that the reporter was at pains to report the case accurately, especially as the court took the important step of "looking at the statute"—usually an occasion of great interest to the compilers of the Year Books. Nor is this case alone in its witness to the existence of this misconception concerning the text of this statute, for we read (also in the reign of Edward II) how STAUNTON, J.

[1] *Anon.*, Y.B. 20 & 21 Edw. I, 31.

[2] *Anon.* v. *Coupe of Canterbury*, Y.B. 32 & 33 Edw. I, 77. The words "vendor ou achator" seem to be an explanatory interpolation in French, either by HENGHAM or his reporter, in a Latin text.

[3] *Anon.*, Y.B. 1 & 2 Edw. II, 93.

[4] *Lefevre* v. *Brockwelle*, Y.B. 6 & 7 Edw. II (*Eyre of Kent*), II. 179.

looked at the statute and said..."The statute supposes that the disseisee brings a suit of *Novel Disseisin* but dies pending the plea; but here you do not say that your ancestor died pending the plea, so the statute does not help you."

Most of the manuscripts report an adjournment; one says that the judgment was that the statute did not apply for the reason stated[1]. Even in the previous reign there are traces of the same notion; thus in the 21 Edw. I we find a tenant arguing that since the demandant's predecessor had not sued the assize, he could not have the benefit of the statute, although it was shown that he died immediately after the disseisin and so could not have sued. Both parties demurred in judgment here—with what result we do not know[2]. We may, however, guess the probable judgment from another case in the same volume and only a year later, where we find a tenant saying that a demandant who was bringing action on a disseisin done to his mother ought not to have the benefit of the statute since she brought no assize against the disseisor. To this the demandant replied that she could not, since she was under age and *coverte*. Nevertheless the writ was quashed for this reason[3]. In this last case, at least, the error can hardly have been the work of a reporter for it is a material point in the case and not a mere side-issue or embellishment upon which less care might be spent. But even if we blame the reporter (and this especially applies to those cases where he professes to repeat the effect of the statute as the judges declared it upon inspection of the text) the fact remains that an enterprising lawyer who undertook to reconstruct a debate in court did not know correctly a most important detail of the statute under discussion, and in writing his Year Book had not the facilities (or if he had, lacked the inclination) for verifying his reference to the statute. The only other possibility is that of the early judges using a text that has since been lost; there is nothing but conjecture in favour of this theory, while the fact that a large number of manuscripts have come down to us without any trace of the variant would be difficult to account for. While not

[1] *Anon.*, Y.B. 2 & 3 Edw. II, 114. STAUNTON is, in fact, attributing to the statute what was really the pre-existing Common Law. See below, p. 107, n. 3.

[2] *Anon.*, Y.B. 21 & 22 Edw. I, 236.

[3] *Anon.*, *ibid.* 350.

altogether impossible, we must regard the theory as highly improbable. A further complication is due to the fact that at least once[1] we find SCROPE, J. and BEREFORD, C.J. expounding the statute correctly, and contradicting the argument of *Herle*, who was putting forward the commonly accepted interpretation as outlined above.

Another point of similar interest also arose concerning the same statute. After the provision upon which the above cases were founded, the statute goes on to state that this shall also apply to "prelates, and others to whom land may come after the death of another person." In other words, a prelate's successor shall be in the same position as a layman's heir[2]. *Friskeney*, however, took the words "to whom lands or tenements may come in any manner after the death of another," misquoted them as "to whosesoever hands tenements may come after the death of another," and then by inserting them in the first part of the chapter used them to prove that the statute applied not only to a layman's heirs, but also to his alienees—a conclusion that did not commend itself to the court[3].

§ 3. *Other Examples of Ignorance of Statutes*

In the course of a discussion on a case of *Nuper Obiit*[4], *Cambridge* argued that "The Statute of Gloucester says that if an

[1] *Attewelle* v. *Attwelle*, Y.B. 8 Edw. II, 200–1.

[2] The translation in the *Statutes of the Realm* is nonsense, and indeed is the exact opposite of what the text says.

[3] *Anon.*, Y.B. 5 Edw. II, I. 108. His attempt was to maintain a writ of Entry *Sur Disseisin* in the *Post* under the statute. Writs *Sur Disseisin* existed before the statute (see several examples in *Bracton's Note Book*, 76, 131, 372, 383, 434, 493, 872, 993, 1405, 1883). Before the statute the plea demurred for the nonage of the heir, and it was to remedy this that the statute was made saying that in certain cases it should not demur. It also made an extension in the scope of the writ which heretofore had only applied in cases where an assize had been brought and prosecuted as far as view at least; after the statute the heir of a disseised person could have the writ if no undue delay had taken place. Only special forms of the writ if in the *per* or *per* and *cui* were accorded the benefit of the statute (2 *Inst.* 257–8). The writ in the *post* was stated at one time to be used only for clergy, since succession is not a degree (*Reg. Br. Orig.* f. 229*b*, fifth and sixth *regulae*). At a later time, however, the writ in the *post* was commonly used by laymen (an example is in 2 Bl. Comm. (1776) App. V). For the relation of the Statute of Marlborough to *Sur Disseisin* in the *Post* see above, p. 80.

[4] Statute of Gloucester, c. 2; *Cauville* v. *Drax*, Y.B. 6 & 7 Edw. II (*Eyre of Kent*), III. 160; this case is discussed more in detail, above, p. 15.

infant under age bring a possessory writ, and a feoffment or some other matter is pleaded against him whereby the judges award the inquest, the mise shall not be delayed for his age." As a matter of fact, the statute only refers to *Ael*, *Besael* and *Cosinage* (and not to *Nuper Obiit*, nor even to possessory writs in general) although the *Statutes of the Realm* translation interpolates a word (without textual authority) which makes it seem to apply to *Mort d'Ancestor* and perhaps *Nuper Obiit* as well. Consequently STAUNTON, J. had to remind him that the statute said nothing of *Nuper Obiit*, and that even if *Cambridge* was right, yet he was not within the statute, for they were pleading in the right and not in the possession.

Another protracted discussion was occasioned by the question as to whether a vicarage was a temporality or not, the court finally reached the conclusion that it was, but might have saved much trouble had it known that the matter was settled already by statute[1].

Acclum v. *Carpenter*[2] is a strange collection of errors. The action was *Sur Cui in Vita* and *Claver* was defending. The case was begun in the early years of Edward II's reign, but the seisin upon which the demandant relied went as far back as the reign of Henry III. *Claver's* argument was that the writ of *Cui in Vita* was created by the Statute of Westminster II, c. 3 (one manuscript says the Statute of Gloucester) and that as the seisin laid was in the reign of Henry III and before the statute, therefore the statutory action did not lie—in other words, the statute was not retrospective. As we have seen, the confusion between the Statutes of Gloucester and Westminster was not infrequent; the belief that Westminster II created *Cui in Vita* is rarer, though equally inexplicable. Numerous examples of the action occur in *Bracton's Note Book*, dating from the early years of Henry III's reign, and as *Hedon* pointed out, the statute itself implies that the writ was not then a novelty. The innovation that the statute actually made was to make *Cui in Vita* available for the recovery of lands lost by default as well of those alienated, and

[1] Westminster II, c. 5; *R.* v. *Archbishop of York*, Y.B. 5 Edw. II, I. 57 ff. and *Introd.* xviii.

[2] Y.B. 2 & 3 Edw. II, 150.

to lay down the lines upon which the writ was to be pleaded when brought to recover losses by default.

§ 4. *Westminster II, c.* 48, *and misnomer of vill*

The reign of Edward III affords what is perhaps the most striking of all the examples to be found in our period[1]. After view was had, a writ was abated for wrongly describing the mode of entry. A new writ was therefore brought and view was again demanded. *Gaynford* was somewhat puzzled:

> The statute [Westminster II, c. 48] says that if a writ abate for misnomer of a vill, "vel huiusmodi" he shall not have the view by the statute, but the statute does not mention the case in which the writ is abated for bad description of the entry.

SHARDELOWE, J. accepted this extraordinary assertion, and it was only by construing the words "vel huiusmodi" as including misnomer of entry as well as of vill that he brought the case under the statute. Both court and counsel seem completely ignorant of the fact that the statute does, in fact, expressly provide for misnomer of entry as well as that of vill in these words:

> In breve etiam de ingressu cassato per hoc quod petens male nominavit ingressum, si petens suscitet aliud breve de aliquo ingressu, si tenens in priori breve habuit visum, in secundo non habebit.

Another judge, SPIGURNEL, based a decision on his belief that the Statute of Westminster II, c. 12 only applied to appeals of homicide, and therefore refused to apply it to an appeal of rape[2]. The statute, however, expressly mentions in the preamble "appeals of homicide and other felonies" and in the operative part "appeals of felony." Again, in a statutory counterplea of voucher the tenant required the demandant's averment to be in a particular form of words: the demandant objected that that form was only used in a writ of Right—"and the statute was read, and found to be as he said." If this is so, the text they used was unique, for as we have it, the statute gives only one form

[1] *Anon.*, Y.B. 12 & 13 Edw. III, 116 (22).

[2] *R.* v. *Anon.*, Y.B. 30 & 31 Edw. I, 521. The same manuscript is again printed in Y.B. 6 & 7 Edw. II (*Eyre of Kent*), I. 111 (MS *T*).

for all writs[1]. In another case a strange decision may be attributed to a corrupt reading of Westminster I, c. 37[2]. Only one case has been found which makes it clear that the reporter is at fault[3]; this was a trespass on the statute against the bailiffs of Northampton for distraining a traveller passing through their liberty in respect of a contract made outside their jurisdiction. The record makes it quite clear that the statute in question is Westminster I, c. 35 but the Year Book alludes to the Statute of Marlborough, c. 15[4].

There are some remarkable features attending the Statute of Marlborough, c. 17 which gives to the heir of socage lands an action to bring to account his "propinquiores parentes" who had his wardship, to ensure that they do no waste, sale or destruction during his minority, without being strictly accountable to him as soon as he reached his age. When an heir[5] brought his writ against the Abbess of Barking, however, *Pole* demanded judgment of his count "because he does not make the Abbess the infant's next friend." SHARDELOWE, J. refused to accept *Pole's* argument, saying that anyone who occupies the wardship is presumed by the law to be "next friend," and told him to plead over. *Stouford* then raised a very pertinent question: "This writ is given by Statute, which says 'Kinsman (*parent*),' but nothing of next friend; judgment of the writ." We are told no details of the discussion of this point—simply that "this was not allowed." It seems clear that *Pole* thought that the statute said "next friend," and it is almost as clear that SHARDELOWE, J. thought so too, for otherwise his declaration that anyone who happed the wardship was constructively "next friend" has no point. *Stouford* knew that the statute really did say "Kinsman" and not "next friend" but his objection was not allowed. We

[1] *FitzWalter* v. *Bodregan*, Y.B. 30 & 31 Edw. I, 226. The statute (Westminster I, c. 40) is very clumsily drawn: it begins with giving one averment to be used in possessory writs, and later on gives a different averment to be used in writs of Right: then follows a statement that the second averment shall also be available in "the other writs aforementioned"—i.e. possessory writs, and writs of Entry.

[2] See above, p. 17.

[3] *St Maur* v. *Bailiffs of Northampton*, Y.B. 13 & 14 Edw. III, 298–9.

[4] And Pike gave the reference as Westminster I, c. 16. Compare the Chapters of the Eyre, *Stats. Realm*, I. 237*a* (25); *Reg. Br. Orig*. ff. 98, 102*b*.

[5] *Anon.* v. *Abbess of Barking*, Y.B. 12 & 13 Edw. III, 321.

may suspect that a textual variant existed in the statute, for the old translation printed in the *Statutes of the Realm* also has "next friend." This, however, is purely conjectural, for no such reading has so far been noticed.

§ 5. *Traditional Misconceptions concerning Statutes*

The Register of Original Writs, which represents the accumulated traditions of the law, contains one very curious example of a misconception about a statute. A writ "quod justiciarii procedant ad captionem assisae non obstante aliquo mandato magni sigilli sive parvi"[1] begins with the recital "Cum in Parliamento Domini Edwardi nuper Regis Angliae avi nostri apud Northampton anno regni sui secundo convocato." The writ is therefore based upon an exemplar at least as late as Richard II, and must refer to a Parliament of Edward III; the Register gives it as the proper form, but with this quaint comment: "Nota quod non habetur aliquod tale statutum prout in isto brevi fit mentio in anno 2 Edw. III apud Northampton editum; sed habetur huiusmodi statutum in anno 20 eiusdem regis. Attamen quaere Articulos super Cartas, si statutum predictum inseratur necne." It is important to note the curious mentality of an age which, although pedantic in the extreme about literal accuracy in legal records, could continue to use a writ based on a statute generally believed to be non-existent. As a matter of history, there was a Statute of Northampton in the second year of Edward III and the writ is founded on its eighth chapter.

Closely connected with this subject is the growth of legends, so to speak, concerning statutes. Such are the notions that the Statute of Merton, c. 10 allows one to appoint an attorney to prosecute and defend actions in various courts[2]; that *Magna Carta*, c. 6 instituted the marriage of male wards[3], and that c. 11 forbids common pleas being heard in the Exchequer[4]; that *Magna Carta*, c. 13 includes *Quare Impedit*[5]; that the Statute of Essoins allows a protection *de Servitio Regis* "For women as necessary attendants upon the Camp, and that in three cases,

[1] *Reg. Br. Orig.* f. 186. [2] Y.B. 6 & 7 Edw. II, xiii; above, p. 75.

[3] Pollock and Maitland, I. 324.

[4] *Memoranda de Scaccario*, Mich. 12 Edw. I, f. 7; Stat. Rothlan (end); *Articuli Super Cartas*, c. 4. [5] *Reg. Br. Orig.* f. 30.

quia Lotrix, seu Nutrix, seu Obstetrix"[1]. Some have been traced to their origins—such as the conversion of "prisone forte et dure" of Westminster I, c. 12 into "peyne fort et dure"[2]; others have not, and among them may be included the theory that the statute *Quia Emptores* prevents the creation of a new manor[3].

In one case a Year Book seems ignorant of the fact that a statute which it mentions had been repealed[4].

[1] Co. Lit. 130; Barrington, 161–2. For protections *Quia Nutrix* see *Anon.*, Y.B. 17 Edw. III, 34; *Staunton* v. *Staunton*, Y.B. 13 & 14 Edw. III, 18.

In *Anon.*, Y.B. 16 Edw. III, I. 176 (11), a woman claimed to be the nurse of the King's son, Richard, and the following dialogue took place:

"*Thorpe*. It is sufficiently of record that the King has no son Richard, so we pray that the essoin be quashed.

HILARY, J. The essoiner cannot be a party to try that issue.

Thorpe. Then we pray that our challenge be entered.

HILARY, J. Why? If the King will warrant the essoin at another day, that will be sufficient...."

However, the challenge was entered.

For the so-called "Statute of Essoins," see Y.B. 32 & 33 Edw. I, xxxiv, n. 3.

[2] Barrington, 62–70; Pollock and Maitland, II. 651–2.

[3] 2 Dwarris, 849. Some light may come from the words of STONORE, C.J.: "In ancient times one could enfeoff of a manor by the description of a knight's fee, and it is so even to-day." (*Ryhille* v. *Umframville*, Y.B. 17 Edw. III, 122.) Compare also *Herle's* statement in *Grymbaud* v. *Huby* (Y.B. 8 Edw. II, 3) that where a manor lies in four or five hamlets "each of them becomes a separate manor in itself by long continuance," and *Denham's* argument in *Furness* v. *Castle* (*ibid.* 34), "May not a third part of the manor of Plashes have become in some way the manor of Rennesley?" In the previous reign METINGHAM, J. had suggested that a vill "may be reputed to be a manor" in the neighbourhood. (*Anon.* v. *Master and Scholars of Merton*, Y.B. 21 & 22 Edw. I, 226.) Further references are given by Mr Bolland in his Introduction. (Y.B. 8 Edw. II, XXIX.)

[4] Y.B. Hil. 2 Hen. IV, 26; 14 Edw. III, stat. 4, c. 2.

CHAPTER IX

THE RETROSPECTIVE EFFECT OF STATUTES

MUCH debate is reported on the subject of whether various statutes are retrospective or not in their operation[1], and the problem seems to have been so insistent as to merit special treatment here. We will begin with its relation to the statute *De Donis* in which connection the difficulty was most acutely felt.

§ 1. De Donis *and Conditional Fees created before the Statute*

The statute reads as follows: "Hoc statutum quoad alienacionem tenementi contra formam doni imposterum faciend' locum habet, et ad dona prius facta non extendit." How is one to expand "faciend'"—as *faciendam* or *faciendi*? We venture to suggest that self-consistency would require the latter, in which case we should translate: "This statute takes effect with respect to alienations contrary to the form of gifts hereafter to be made, but does not extend to gifts made before." Moreover, what are "dona"? Are they the gifts creating the entail, or are they the gifts discontinuing it? The statute seems to have attempted to be consistent by always using "donum" in the former sense and "alienatio" in the latter; this can easily be verified by examining the use of the words "donum" and "alienatio" and their respective derivatives. This will leave no doubt that, apart from this particular clause, the use of the two sets of terms was consistently governed by this principle throughout the rest of the chapter. We therefore see no alternative to the assumption that the same principle applies to this sentence also. Otherwise we have the amazing anomaly that when the statute says "contra formam doni" in one line, and "ad dona prius facta" in the next, it means one thing by the first "donum," but a totally different thing by the second.

It must be confessed that practically all authority is against this construction, save perhaps a cautious hint by Maitland[2],

[1] For the Canon Law of the subject, see above, p. 37.

[2] Y.B. 3 & 4 Edw. II, 72, n. 1.

who suggested that the traditional view as expressed by Coke was not easy to justify from the text of the statute, although on the other hand he did not commit himself to the view of the meaning of "dona" expressed above. Coke[1] found two explanations necessary before the statute could be reconciled with the law as he knew it. First, that "dona prius facta" means alienations by the tenant in tail; this we have shown to be inconsistent with use of the word in the rest of the chapter. Secondly, these "dona" are only those gifts made *post prolem suscitandam*, because a tenant of a conditional fee before the statute only acquired the power of alienating it if he had had issue and thereby fulfilled the condition. These two constructions having been accepted, Coke deduces that the statute does extend to gifts creating entails before the statute—a result which is the opposite of what the statute states, if read in the light of the above suggestions.

We are, therefore, faced with two constructions: either *De Donis* does extend to entails created before the statute, or it does not. It now remains to be seen how this problem was handled in practice.

The first notice we find is hardly a case, so much as a poser by some eminent lawyer, whose solution interested the reporter. Its date cannot be definitely proved; its presence in a Year Book of 1292 raises a presumption, however, and there seems no evidence to the contrary. As it stands, it deals with the following facts[2]. *A* gives a tenement to *J* in frank marriage with his daughter. Before the statute *J* alienates it; after *J*'s death and after the statute his widow confirms the deed. The writer of the note argues that:

(1) After the husband's death and after the statute, she could have had recovery by the *Cui in Vita*.

(2) And therefore "I am advised that the issue could probably recover" (by Formedon).

(3) A fine, "which is the highest thing in the court," levied after the statute is void if contrary to it; therefore the confirmation is void *a fortiori*.

[1] *Inst.* 336.

[2] *Anon.*, Y.B. 20 & 21 Edw. I, 300.

It will be noticed that none of these deductions is tenable except on the assumption that the statute applies to entails created before the statute was passed—an assumption not easily made, as we have shown, in view of the wording of the statute. The legal theory beneath all this is to be found in the next year when a case arose with the following facts[1]. A demandant sought to recover by Formedon in the Descender lands given to his father and mother in frank marriage. The tenant's exception to the writ was that the donees died ten years before the statute and that therefore a statutory writ does not lie. BEREWYKE, J. advised him to be more explicit:

if you wish to set up the statute you must take all the words of the statute. Although the donees died before the statute, nevertheless his action remains by virtue of the statute unless you can say that they to whom the gift was made alienated before the statute.

And again:

The statute was directed against alienations to be made of tenements so given, and does not extend to gifts made before, so your argument would be good enough if you had said that the donees alienated before the statute.

BEREWYKE reads "dona" as meaning alienation, be it observed, which is a necessary consequence of having read "faciendam" instead of "faciendi." The tenant replied that there was nothing in that which answered his objection, which was to the writ and not to the action, for he maintained that whatever action the plaintiff might be entitled to, he could not bring Formedon. BEREFORD then intervened with a characteristically original point of view in support of the writ:

When you say that the writ originated in the statute you are quite right. But the statute was to provide for a case occurring before the statute;...even if the gift were made forty years before the statute, he would have a remedy by the statute, for by the form of the gift a right accrued to him immediately, although his action remained in suspense until the donee's death. Moreover, when the writ of *Mort d'Ancestor* was provided it served in case my ancestor was previously dead[2]. Similarly when one comes to chancery and prays remedy in

[1] *Anon.* v. *Waltham*, Y.B. 21 & 22 Edw. I, 320.

[2] How does BEREFORD know this? Was there some tradition among the Judges to this effect? *Mort d'Ancestor* dates from 1176—over a century earlier. (Pollock and Maitland, I. 147.)

a case which has happened to him where there was no remedy before, then so that he may not quit the court in despair, the chancellor shall give him a writ which shall serve for his case which before the making ["confeccion"] of the writ was unprovided for, so your argument does not hold good.

To this the tenant objected that if the donees died before the statute, then the action also accrued before the statute, and therefore the plaintiff cannot use a writ founded on the statute. He was, however, prepared to admit that if the donees had died after the statute, then the statute would have applied. To all this BEREWYKE curtly answered, "And we think the contrary." The tenant therefore answered to the writ, and it appeared that he had good reason for not pleading as to the date of the alienation by his ancestors, the donees, for the inquest found that the donees had never been seised by the form of the gift. Summing up the results of the case, it will be seen that BEREFORD's speech is the key to the situation. We are tempted to be too dispassionate in handling what must have been at the time a hotly contested question. The donee of a conditional fee could indeed alienate the land after issue born, with perfect impunity to himself, the complete disinheritance of the issue, and a good title to the purchaser. But all the same it was felt that it was a dishonest transaction, and the heir was believed to have suffered a wrong. But for this wrong there was no legal remedy until the statute, which came like a special providence of the chancery, and gave a writ and a remedy where previously there was none. It soon became, and indeed already was, the custom to regard the statute as removing an abuse from the law of conditional fees, rather than as creating a new branch of law dealing with entails. That the wording of the statute will not bear this interpretation, is clear; but it is equally clear that hundreds of disinherited heirs had the public's sympathy, and that of the Bench, too, while many others must have been apprehensive, knowing that the present tenant could, under the existing law, disinherit them. There was therefore a natural desire that existing conditional fees should have the same protection as the statute only strictly gave to entails created after the act, although it was also recognised that the *bona fide* purchaser who had a good title under the old law could not reasonably be disturbed under the new. This was a possible settlement of the matter; but it is not the settlement laid down in the statute. How then can the one be read into the other? BEREWYKE shows us. We shall have to read "faciendam" instead of "faciendi," and make "dona" mean the same thing as the "alienacio," but a different thing from the "doni," which both occur in the previous line.

BEREWYKE's view was not destined to hold the ground very long, for in 1302 the contrary decision was given[1]. Roger Haye had given to Robert Bussard a tenement in frank marriage (as was alleged) with his daughter Joan. Bussard committed felony, fled the country and died leaving no issue. Joan married secondly William Seygnour who had issue and remained seised of the tenements after Joan's death as by the curtesy for ten years. Then Walter, the heir of Roger Haye the donor, entered upon the land as reversioner and so disseised William. William recovered his seisin by assize and Walter was driven to his Formedon in the Reverter. In this action issue was taken as to whether the gift was in frank marriage or in fee-tail, and the inquest found that it was in tail[2], so William recovered his seisin. This, however, was not completely satisfactory, for William's position as second husband was still uncertain. He therefore brought a bill in the eyre alleging that the tenements were given before the statute, and that consequently he ought to hold them for his life (a privilege which the statute abolished). The inquest was recalled and said that the gift in tail was before the statute, but that Joan died after the statute. *Middleton* now argued that as Joan died after the statute therefore the statute would apply—and William as second husband was not entitled to the curtesy. But BRUMPTON, J. adjudged that since the gift was made before the statute that therefore the statute did not apply, and so he allowed William his curtesy, with reversion at his death to Walter. This is the first reported example of the statute being applied in exact accordance with its provisions on the point.

[1] *Haye* v. *Seygnour*, Y.B. 30 & 31 Edw. I, 122–6.

[2] "This is the difference between Formedon and Frank Marriage; in a gift in Frank Marriage the reversion is always saved and supposed, but in a gift in tail the reversion is not saved if the reversion be not expressly saved in the charter. *Per* Toutheby." Y.B. 30 & 31 Edw. I, 384 (cf. 250).

Brumpton came near to affording us another example in the same year, but a demurrer on another point cuts short the report[1].

In the reign of Edward II there was the notable argument in *Maners* v. *Randolf*[2] where *Scrope* said "Sir, we hold that the statute extends as well to gifts made before it as after, if the tenements were not alienated before the statute": but the tenant waived his first plea and vouched to warranty, so that judgment was not given on this point[3]. After this only one other case occurs bearing at all upon the point, and that proves little[4]. It was, of course, impossible for the question to arise except within a very few generations of the passing of the act. There are, however, several anonymous cases which, taken together, seem to show that the courts were forming the habit of applying the statute to gifts made before it was passed, but allowing issue to be taken on the exception that the donee in tail alienated before the statute[5].

§ 2. *Retrospective Application of other Statutes*

De Donis was not the only statute that raised this problem. The Statute of Gloucester, c. 1 enacts that henceforth in actions of *Ael* damages shall be awarded, and a special explanatory note was published by the king and some of his judges to say that this means only such damages as were sustained since the passing of the act[6]. In a case[7] on the Statute of Westminster II, c. 40, Metingham, J. adjudged that "Forasmuch as the statute makes no mention of alienation before or after the statute, we will hold the old law" in this case where the alienation was before. In another case[8] on the same statute, *East* argued: "The statute ought only to have relation to things done since the statute and not to things done before," and Bereford, J. corroborated this,

[1] *Traneryon* v. *Traneryon*, Y.B. 30 & 31 Edw. I, 129–130.

[2] Y.B. 3 & 4 Edw. II, 40.

[3] The editor's headnote implying a decision is hardly justified by what appears to be only counsel's opinion expressed in argument.

[4] *Anon.*, Y.B. 11 & 12 Edw. III, 545–6.

[5] Y.BB. 30 & 31 Edw. I, 384; 32 & 33 Edw. I, 188; 11 & 12 Edw. III, 345–6.

[6] *Expositio Statuti Gloucestr.* (*Stats. Realm*, 1. 50); it will be noticed that this exposition is in complete harmony with what has been here suggested in connection with *De Donis*.

[7] *Anon.*, Y.B. 21 & 22 Edw. I, 476.

[8] *Rote* v. *Anon.*, Y.B. 32 & 33 Edw. I, 480.

remarking that at Common Law (i.e. before the statute) none knew that the law would be different in the future.

The Statute of Marlborough, c. 9 provides that if land is partitioned among co-heiresses, then the suit of court due to the lord shall be done by one of them, the rest contributing towards the cost, the object being to stop the harsh custom hitherto prevailing of the lord exacting the whole of the suit from each parcener. One such parcener in 1311 brought the statutory action *De Contributione Facienda* against his fellow-parcener[1]. The defendant stated that his father did not contribute "and died seised of that estate," and that he himself was under age and could only continue his father's estate until his majority. The court awarded that he should answer immediately, so he offered the following defence: their common ancestor (on whose death partition was made) was seised, and died, in the reign of King John—over half a century before the Statute of Marlborough—and also that his ancestor held his share without contributing to the plaintiff's ancestor in the same reign; they were discharged of contribution before the statute, and demanded judgment whether the plaintiff could charge them by this statutory writ. *Miggeley* made a very original deduction about the relations of statute to Common Law[2], but Bereford, C.J., ordered him to defeat their seisin of the estate of not contributing, if he hoped to charge them, and accordingly an issue was reached on these lines. In short, Bereford held that the statute was not retrospective.

In a Court Baron a woman demanded dower, and the tenant rebutted her by showing that in her husband's lifetime she had dwelt with an adulterer and had never been reconciled. The Court of Common Pleas held that there had been error in the court below because it had not enquired whether this was before the statute or not[3]. Parties also demurred in judgment as to whether Westminster II, c. 5 was retrospective or not, but nothing seems to have been decided[4]. So also a case[5] arose upon the

1 *Kellestekmur* v. *Lanbrunmur*, Y.B. 4 Edw. II, 143.

2 Noticed below, p. 136.

3 *Anon.*, Y.B. 5 Edw. II, II. 228; Westminster II, c. 34.

4 *Heslartone* v. *Saluayn*, Y.B. 6 Edw. II, 48–59. See also *R.* v. *Bishop of Coventry and Lichfield*, Y.B. 14 Edw. III, 138, discussed above, pp. 42–43.

5 *Anon.*, Y.B. 30 & 31 Edw. I, 348.

Statute of Westminster II, c. 3, which gives a widow recovery of lands lost through her husband's default. In this case the defence was that the default in question was before the statute, and that therefore the judgment upon it could not be undone by the statute. The pleading shifted to other grounds, however, and no decision was given on the point.

We may say, in conclusion, with a fair amount of certainty, that though statutes were not in general applied retrospectively, yet in one very important instance, that of *De Donis*, the courts did habitually construe it in such a way as to make it retrospective, although the wording of the clause clearly implies the reverse.

CHAPTER X

JUDICIAL DISCRETION

§ 1. *The Separation of Law and Equity*

THE attitude of the courts towards statutes was partly determined by the fact that during our period equity was not strictly separated from law, but both were administered together by the same courts which enjoyed a very wide discretion[1]; it is no coincidence therefore that the rule "statuta sunt stricti juris" should appear at about the same time as the beginnings of the separation of equity from law[2]. Of course the change not only affected the interpretation of statutes, but extended also to the Common Law which was gradually becoming more rigidly protected from innovation. The beginnings may be seen in the words of BEREFORD in 1310: "We ought to maintain ancient writs wherever it is possible, rather than new ones"[3]—and can be traced to the finished dogma as stated in 1341–2 by HILARY, J.: "We will not and *cannot* change ancient usages"[4]. The closeness of the dates is remarkable: this dictum of HILARY in 1341–2, the first clearly expressed contrast in the Year Books between "law" and "equity" in 1342, and the dictum "statuta sunt stricti juris" in 1342–3. The process certainly was slow and gradual, but obviously 1342 is a useful date and a well-defined turning point in the development of the new policy of the

[1] See Y.B. 2 & 3 Edw. II, xiii; Hazeltine, "Early English Equity" (*Essays in Legal History*, 262). Discretion was even wider still a century before our period; Hazeltine, *Judicial Discretion in English Procedure of Henry the Second's Time* (Festschrift Otto Gierke, 1055–1068).

[2] The two first appear contrasted in the Year Books in *Cheverestron* v. *Teukesbury*, Y.B. 17 Edw. III, xl, 370; it is also about this time that Chancery appears as a separate court, Baldwin, *Cases before the King's Council*, xxiv.

[3] *Box* v. *Palmer*, Y.B. 3 Edw. II, 92.

[4] *Anon.*, Y.B. 16 Edw. III, I. 90 (26); cf. *Anon.* v. *Prior of St Swithin's, Winchester* (Y.B. 11 & 12 Edw. III, 266) where a pleader omitted to "lay the esplees"—a matter of form only—and SHARESHULLE, J. said: "It shall be forgiven him this time, but let everyone take care for the future, for whoever counts like this, his count shall abate, for we ought to maintain our ancient forms." There is an interesting list of such judgments after the Preface of Jenkins' *Centuries*.

Common Law courts. A few examples of judicial discretion exercised in the interpretation of statutes may now be considered.

§ 2. *The Use of Discretion in the Application of Statutes*

A writ of Dower was brought against a man and his wife who were jointly enfeoffed; the man pleaded in person, the wife by attorney. At length the wife prayed to be received to defend her right alone as her husband was pleading faintly and badly; but KAVE, J. refused on the ground that she had pleaded together with her husband—if she had not done so, she would have been admitted by the statute. KAVE evidently believed that she was within the statute but deliberately denied her the benefit of it, since either her previous plea or else her prayer for receipt must have been in deceit of the court[1]. It is not likely that the annotator's comment "Et hoc de equitate et de jure et bene" is contemporary with the case. Again, HENGHAM intimated that a wife would not be received by the statute, if her husband's default was done with her connivance[2]. Once in the reign of Edward I we even find the Court setting aside a statute "by favour," the only discoverable reason being a desire to oblige the demandant who was Earl of Gloucester and Hereford[3]. During an eyre the court gave judgment against a party in an assize of *Novel Disseisin*, advising him that although he could not lawfully enter, yet he could bring Formedon in the Reverter instead if he desired, which he thereupon did. Exception was taken, however, on the ground that the second writ was issued after a date fixed as the latest limit in accordance with the Statute of Westminster II, c. 10. To this BEREWYKE, J. replied, "This writ was given by the court and therefore the court will maintain it"—"mirum tamen videtur, ex quo non est in casu statuti, quod non tulit breve ante," adds a commentator[4]. The statute said that if a plaintiff's writ was abated, he could bring a new one although the date fixed by the proclamation had passed. But

[1] *Anon.*, Y.B. 20 & 21 Edw. I, 106; Westminster II, c. 3.

[2] *Anon.*, Y.B. 30 & 31 Edw. I, 294.

[3] *Earl of Gloucester etc.* v. *Anon.*, Y.B. 21 & 22 Edw. I, 524. The statute is Westminster I, c. 39 (not Westminster II, c. 48, as stated by the editor).

[4] *Haye* v. *Seygnour*, 30 & 31 Edw. I, 127. The commentator's remark becomes more intelligible by thus reading "in casu" instead of "nisi causa."

in this case nobody's writ was abated, and the second writ was brought not by the original plaintiff, but by the defendant who had attempted to assert his right by Entry, but had been defeated in the assize and was therefore put to his Formedon. The reporter is justifiably surprised because the privilege of the statute was extended by the court in its discretion to one who had not brought a writ before.

A still more remarkable example of discretion is the following. A writ of Entry *Sur Disseisin* in the *Per* was brought against one Avelyne alleging a disseisin done by Hugh[1]. Avelyne vouched to warranty one J., a stranger, and the demandant immediately counterpleaded the voucher by the statute, which said that in such a case none could vouch out of the degrees[2], or in other words, the only person Avelyne could vouch was Hugh. Avelyne then stated the facts, which were that the tenements had been in Hugh's seisin, and on his death were assigned by Isabel his heiress to Avelyne as dower. Isabel and her husband had then granted by fine the reversion to this J., the vouchee, who brought *Quid Juris Clamat* making Avelyne attorn to him, and binding himself to warrant her. It was a hard case, for the statute was perfectly clear in forbidding the voucher, and yet it was just as clear that great injustice would be done to Avelyne if she were deprived of J.'s warranty. STAUNTON, HENGHAM and HOWARD, JJ. were equal to the occasion, however:

"Whatever the statute says, because of the hardship which would otherwise ensue, the voucher is receivable" they adjudged "and it shall not destroy your writ, but it shall always be in the *per*, for this J. is the assign of the heir[3] of him[4] who is within the degrees and they shall be as one degree";

which reason was put on the roll.

Very similar is a case early in the next reign[5] dealing with the Statute of Westminster II, c. 40 which came before the court for interpretation. In Entry *Sur Cui in Vita* in the *Post* the tenant vouched the infant heir. The woman demandant prayed that

[1] *Anon.* v. *Husee*, Y.B. 33 and 35 Edw. I, 380.

[2] "En touts maners des briefes Dentre queux font mention des degrees, purvuew est que nul desormes vouche hors de la line." Statute of Westminster I, c. 40.

[3] Isabel. [4] Hugh. [5] *Anon.*, Y.B. 2 & 3 Edw. II, 33.

her suit be not delayed until the infant vouchee attained his age, but that she be awarded seisin at once by the statute, which says, "expectet emptor," etc. The tenant argued very plausibly that he could not be regarded as "emptor" (generally understood of buyers at first hand) since the demandant herself had brought her writ in the *Post*, thereby implying that the property had changed hands several times. The point was difficult, and so BEREFORD, J. looked at the statute and said "We will not now determine the meaning of the statute, but in the present case, because of the hardship which might otherwise ensue...let the voucher stand."

Another case also involving a considerable hardship was an action of Dower *Unde Nihil Habet* concerning which the Statute of Westminster I, c. 49 enacted: "In Dower *Unde Nihil Habet* the writ shall not abate by the exception of the tenant that she has already received dower at the hands of another man, unless he can show that she received part of the dower from himself and in the same vill." In the present case, the husband had enfeoffed his heir of some land, and the woman had already received dower of the lands that were left—i.e. those that had descended to the heir, and now claimed dower of those he had by purchase (the feoffment of his father). As both were in the same vill the tenant was able to offer an exception in the precise words allowed by the statute. Nevertheless STAUNTON, J. refused to let the woman be debarred from her dower by this trick, and by distinguishing between the heir's inheritance and his purchase was able to do her justice[1].

§ 3. *The Restriction of Discretion under Edward III*

From the reign of Edward III come a few examples of discretionary judgments but accompanied by others in which the courts refused to mitigate rigour of the law. The Statute of Westminster II, c. 25, for instance, enacts that if a defendant in *Novel Disseisin* vouches the rolls of the court to warranty and fails in the voucher then he shall lose the land, pay double

[1] *St Amand* v. *St Amand*, Y.B. 4 Edw. II, 25–6. The tenant's counsel, *Passeley*, seemed none too pleased with this decision; the reporter tells us, "Afterwards I asked *Passeley* the reason for STAUNTON's statement, and he said the judge had some reason of his own."

damages, and go to prison for one year "for his falsity." A defendant had vouched the rolls but could not get access to them because a judge had taken them to Wales with him; he therefore prayed another day to be given him, but the court refused: he was not imprisoned, it seems, but he lost the land[1].

A knight[2] was in prison for the non-payment of a debt by statute merchant, and prayed to be released on mainprise (the mainpernors making themselves responsible for the debt) pending the trial at *Nisi Prius* of an issue that had been reached on the genuineness of a certain bond. HILARY, J. refused to allow this, and the knight's counsel pointed out the hardship of being in prison for a debt which he pleaded was paid. Moreover, the trial of this issue might never be taken at Westminster, "for he will never as long as he is in custody, succeed in causing jurors to come from so distant a county"[3]. Yet the court refused to let this jury be taken in the county because the knight had to remain in prison according to the statute until the debt was paid. In similar cases, the reporter tells us, he remembers the prisoner having been mainprised and the issue taken at *Nisi Prius*, but now HILARY, J. was obdurate: "We cannot," he said, and so the luckless knight was again remanded.

A very interesting attempt to misuse the law is seen in an action of Ravishment of Ward given by Statute of Westminster II, c. 35. The circumstances were curious; the defendant admitted the facts alleged against him, but said that while the ward was in his custody he allowed the plaintiff to offer a marriage to the ward and that the ward accepted it. The defendant confessed that he was technically a ravisher but showed that the plaintiff had nevertheless enjoyed all the profits of the wardship. The judgment enrolled reveals the plaintiff's reason for bringing the action to have been the recovery, if possible, of damages, but he was certainly unsuccessful, the court considering that it was "not consonant to right that he have damages as well as profit"[4].

[1] *Anon.*, Y.B. 15 Edw. III, 386 (51).
[2] *Stifrewas* v. *Wedone*, Y.B. 15 Edw. III, 50–2.
[3] Compare Mr Bolland's Introduction to Y.B. 8 Edw. II, i.
[4] *Hakebeche* v. *Rycheford*, Y.B. 16 Edw. III, II. 346 (Note from the Record); another report of the same case is in Y.B. 20 Edw. III, I. 542–6.

Pleaders seem to have found increasing difficulties, however, in persuading judges to grant relief out of the usual course of law, judging from the long argument that one gave showing that discretion had been exercised before in altering a process which would work mischief and praying for a similar relief in his own case, but unsuccessfully it seems, for no decision is known to be made[1]. A similar point of view was adopted in the parliament of 1348 when it was said that "law had and used in time passed and the process thereupon used heretofore cannot be changed without making a new statute"[2]. It will be observed that this is nearly contemporary with a remarkable case where the process in an action of Debt had been so abused that it had lingered seven years and might continue indefinitely without a plea ever being made, the defendants "fourching by essoins." There were several defendants; one would be essoined, whereupon the others would be told to appear on the same day as had been given to him (technically known as *Idem Dies*). When the day arrived, another of them would be essoined, and again the rest would be given *Idem Dies*. The pleading could not begin until all were present in court together, which well might never be, for fourching could continue indefinitely, the Common Law being that if a man appeared in court once, he could be essoined at the next day, and every appearance he made entitled him to an essoin afterwards. The court refused to stop this procedure and take the case at once, since they could not alter the process—"Ceo ne poms faire saunz estatut," said HILARY, J.[3]

In one instance the judges seemed unfavourably impressed

[1] *Tornerghe* v. *Abbot of Furness*, Y.B. 17 Edw. III, 98; Westminster II, c. 9.

[2] *Rot. Parl.* II. 203 (30): the King went on to explain that he could not do this at present (i.e. in Parliament), but would ordain a remedy with the Great Men and the Council. The King's reply has the additional interest of clearly showing the absence of a juridical distinction between a statute and an ordinance as well as the indefinite nature of the small circle which exercised the legislative power. The text will be found below, Appendix, p. 192.

[3] *Gisors* v. *Anon.*, Y.B. 19 Edw. III, 12 (4). Contrast above, p. 22.

Fourcher by essoins was abolished by the Statute of Westminster I, c. 43, where the defendants were parceners or tenants in common, and the Statute of Gloucester, c. 10, forbade fourcher by a husband and wife, but defendants in the action of Debt were apparently not within these statutes, as they were not "tenants."

by the tenant in an action of *Cessavit* who just managed to redeem his land by paying his arrears. They therefore gave this unusual judgment: "...for security [for the payment of arrears and damages] we adjudge that in case in time to come it may be found in this court that you again cease for two years, the land shall be forfeit for ever[1], so that you do not have the benefit of the statute"[2]. By this time too, the courts did not find it so easy as formerly to sweep aside a statute in a particular case, for one technical irregularity might have quite unforeseen consequences in later proceedings before a less courageous Bench. As example we may take a case where a defendant in *Novel Disseisin* fraudulently caused a writ of Right to be issued against himself in the plaintiff's name, and thus hoped to abate the assize by the exception that "a writ of higher nature" was pending[3]. The plaintiff exposed the fraud to the court, who being sympathetically inclined, cancelled the record of the writ of Right and proceeded with the assize, the plaintiff giving security that he would sue the deceiver[4]. Next term he therefore brought his judicial writ of Deceit, but then the trouble arose; a writ of Deceit should be issued "out of" the deceitful record but in this case none such existed, for in the previous plea the judges had cancelled it. The prosecution broke down and the parties "concordati sunt." If the case had been left to follow the usual course, i.e. abatement of the assize, followed by a writ of Deceit out of the record of the writ of Right, the defendant's *narrator* would have spent one year and one day in prison and have been debarred from practice ever after[5]. This punishment he escaped, thanks to the short-sighted discretion of the court.

[1] "Encoru au remenant." The editor's rendering, "liable as to the rest," will not fit in with the clear use of the words in the Statute of Gloucester, c. 4 (end), and in Y.B. 32 & 33 Edw. I, 450. See Ducange, s.v. *Incurramentum*.

[2] *Prior of Plympton* v. *Anon.*, Y.B. 17 & 18 Edw. III, 234.

[3] *Audele* v. *Anon.*, Y.B. 17 Edw. III, 204.

[4] *Anon.*, Y.B. 17 & 18 Edw. III, 136–8.

[5] Westminster I, c. 29; for such a sentence, see Y.B. 13 & 14 Edw. III, 350 (71).

CHAPTER XI

STATUTES AND THE COMMON LAW

THE relation between a statute and the pre-existent Common Law was a question of great urgency and no little difficulty during our period. Various opinions were held and conflicting decisions are therefore to be found at different times, and it is only at the end of the period that a settled policy begins to appear.

§ 1. *The Relation of Trespass to Replevin*

For instance, the regular Common Law method of securing a decision on the lawfulness of a distress was the action of *Replegiari*. Now the Statute of Marlborough, c. 4 had forbidden a distrainor to drive beasts of the plough taken in distress outside the county in which it was taken, and upon this statute a special writ of Trespass had been framed in the chancery although the statute does not actually specify the form of the writ[1]. A party brought *Replegiari* against a distrainor for driving his beasts out of the county, but the distrainor objected that he should have brought the writ on the statute. To this the plaintiff replied that it was in his election to bring either the statutory or the Common Law writ and the court agreed[2]. The principle of the decision, therefore, is that where a statute ordains a new remedy for a wrong, but specifies no particular action to secure it, a plaintiff can choose between a previously existing Common Law action if it affords an opportunity of raising the question, and a special action on the statute. This was affirmed in the next reign[3].

This same statute, however, imposes an extraordinary penalty for arbitrary distress, viz. to be in the king's ransom. But the action of Replevin issues naturally in damages only; can one therefore exact the statutory penalty by means of the Common Law action, or must the special writ upon the statute be used? In the two cases just mentioned there is no evidence as to what

[1] *Reg. Br. Orig.* f. 97.
[2] *Anon.*, Y.B. 21 & 22 Edw. I, 26.
[3] *Prior of Lewes* v. *Butler*, Y.B. 5 Edw. II, 1. 84 (16).

penalty was imposed, but some thirty years later *Gaynford* contradicted the incidental remark[1] of BASSET, J. that ransom was due in *Replegiari*, while not long afterwards a Replevin case arose[2] where the verdict of the inquest was that the lord had distrained outside his fee. "Then by statute he must pay ransom," said HILARY, J. *Pole* denied this, saying that ransom could only be imposed in a writ upon the statute, and that as they were in Replevin only damages were due. STONOR, J. then put the question clearly: "The statute speaks generally," he said, "that the lord must pay ransom; is it reasonable that you should escape punishment because a particular writ was not used?" "Yes," replied *Pole*, "that has always been the practice since the statute was made." No decision is reported and so the question, important as it was, still remained undecided at the end of our period. Nevertheless, the main position that the party could choose between *Replegiari* and trespass on the statute remained unaffected by the doubt as to whether the penalty of trespass would apply if he brought *Replegiari*.

There is a similar difficulty in dealing with the Statute of Marlborough, c. 9, but in this case the court after a period of uncertainty adopted the policy of compelling the party (although in the Common Law action of Replevin) to plead according to the rules laid down for the statutory action of *Contra Formam Feoffamenti*[3].

§ 2. *The Views of* BEREFORD, C.J.

The same question arose in connection with other statutes. There was at Common Law a writ of Entry to recover lands which a guardian had alienated in fee, but the Statute of Westminster II, c. 25 extends the scope of *Novel Disseisin* to cover this case. In 4 Edw. II the old Common Law writ was brought and exception was taken to it on the ground that the statute gives *Novel Disseisin* and that therefore no other writ was available[4]. After much argument STAUNTON, J. was convinced by these reasons and abated the writ accordingly. BEREFORD's speeches in the case are most interesting:

1 *Stevene* v. *Causton*, Y.B. 15 Edw. III, 308 (9).
2 *Tryvet* v. *Audele*, Y.B. 18 & 19 Edw. III, 320.
3 These complicated cases are discussed together in pp. 91–100 above.
4 *Sampson* v. *Grene*, Y.B. 3 & 4 Edw. II, 112–5.

"If statute ordains another writ," he declared, "then it abolishes this one; the cause of the statute was that this writ was not founded upon reason[1], so another was ordained instead of it, for a writ is against reason if it supposes that the guardian can alienate and that the alienation is not recoverable until the ward has attained his age.... The words of the statute *De Donis* do not abolish *Mort d'Ancestor* but give a special writ in the descender; but think you that the *Mort d'Ancestor* lies now? No."

Again, the Chief Justice said,

The statute was not made for nothing, but because a remedy in accordance with the law was not ordained by the old law. Therefore insomuch as a statute gives a remedy in the aforesaid case, you must understand that that remedy is more according to law[1].

So strongly did he feel on the matter, that when *Denham* urged that he could elect between the Common Law and the statutory remedy, BEREFORD exclaimed: "I have been here fifteen years and never saw such a writ. If my companions were here I would not go hence until judgment had gone against you."

BEREFORD's contention that the old action was unreasonable in deferring the heir's recovery until his majority is perfectly sound, and the statute having ordained a speedy assize instead of the slow writ of Entry, must have had the effect of driving the old writ out of use—hence BEREFORD's statement that in fifteen years' experience he had never seen it before. Why any one should have revived such a clumsy writ is not clear[2]. But the ground of the court's decision was not that the old writ was obsolete but that the statute in ordaining a new remedy had *ipso facto* abolished the old one. There is no evidence by which to verify BEREFORD's statement that *Mort d'Ancestor* cannot be used where Formedon in the Descender lies[3]; even if such were the case it would be unsafe to attribute the effect solely to the operation of the statute *De Donis*, since there is good reason to believe that there was a writ in the Descender before the

[1] The use of these terms is noticed above, p. 35.

[2] If the writ had been held good and the debate had been continued further, we might have found that some technical point of procedure supplied the motive.

[3] See the doubts expressed in F.N.B. 196. In *Anon.*, Y.B. 6 Edw. II, 44, BEREFORD quoted a precedent in support of this view.

statute[1]. This decision is unique in our period and the doctrine of the brilliant but erratic BEREFORD found little favour. Indeed it will be noticed that it is almost contemporary with some of the decisions on the Replevin cases already noted in which it was consistently allowed that parties could elect between Common Law and statutory remedies.

§ 3. *The Principles more generally applied*

There is ample evidence to support the view that the settled opinion of the courts was that a new statutory remedy did not involve the abolition of the previous Common Law on the matter. Thus Westminster II, c. 25 gives an assize of *Novel Disseisin* for the recovery of certain types of annuity, but SHARESHULLE, J. stated that "Even though I grant you an annuity out of certain land, it is at your election if you are not paid the rent to bring an assize [by the statute] or an action of annuity [the previous Common Law remedy]"[2]. Similarly, the granting of an assize to recover estovers did not abolish the older action of *De Estoverio Rationabili*[3]; and *Stouford* argued that the provision of a statutory counterplea did not prevent one from electing to use a Common Law counterplea that existed before the statute[4]. So also STAUNTON, J. admitted a woman to defend her right although her case was not covered by the Statute of Westminster II, c. 3, because she would have been receivable before the statute at Common Law, and decided against *Herle's*

[1] Maitland, "History of the Register of Writs" (*Anglo-American Legal Essays*, II. 586 *n.*). Cf. *Maners* v. *Randolf*, Y.B. 3 & 4 Edw. II, 41:

"*Toudeby*. There was no tailed form before the statute. BEREFORD, C.J. Yes, there was; long before. *Toudeby*. But there was no recovery save in the remainder or reverter. BEREFORD, C.J. That is a different matter."

Professor Maitland, however, found no evidence of Formedon in the Remainder before the statute, and later grew somewhat less certain of the existence of the writ in the Descender before the statute, inclining to the belief that *Mort d'Ancestor* was pleaded in a particular way which made it serve the purpose of Formedon in the Descender (Pollock and Maitland, II. 28). Cf. above, p. 79.

[2] *Heselhawe* v. *Bishop of Bath and Wells*, Y.B. 17 & 18 Edw. III, 538.

[3] *Reg. Br. Orig.* ff. 155–66; f. 76 does not quite cover the same ground as Westminster II, c. 35.

[4] *Isle* v. *Archbishop of Canterbury*, Y.B. 11 & 12 Edw. III, 511; Westminster I, c. 40. He demurred here, but no judgment appears.

argument that none could be received unless in the case of the statute[1].

§ 4. *The Statute of Merton, c.* 6, *and Forfeiture of Marriage*

That this method of interpretation worked in the interests of justice can be seen in such cases as the following where the lack of a scientific legislative technique would have worked great hardship if BEREFORD's doctrine had been followed. Before the statute, if a lord offered a competent marriage to his ward and the ward refused to accept it, then a writ of Forfeiture of Marriage lay whereby the lord could recover from the ward double the value of the marriage. The Statute of Merton, c. 6, however, made the provision that in such a case the lord could retain the heir's lands after the heir comes of age until he has recouped himself to twice the value of the marriage. In the majority of cases it is obvious that the statute would materially assist the lord in the collection of his due forfeiture, but in 1344 there arose a case where the statutory remedy was useless. The heir's marriage was valuable, but he held only an insignificant amount of land in demesne, the rest being in service. As there was no land worth holding from which to collect the double forfeiture, the lord brought the old Common Law writ to recover directly from the heir. It was argued that the writ was bad, but the lord replied that the marriage might be worth £1000 and yet the heir have only one acre of land, or even none at all, and that therefore the lord could have his election between the Common Law and the statutory action. WILLOUGHBY, J. agreed and the writ was adjudged good[2].

Exactly the same state of affairs had arisen a generation before, and was met in the same way, although the arguments upon it are not so fully reported[3]; there is no doubt upon the Court's decision and the reason for it, however, for the words of SCROPE, J. are perfectly clear: "It is possible that the land held of him is worth but twenty shillings and perhaps the marriage is worth twenty pounds. So he can elect between land and forfeiture."

[1] *Anon.*, Y.B. 33 & 35 Edw. I, 400.
[2] *Holland* v. *atte Bridge*, Y.B. 18 Edw. III, 108.
[3] *Barre* v. *Haughton*, Y.B. 1 & 2 Edw. II, 188.

§ 5. *The* Dicta *of* Staunton, J.

Perhaps the clearest statements of the principle in general terms are those made by Staunton, J. under the following circumstances. Edmund Wandsworth[1] executed a bond under the Statute of Merchants in favour of John Bakewell, and failing to pay his debt, Bakewell took possession of his lands under a writ of *Elegit*, and enjoyed the freehold estate in them expressly given him by the statute. Then came the debtor, and disseised the creditor, who therefore brought against him the assize of *Novel Disseisin* to which also the statute entitled him. The tenant, i.e. Wandsworth, the original debtor and present disseisor, pleaded in abatement of the writ that he had nothing in the lands save jointly with his wife who was not named in the writ. *Spigurnel* explained that the Common Law was quite clear: Wandsworth had by his bond alienated temporarily his wife's right, and had then disseised the alienee, and so the alienee must name the wife in the writ by which he seeks to regain seisin. In vain the demandant pleaded the peculiar form of freehold defined in the statute. Staunton, J. laid down a principle which he refused to depart from, and, finally the demandant was glad enough to be allowed to get a better writ instead of having the present one abated. According to one report Staunton said:

> a statute does not restrain the common law outside the words of the statute; and although the statute gives you seisin[2] of half the lands until [the debt is paid], and the assize to recover [them by if you are disseised], yet it does not follow that your recovery will not be pursued according to the common law [procedure].

In another report we read, "A statute does not change common law process unless it gives a special process."

§ 6. Exigent *and the Writ of Debt*

An interesting example of the application of the principle to a difficult point of process occurred in 1340. The old Common

[1] *Bakewell* v. *Wandsworth*, Y.B. 6 & 7 Edw. II (*Eyre of Kent*), iii. 75. This is undoubtedly the same case as the one printed in the same volume, *Anon.*, *ibid.* 134.

[2] *Assize*—ms, which does not make sense; the lands were obtained by *Elegit*, not assize. The emendment of "seisin" for "assize" may be supported from the report, *ibid.* 135, which has in this place "franc tenement."

Law action of Account, like the action of Debt, could be begun in any county where the debtor could best be brought to answer, thus forming an exception to the general rule that an action must be brought in the county in which the cause of action lies. Now Westminster II, c. 11, in order to make Account more speedy, enacted that the process should be by *Exigent*, i.e. arrest of a debtor's body, and the possibility of outlawry, where the old process was nothing more drastic than distress[1]. In the case referred to, the defendant took exception to the writ since the *Exigent* was brought in Middlesex while the plaintiff laid his cause of action in London; since the statute gives *Exigent*, he argued, the action must be treated like trespass (of which *Exigent* is the typical process), and brought in the same county as the cause of action. To this the plaintiff replied that the action was at Common Law, and that at Common Law it could be brought in any county where the debtor could best be found; the statute, indeed, gives *Exigent*, "but it does not oust the Common Law at this point." "After good consideration," the court adopted this interpretation[2].

The general attitude seems one of jealousy for the Common Law, which was not to be modified by statute more than could be avoided. This is recognised even in the statutes themselves, for they occasionally go into lengthy disquisitions to explain exactly how much and how little of the Common Law is to be superseded[3]. Where the statute clearly superseded the Common Law, however, there was frank acknowledgment of the fact. As *Inge* said in the course of an argument, "this statute was made to stop wrongful distress; as one canon defeats many laws, so also a statute defeats many things that are at common law"[4].

§ 7. *The Assimilation of Statutes into the Common Law*

A few examples may be considered here of a curious phenomenon, namely, the gradual assimilation of statutes into the Common Law. We shall discuss later, for instance, a case which gives one the impression that at least one provision of *Magna*

[1] Compare the Statute of Marlborough, c. 23, and above, p. 84.
[2] *Anon.*, Y.B. 14 Edw. III, 10.
[3] See for example Westminster II, c. 2 and c. 9.
[4] *Venour* v. *Blund*, Y.B. 3 & 4 Edw. II, 162.

Carta has been forgotten in its original connection and is remembered as merely custom[1]. So also, we find a widow claiming not a third, but a half, of her husband's lands, pleading that such was the local custom. To this the tenant replied: "The Great Charter says that a wife is to be dowered with one third of the tenements which were in the seisin of her husband; therefore your claim is against common law"[2]. But *Magna Carta* is in many respects a thing apart, and cannot be considered as merely a statute; besides, it has the additional peculiarity of having been solemnly confirmed and imposed upon the courts "as common law"[3]. The following, however, will show that it was not alone in becoming absorbed into the Common Law.

The Statute of Westminster I, c. 16 made it a trespass to distrain cattle on the king's highway. A plaintiff brought his writ reciting this provision and the defendant's alleged offence, and concluding with the phrase "contra legem et consuetudinem regni." This form was challenged on the ground that properly it belonged only to Common Law writs, and that this writ being statutory ought instead to say "contra formam provisionis predicte." *Shardelowe* supported his writ by the reason that when a statute had ordained law, that law was henceforward part of the law and custom of the land[4]. This theory only became a permanent part of our law in a peculiar form, namely, that "statutes"[5] made before the time of memory are incorporated in the Common Law[6]. Needless to say, some such theory as this is a logical necessity in view of the fact that the texts of these ancient enactments are in almost every case lost, or at least buried among inedited archives. It is also highly interesting to find that the Common Law, which we usually regard as immemorial custom, has preserved a tradition attributing its origin, in part at any rate, to legislative enactment, a tradition which may very well have a firm foundation in fact. Although

[1] See below, p. 151.

[2] *Beaumont* v. *Bishop of Coventry and Lichfield*, Y.B. 6 & 7 Edw. II, 34–6.

[3] *Confirmatio Cartarum*, c. 1.

[4] *Anon.* v. *Abbot of Abingdon*, Y.B. 19 Edw. II, 624. *Reg. Br. Orig.* f. 98 implies more assent by the court to *Shardelowe's* proposition than the printed Year Book seems to warrant.

[5] This is further discussed below, pp. 165–6.

[6] 1 Dwarris, 2; Hale, *History of the Common Law*, 3–5.

our early archives have not yet been systematically searched for this purpose, enough is known about their contents to warrant us in regarding the tradition as containing a considerable element of truth[1].

§ 8. Miggeley's *Fallacy*

In a few cases, the contrast between statute and Common Law was made the subject of some startling ratiocination. In 1311 a litigant was striving hard to obtain the benefit of a statute, although his right to come within its provisions was doubtful. His counsel, *Miggeley* by name, offered the court an ingenious argument in the following form:

The statute was made in aid of the common law, [rather than in defeasance of it]. We are now at common law, therefore the statute will aid us, seeing that we are not in the case of the statute, but the reverse.

We have no report of any discussion of this proposition save the brief comment "*Miggeley* was not allowed to say this"[2]. The editor, not unnaturally, seems to have had doubts about this speech, and in the first footnote to page 147 of the Year Book warns the reader to compare it with the version in the first of the two reports (printed on page 145). But the only result we can reach from this is that the first report states *Miggeley's* premise that the statute is in aid, not defeasance, of Common Law, but proceeds immediately to his conclusion that his client is entitled to the benefit of the statute. The second report gives two versions of the speech (pages 146, 147), as we have quoted it, filling in the steps of the argument. Moreover, the first version of the speech is unintelligible as it stands, showing no connection between the one premise given and the conclusion; without the second report the first is meaningless. Historically, the evidence is therefore indicative of the genuineness of the speech. But even if we put the minimum of stress upon the evidence for *Miggeley* having used the argument, the fact remains that the reporter (or his redactor) thought the argument a probable (or possible) one in the Court of Common Pleas, and deemed it

[1] Pollock and Maitland, I. 180.

[2] *Kellestekmur* v. *Lanbrunmur*, Y.B. 4 Edw. II, 147; Statute of Marlborough, c. 9; above, p. 119.

worthy a place, either as example or warning, in his Year Book. It must not be supposed, however, that *Miggeley* was the only one to employ this device. As late as 1346 it appears in an action of *Mesne*[1] brought by a tenant by the curtesy upon the Statute of Westminster II, c. 9. The statute expressly states that it does not apply to tenants by the curtesy, but *Derworthy* argued that

the statute is made for the advantage of the tenant against the *mesne*. So tenants in dower and such like are excepted by the statute itself; therefore since the statute was made for our benefit, whatever estate we have, it will not toll our suit ordained for our advantage.

There is no discussion of this argument reported, as other points arose, but the fact that it was thought worth while to report it at all is significant[2].

[1] *Wynbury* v. *Claville*, Y.B. 20 Edw. III, II. 408.

[2] As an additional illustration of the relations of Statute and Common Law, see *Anon.* v. *Earl of Warren*, Y.B. 21 & 22 Edw. I, 527–531, the text of which is given below, p. 193.

CHAPTER XII

STATUTES AND THE ROYAL PREROGATIVE

Occasionally there were interesting conflicts between the royal prerogative and statute law, but the result in political theory was surprisingly small; it may well be suspected that the power of the crown was still too near and too immense to be a safe subject for abstract speculation in the courts during our period. Indeed, so much were the legislature and the judiciary bound together in the personal monarchy, that it may even be doubted whether there was much opportunity in early times for a serious conflict between statutes and the prerogative, which were in fact merely two aspects of the King's power.

Within our period the crown certainly received a preferential treatment in the courts—and even in the drafting of statutes, as for instance, the 50th chapter of Westminster I, which is an express saving of the King's rights[1].

§ 1. *The Relation of Statutes to Royal Charters*

Frequently cases involving royal charters revealed a conflict between them and a statute. Thus the town of Cambridge[2] claimed by virtue of a royal grant the liberty of distraining clerks for debt anywhere within their liberty. The Statute of Marlborough, c. 15, on the other hand, forbids distress "ex quacunque causa" on the King's highway; in this case Gislingham, J. upheld the statute against the charter. Not only statutes, but the King's interests in general were maintained against his own charter; thus the burgesses of Yarmouth claimed by charter the right of holding certain pleas, citing records of cases in which the King's justices had allowed their rights. Their counter therefore "prayed his franchise as largely as our lord the king had granted it."

[1] No discussion, or even mention, of this chapter has been found in the Year Books of our period; its value, therefore, as a safeguard of the royal power, is difficult to determine.

[2] *Chamberleyn* v. *Anon.*, Y.B. 21 & 22 Edw. I, 56.

METINGHAM, J. "It is too large"[1].
Gosfeld. "That is nothing to you."
METINGHAM, J. "Answer over."

If royal grants fared so badly in court, there is nothing surprising in a reporter's note upon a certain decision that "The judges did this more for the king's profit than for the vindication of law, and they did it through fear"[2].

An interesting point is raised by Edward I's charter to the citizens of Chester, dated 1300, for its eighth paragraph concedes that the King will not confiscate the goods of deceased citizens[3]; *Magna Carta*, on the other hand, reserved this right to the King when he was the deceased's creditor. How far the men of Chester could maintain their charter against *Magna Carta* is a question which unfortunately we have not found discussed.

§ 2. *Royal Interference with Litigation*

The use of prerogative writs—often under minor seals—of *Supersedeas* and *De Procedendo*, was the most striking example of royal interference with justice, and produced some sharp debates and eventually parliamentary legislation. Not only were these writs freely employed in suits involving the King's rights[4], but private litigants were at liberty to obtain them—if they had sufficient court influence. The long case of *Scoland* v. *Grandison* is an excellent illustration of this. The two Justices in Eyre had proclaimed a date, after which they would refuse to accept original writs, in accordance with the Statute of Westminster II, c. 10. A writ was brought after the day fixed, but the court claimed to have special instructions from the King ordering them to receive it although it was of a later date than they had

[1] *Burgesses of Yarmouth*, Y.B. 21 & 22 Edw. I, 230.

[2] *Rex.* v. *Anon.*, Y.B. 6 & 7 Edw. II (*Eyre of Kent*), I. 104.

[3] "Et si ipsi cives vel eorum aliqui testati vel intestati decesserint nos vel heredes nostri bona ipsorum confiscari non faciemus quin eorum heredes executores aut amici sui propinquiores ea integre habeant quatenus dicta catalla ipsorum fuisse constiterit defunctorum dum tamen de dictis heredibus executoribus vel amicis noticia seu fides sufficienter habeatur." Rupert H. Morris, *Chester*, 491; *Magna Carta*, c. 18. (Note that paragraph 1 of the Chester Charter shows that the citizens are crown tenants and therefore clearly within *Magna Carta*.)

[4] There is a translation of one in the Note from the Record of *R.* v. *Walsay*, Y.B. 4 Edw. II, 180.

fixed[1]. The following remarkable discussion took place upon *Stonore's* exception to the writ as being too late[2]:

ORMESBY, J. "You are only challenging and disputing the king's authority, and that neither we nor you can do."

Passeley. "The statute says that if a writ is received after the date proclaimed, then the process upon it shall be null."

STAUNTON, J. "We have the king's warrant, and so we must go on; if you think it is wrong, then sue error afterwards."

Another MS[3] records the controversy still more fully:

STAUNTON, J. "We have a later warrant from the king, and that is as high as the statute."

Stonore. "The answer we put forward is fully warranted by the statute and no one can go against the statute."

SPIGURNEL, J. "You would be correct if the sheriff had taken the writ after the proclamation, but we have received it by the king's command and by a new authority that is as high as a statute."

Passeley. "Sir, the statute is given by common counsel of the realm and that cannot be defeated by the king's simple[4] command; wherefore it seems that such a command ought not to exceed the bounds[5] of the statute."

ORMESBY, J. "When the king commands, one must suppose that it is by common counsel, and besides, no one may counterplead the king's deed"[6].

Costone[7]. "You have it in the statute, Sir, that writs delivered after the proclamation are null and that all the process is utterly undone, and moreover, by the New Ordinances [c. 32] you have it that no law shall be changed by the king's command under the targe[8], so we pray a bill of exceptions or else that you will enrol our challenge."

STAUNTON, J. "We will make no bill but [you have[9]] the testimony of the whole court; take your challenge when you will."

[1] Such an order may be seen in *Cal. Close Rolls*, 1313–8, 36.

[2] Y.B. 6 & 7 Edw. II (*Eyre of Kent*), I. 161.

[3] *Ibid.* 175. The relation between these two reports may be seen from the *variae lectiones* on p. 161.

[4] "Simple counsel and command," *aa*, *β*, which implies a noteworthy distinction between the King's common counsel, and his "simple" counsel.

[5] MS "passer les poynts del statut." Cf. "the points of the assize."

[6] Some manuscripts say his "estate."

[7] Attorney for Grandison.

[8] "De south la targe" (MSS *aa*, *β*, *ζ*). Not "to the delaying of justice" as in the editor's translation (which is also much more free than that given above). The targe was a small seal bearing the royal arms on a *targe* or shield (not connected with the verb *targer*, to be delayed); Tout, *Administrative History*, II. 283, n. 3, shows that "targe" was simply another name for the privy seal.

[9] The sense seems to require this addition.

Perhaps the most remarkable feature of this case is its witness to the fact that the Crown was hardly yet an institution. All the functions of the Crown were still thought of as being the personal acts of a personal monarch. A statute is the King's command, but his missive under a small seal is "a new authority that is as high as a statute"; the Court seemingly was unable to find any difference between these two expressions of the royal will. *Passeley*, it is true, drew a notable distinction between the King's act by common counsel, and his act by simple counsel[1], but even this elementary piece of political science was too much for the Court which preferred its old habit of thinking in terms of real property law; as ORMESBY said, the privy seal was the King's deed[2], and everyone knew that it could not be counterpleaded.

The following case[3] is less clear though none the less interesting. Thomas Hothwayt was impleaded by *Quare Impedit* by one Hugh Courtenay, and also by the King, in respect of the same church. Courtenay was the first to win against Hothwayt and had his writ to the Ordinary, but the Ordinary was afraid to admit his presentee, in view of the King's suit still proceeding; so Courtenay petitioned "in the king's common parliament" to be allowed to plead his right. The King ordered the record of his own plea against Hothwayt[4] to come before BRABAZON, C.J. in the King's Bench[5], where he ordered Courtenay's petition to be tried also. The King claimed the advowson "as the right of his crown and of his prerogative" (although in the previous plea he claimed as "Edward, a strange purchaser"), deriving his title from one Isabel, tenant in chief, who had successfully made a presentation to the church, and so died seised, whereby the advowson fell into the King's hands by his prerogative; and in her right he claims to present, without replying to the title

[1] It is also in the reign of Edward II that we find the first examples of the Crown being distinguished from the person of the King.

[2] Compare p. 8 above, where legislation in the forms of conveyances of real property is noticed.

[3] *Courtenay* v. *the King*, Y.B. 5 Edw. II, I. 130.

[4] Not of *Courtenay* v. *Hothwayt* as in the translation on *ibid.* p. 130; the actual writ is printed on p. 133.

[5] This is the plain meaning of the text; the editor's translation erroneously suggests that there had been previous pleading before BRABAZON and that the records of this were brought into the King's Bench.

set up by Hothwayt and Courtenay, both of whom claimed substantially the same title as against the King. To this Hothwayt replied by pleading that the presentation by Isabel was made while he was under age and therefore by the Statute of Westminster II, c. 5 ought not to prejudice him. Then *Hartlepool* made a remarkable claim for the King: "Statute does not lie against the king's prerogative." Hothwayt's argument that his answer would have been good against Isabel, and that the King ought not to be in a better position than she, through whom he claimed, was fruitless and BRABAZON gave judgment for the King, impliedly confirming *Hartlepool's* doctrine, although there is no foundation for it in the statute[1].

§ 3. *The Statute of Northampton and the Minor Seals*

In the second year of Edward III a statute[2] ordered that justice should not be delayed by writs under the privy seal, but it seems to have been of little avail. Thus in a case of 1339 Bodenho brought *Novel Disseisin* against Derby for tenements which all confessed were appurtenant to a chapel on Bedford Bridge. Derby professed to be in by the King's collation and produced a writ of *Supersedeas* under the privy seal. The case was therefore adjourned for the King to be consulted. Bodenho now got a *de Procedendo* under the great seal. The King, however, had taken the chapel into his own hands and collated a third person, and more writs followed upon further *ex parte* statements before the council. Eventually a writ of Error was brought, which transferred the case to the King's Bench where it finally evaporated, leaving no trace on the *Coram Rege* Roll[3].

Writs interfering with the course of justice seem to be as frequent after the statute as before; thus we find STONORE, J. saying "the king had commanded us by writ that notwithstanding all the challenges, we make the note and engross the fine—so sue to have the note made, and if you suffer wrong, sue elsewhere"[4]. Once we find that a *Supersedeas* under the privy

[1] Westminster I, c. 50 contains an express saving of the royal rights, but none such appears in Westminster II.

[2] Statute of Northampton, c. 8.

[3] Y.B. 12 & 13 Edw. III, xcv, 370 ff.

[4] *Anon.*, Y.B. 12 & 13 Edw. III, 186; cf. *Anon.*, Y.B. 18 Edw. III, 44.

seal (*targe*) was cancelled by a writ close which actually recited the Statute of Northampton[1], while in one case at least the judges boldly withstood the King's writ, and hanged "one of the chiefer barons of the Cinque Ports" for robbery, *Supersedeas* notwithstanding[2].

§ 4. *The Operation of Statutes of Liberty*

In letters patent enrolled on the statute roll granting liberties to the church, Edward III had surrendered his right to bring action for an advowson at any time, however long delayed after the vacancy, and declared that from henceforth if he did not sue within three years of a vacancy, no one should afterwards be compelled to answer him. Four or five years later when this statute was pleaded in court[3], THORPE, J. said, "Some people hold that statute to be of no value to foreclose the king for it was never put into operation," and SCOT, C.J., K.B. agreed and ordered the party pleading it to "say something else." It is not clear whether THORPE meant that no statute was valid until it had been put into operation, or whether he only referred to statutes affecting the rights of the crown. In either case the authority responsible for applying the statute for the first time (in this particular instance, SCOT and THORPE) obviously had a virtual veto upon it. As far as this period is concerned the doctrine does not appear to have been applied in any other case, and it is therefore not only difficult to determine its exact significance, but doubtful whether it can be regarded as anything more than an anomaly[4].

The notion reappears in 1410 when it was argued that the Statute of Provisors had never been put into execution, but we are told that the Judges took no notice of this[5]. A comparison may be suggested between this doctrine and the custom of

[1] *R.* v. *Wigton*, Y.B. 18 Edw. III, liii, 185.

[2] Y.B. 5 Edw. II, II. 17.

[3] *R.* v. *Bishop of Lincoln*, Y.B. 19 Edw. III, 170; statute 14 Edw. III, st. 4, c. 2.

[4] See *R.* v. *Bishop of Bath and Wells*, Y.B. 14 Edw. III, 122, and *R.* v. *Bishop of Coventry and Lichfield*, *ibid.* 138, in both of which cases it was held that the statute did not apply, the litigious presentations and the original writs having been in both cases before the statute. (See above, p. 43.) It was repealed by 25 Edw. III, st. 6, c. 2.

[5] *R.* v. *Bishop of St Davids*, Y.B. 11 Hen. IV, f. 38.

"laying esplees" whereby a dispossessed tenant would allege that he had actually received profits from the land. Similarly, holders of liberties when challenged by the justices had to show that they had exercised the privileges alleged: the mere production of the King's charter of grant was not sufficient unless accompanied by this proof of seisin, as it were. So also, perhaps, a statutory grant of relief from the King's rigorous prerogative may have been regarded in the same light, but a still further stretch would be required to fit the theory to the Statute of Provisors.

§ 5. *Licenses to amortise lands*

Finally, it may be observed that licenses to alienate in mortmain are not authorised by the statute, and had no legal basis outside the royal prerogative until the statute 18 Edw. III, st. 3, c. 3, enacted that a license and an inquest *Ad Quod Damnum* would be a sufficient bar to an action upon the statute[1].

The well-known case of Edward III's prerogative repeal of a statute on the grounds that his royal assent was dissembled need not detain us, belonging as it does to the category of *coups d'état* rather than of constitutional or legal science[2].

[1] License was apparently a bar to forfeiture in *R.* v. *Master of St Giles' Hospital, Norwich*, Y.B. 14 Edw. III, 334 (56), a case dating from before the statute. As early as 20 Edw. I restrictions were imposed in parliament upon the issuing of inquests *Ad Quod Damnum* (which were the normal preliminary to the issue of a license to alienate). Thus it is evident that within the short space of thirteen years of the passing of the statute *De Religiosis* the frequency of licenses to evade it had caused some alarm. *Stats. Realm*, I. 111.

[2] Stubbs, *Constitutional History*, II. 425, 632; 15 Edw. III, stats. 1 and 2.

CHAPTER XIII

STATUTORY WRITS

In the present chapter we shall consider the relation of statutory writs to the statutes upon which they were founded. Form and formula by the end of the 14th century had assumed a tyranny almost—but not quite—absolute; the slight qualification of this general statement can only be due to the lack of a completely logical theory of the Statute, for if there had been evolved a clear consistent notion of its legal nature, there could hardly have been room for the hesitation and indecision which make the following cases so remarkable.

§ 1. *Formalism in Common Law Writs*

In every action the text of the original writ was of fundamental importance; generally speaking[1], the plaintiff would have to maintain every word[2] and every letter[3] of it as true fact and good law—or even as good Latin, upon occasion[4]. Time after time a defendant would "demand judgment of the writ," as he discovered first one, then another defect of form or spelling, or perhaps insisted upon the literal fulfilment of some obsolescent piece of common form[5]. In the case of Common Law writs

[1] See for example such remarks as "Not every word spoken in court is to be weighed, for they are only words of court" (*Lowther*, in *Lucy* v. *Anon.*, Y.B. 20 & 21 Edw. I, 280), while a plaintiff who alleged broken hedges in a writ of trespass explained that "we only say that to serve our writ" (*Anon.*, Y.B. 1 & 2 Edw. II, 36.)

[2] *Beyville* v. *Audele and Shayl*, Y.B. 14 Edw. III, 274; the writ was abated as for Audele because he was not mentioned as "Earl of Gloucester." The words "Wednesday after the Feast of St John" caused an outlawry to be reversed for uncertainty; the word "next" should have been before "after." (*Anon.*, Y.B. 12 & 13 Edw. III, 368.) Cf. *Richer* v. *Vavaceour*, Y.B. 11 & 12 Edw. III, 112.

[3] "Avia" instead of "Avie" abated a writ, *Anon.*, Y.B. 12 & 13 Edw. III, 110 (18).

[4] *Anon.*, Y.B. 16 Edw. III, II. 17 (7), 64 (21); *Pavely* v. *Pouer*, Y.B. 18 & 19 Edw. III, 142.

[5] Especially the production of "suit," *Anon.* v. *Warreyn*, Y.B. 17 Edw. III, xxii, 72. Sometimes as in Admeasurement of Pasture, on the other hand, a demandant counts of damages, but by custom he cannot get them, while at other times he will get damages although he has not counted of them. Hengham, C.J., in *Anon.*, Y.B. 4 Edw. II, 140.

their every detail was determined by a tradition created and preserved by an indistinct group of Judges, Sergeants, and Chancery clerks. This did not entirely preclude the possibility of occasional changes both in the form and substance of the writs, for the Chancery was allowed a certain amount of discretion[1], but even this slight freedom was afterwards curtailed by statute[2].

§ 2. *Statutory Forms of Writs*

Statutory writs were felt to be on a somewhat different basis. The exact nature of that difference was not at once determined, but that it was in the direction of a fairly strict limitation of the writ by the statute seems to have been generally recognised. More particularly was this the case when the statute explicitly set up a form of words to be used in the writ, but the fact that this was by no means a general practice shows how little serious attention had as yet been given to the question[3]. Even in the simple case where the statute contained a special form of words, the courts had no consistent policy towards writs which deviated from that form. Thus in the action of *Cessavit de Cantaria* the statute prescribes a writ containing these words: "Precipe A. quod reddat B. tale tenementum quod A. de eo tenuit per tale servitium," but a writ which omitted "quod de eo tenet" was nevertheless held good[4], and it seems as though the omission later became the regular custom, in spite of the statute[5].

§ 3. *The Views of* Bereford, C.J.

Only three years later, however, we find a contrary decision. The wording of the writ of Ravishment of Ward was contained

[1] See for example the note in *Reg. Br. Orig.* f. 200 that "Istud breve fuit concessum de assensu W. de T(hirning) capitalis justiciarii et aliorum justiciariorum de Banco et clericorum de cancellaria." See also above, p. 83.

[2] Westminster II, c. 24; Baldwin, *King's Council*, 238–9.

[3] Several miscellaneous examples are given in Theloall, *Digest Des Briefs Originals*, 117–8.

[4] Westminster II, cc. 21, 41; *Anon.*, Y.B. 2 & 3 Edw. II, 18. An early instance of the same question being raised in a parallel case occurred in *Anon.*, Y.B. 33 & 35 Edw. I, 174, where a count was challenged for not alleging seisin as required by the statute. Discussion of the principle was prevented by the discovery that the statute (Westminster II, c. 35) said nothing of the sort. Compare *Hardegrey* v. *Swan*, Y.B. 18 & 19 Edw. III, 66 (note that the words "keeper of the prison" were commonly misquoted as "sheriff." *Anon.*, Y.B. 12 & 13 Edw. III, 130, 355; *Reg. Br. Orig.* f. 98*b*.

[5] *Reg. Br. Orig.* ff. 237*b*–238*a*.

in the Statute of Westminster II, c. 35, but in the present case[1] the writ contained the additional words "vi et armis" frequently found in such writs of trespass. The writ was challenged by *Scrope* who argued that "the clerks of the Chancery cannot change the form of a writ that is given by statute where certain words are given in the writ as recited in the statute. It is otherwise with common law writs." The Bench gave judgment on these lines, BEREFORD, C.J. (or in some manuscripts, STAUNTON, J.) stating that "if additional words are put in a writ the form of which is given by statute, then the writ errs; so you may get a better one." We have already had evidence which would suggest that BEREFORD was quite capable of embodying original ideas upon law in his judgments, and we shall be certainly doing him no injustice by attributing this decision also to him rather than to STAUNTON. Indeed, it has the merit of being logical (from a modern point of view), and implies that the Chief Justice had formed a fairly clear opinion about the authority of a statute. On the other hand, we have the reporter's laconic remark, "The contrary of this is law." BEREFORD was in advance of his time but succeeded in spite of general disapproval in imposing his own opinion—as he also did in the much-argued cases of Entry *in Consimili Casu*, where he again insisted on a statutory writ being strictly limited to the scope prescribed in the authorising statute[2].

§ 4. *Later Inconsistencies*

If, as is most probable, the many notes and comments embodied in the printed *Registrum Brevium* are later than our period, then we have evidence that the problem remained unsettled until a later date, for opposite rules appear in the same book of authority. Thus in a writ of *Quod ei Deforciat*, the word "injuste" (usual to such writs) is omitted, the reason given being that "'injuste' non habetur in statuto"[3]. On the other hand we find that the form of a writ of Mainprise commonly used contains the important conditions "dum tamen bone fame sit" and

[1] *Anon.*, Y.B. 5 Edw. II, II. 94–6.

[2] Above, p. 83.

[3] *Reg. Br. Orig.* f. 171 *b*; Westminster II, c. 4; but note that the last form at the end of the statute does say "injuste" but the translation beside it omits it.

"si de aliis latrociniis prius rettati non fuerint" which (it was believed) were not supported by the statute[1]. That this writ was in the Register shows that it was good enough to pass the Courts, but the annotator's doubts show that a new way of looking at statutory actions was in fashion[2].

Similar to this question was the one whether a statutory writ should or should not rehearse the authorising statute in its preamble. Here again the *Registrum Brevium Originalium* has preserved inconsistent practices; we learn that the Statute of Westminster II, c. 14 ought to be rehearsed[3], but c. 22 ought not[4]; the Statute of Marlborough, c. 23 must be recited[5], but not c. 9[6].

[1] At least this is what the annotator in *Reg. Br. Orig.* f. 269, said. As a matter of fact the phrases are well within the statute (Westminster I, c. 15).

[2] For further doubts, see *ibid.* f. 270*b*.

[3] *Reg. Br. Orig.* f. 72*b*.

[4] *Ibid.* f. 76.

[5] *Ibid.* f. 73*b*.

[6] *Ibid.* f. 172*b*. The annotator was doubtful whether the writ would be bad if the recital were made.

CHAPTER XIV

THE INTERPRETATION OF PARTICULAR STATUTES

THE following examples are arranged in the chronological order of the statutes, and are collected here as having some particular interest, either in the method of interpretation, or the subject-matter of the statute concerned, or the general historical or constitutional importance of the case.

§ 1. *Magna Carta, c.* 28, *and Suit*

We will begin with c. 28 of *Magna Carta*[1]. Receiving its present form in 1225 and re-enacted in 1297, there was already doubt as to its meaning in the early 14th century, which is well illustrated in an interesting little Latin note[2] to the following effect:

> There are two interpretations. It seems that none may be put upon a jury unless he were summoned *ad hoc* by faithful summoners, and the summons testified. The other interpretation is that a defendant in a writ of Debt or other similar writ shall not be received to wage his law without witnesses brought for the purpose. Another and better meaning is that the defendant in a writ of Debt or other similar writ shall not be put to his law unless the plaintiff has arraigned suit against him.

The remarks relating to jury service are obviously based only upon the mis-interpretation of "juramentum" in the text as "jury"[3], and need not be considered further. The second construction is nearer the truth, for the Charter does in fact relate to the wager of law, which was by this time almost confined to the Debt-Detinue group of actions. The annotator's third suggestion is the best, however, and has the valuable authority of Fleta[4] on its side, who says of a writ of Debt: "None shall answer a bare word, but if the plaintiff produces suit the defendant can wage law against him and his suit, by the statute."

[1] "Nullus ballivus ponat de cetero aliquem ad legem manifestam nec ad juramentum simplici loquela sua sine testibus fidelibus ad hoc inductis."

[2] Y.B. 32 & 33 Edw. I, 516.

[3] The official Latin for a jury is "jurata."

[4] Fleta, II. 63, §§ 9, 10.

It is, then, one of the several conservative provisions to be found in the Charter and has for its object the preservation of that already obsolescent institution, the suit of witnesses. But it is noteworthy that the Charter had good reason for this enactment, and that it only specifically mentions "bailiffs," that is to say, those who sue in the court baron. Of all courts, this was the most conservative, and the bailiff who used it might easily convert it into a formidable engine of tyranny if he acquired the privilege of compelling a man to wager of law merely on his own bare accusation unsupported by suit; but Fleta tacitly assumes that the provision applies equally to all courts.

This view was undoubtedly fostered if not originated by the recent re-enactment of the multifarious provisions of the Charter *en bloc*, thus giving some of them an altogether exaggerated publicity. In this case one effect seems to have been the artificial preservation of the institution of suit even in the Royal Courts, for in 1313–4 we find a plaintiff in an action of Debt still using the formal words producing suit although in fact he had none, doubtless regarding it as unnecessary. The defendant, however, had heard of this chapter and quoted—or rather misquoted—it as saying "nullus ponatur ad legem manifestam," etc., with the contention that the plaintiff has produced no suit and that therefore the defendant should not be put to his wager of law[1]. The case was not in a manorial court but in eyre, and no bailiff was involved; hence the misquotation became necessary (and is indeed also implied in Fleta's words). The Year Book reports an explanation by BEREFORD of how the case should have been pleaded, but no judgment is reported.

§ 2. *Magna Carta*, c. 39, *and Trial by Peers*

Passing to the thirty-ninth chapter of *Magna Carta*, we must be content to leave aside the many questions that have arisen around trial by peers; the only remark that we shall base upon the Year Books will be to point out that knights seem to have been the class most interested in it[2]. One very illuminating

[1] *Anon.*, Y.B. 6 & 7 Edw. II (*Eyre of Kent*), II. 35.

[2] See the illuminating remarks in Pollard, *Evolution of Parliament*, 72, n. 1, published since the above was written. See also Y.B. 14 & 15 Edw. III, xlviii ff. and Y.B. 15 Edw. III, xliii.

report[1] gives us a fairly full record of the dialogue in court at the trial of a knight for rape. Among other objections he raised was one to the effect that he was a knight and claimed trial by a jury of knights; the court granted his claim, the previous jury being discharged and a new one formed consisting of knights. A significant feature of the next case[2] is that *Magna Carta* was not quoted, the court simply remarking that the challenge is "usual" and "often happens." The Charter has seemingly ceased to be statutory in its nature and has become instead a portion of the Common Law, as it were. At the same time we also see that the privilege was claimed by a bishop as a "peer of the land," but granted by giving him a jury of knights and the best people of the county—and this not in a criminal case but a civil plea of *Quare Impedit*.

§ 3. *The Statute of Merton, c. 4, and Approvement of Common*

Chapter 4 of the Statute of Merton dates from 1236 but was occasionally used as late as the second half of the 18th century[3] when it played a part in the enclosure movement. It enables the lord of a manor who has sub-tenants with rights of common in common land which is appendant to the manor, to enclose a portion of the common for his own use, provided that sufficient is left for the tenants, this enclosure being technically known as "approvement." The right was extended by Westminster II, c. 46, which allowed approvement against neighbours as well as tenants. Several interesting propositions are to be found in the Year Books upon these two statutes; thus we find *Scrope* arguing that "once a lord has been admeasured he has for ever lost every kind of approvement which is given to him by statute"[4]. There is nothing about this in the statute, and the report does not contain any discussion of the point. Admeasurement is an action that lies between freeholders who have common of pasture appendant to their freeholds, and can be brought by one commoner to prevent another from putting more than his just

[1] *R.* v. *Anon.*, Y.B. 30 & 31 Edw. I, 529–532.

[2] *Helygan* v. *Stapleton* (*Bishop of Exeter*), Y.B. 12 & 13 Edw. III, 290–2.

[3] Barrington, 38–9; see in general, Scrutton, *Commons*, 42–73.

[4] *Maltalent* v. *Romyly and others*, Y.B. 32 & 33 Edw. I, 230; cf. *Toudeby* in *Anon.* v. *Malcovenant*, *ibid.* 240.

number of beasts upon the common. But this action does not lie for or against the lord[1]. If the lord overcharges the pasture, the tenant's remedy is the assize of common whereby he may recover his rights; if the tenant is the offender, the lord can only help himself by distraining the tenant's surplus beasts. It is probable, therefore, that the lawyers would have regarded it as a valid presumption that if a person was a party to admeasurement, then that person could not have been lord. From this it would follow that one who has been admeasured could not approve, for only a lord can approve. Difficulty attended this rule, however, since it seems that in the reign of Edward I admeasurement could be brought against a lord[2]. Consequently a rule depriving him of his right to approve, on the ground that he had been admeasured, was hardly just. Doubtless this dislocation of the law of approvement was due to the change going on in the law of admeasurement; but the injustice was only temporary. As soon as the new notion that a lord could not be admeasured was firmly established, then the rule would have worked satisfactorily.

Moreover, the statute does not state very clearly that appendancy of the common to the lord's manor is essential; it merely speaks of the lord granting small holdings and then being unable to make his profit out of "the residue"—this phrase being the only warrant we have observed for the rule that there must be appendancy. A curious example of the working of this rule may be seen in a case of 1303[3] where a tenant controverted a lord's right to approve on the ground that the common in question was not appendant to the lord's manor. On reading the deed of gift by which the lord obtained the manor, it was found that the donor had said "dedi...manerium de Petit Bortoun...cum pertinenciis...et communam pasture...." If the deed had said "communa" then the common would undoubtedly have been an appurtenance of the manor, but as it stood in the deed two things were given, the "manerium" and the "communam," and so BEREFORD, J. held that the common was in gross and not

[1] F.N.B. 125. [2] Fitz. *Admeasurement*, 16.
[3] *Wautone* v. *Richard of Little Bortoun*, Y.B. 30 & 31 Edw. I, 326–8.

appurtenant; a single letter in a deed therefore sufficed to debar the lord from approvement.

Rightly or wrongly, appendancy became an important element in the law of approvement, and a curious notion arose that appendancy could not exist if the tenement and the common had once been in the seisin of the same person. When we first find the doctrine[1], SHARESHULLE, J. criticised it, saying,

> That would be against the Statute of Merton which states that whereas great lords enfeoff others of little holdings in their manors, they may approve saving their tenants enough common; Thereby it is supposed that although both lands be in one hand yet the common remains.

Nevertheless, it seems that the parties took issue upon the allegation of the former unity of the tenements. The same argument was used at the close of our period and was disputed by *Seton* on the same grounds as SHARESHULLE, but in this case an adjournment is all that we are told of the result[2]. As an example of the complications possible under this statute we may cite the following case[3]. A man was enfeoffed of a manor on condition that the feoffor should have common of pasture there and that the feoffee should not approve without the feoffor's consent. The original parties to this arrangement being dead, the feoffee's heiress approved the common of pasture against the feoffor's heiress, and as the latter disturbed her, she brought *Novel Disseisin* against her. The feoffee's heiress, Isabel, pointed out that she had the fee and the right in the manor; why should she not approve? To the defendant's reply claiming the higher estate she retorted that that was only fee in service. The judge seemed doubtful; "the statute does not operate so extensively that the tenant can approve against the lord" he remarked. The main puzzle, of course, was who to regard as the lord, the lord in fee or the lord in service—it being noted that the feoffment was most probably before the statute *Quia Emptores*. No decision is reported, nor is there any discussion given on the question whether parties could contract themselves out of the statute.

[1] *Anon.* v. *Hodyng*, Y.B. 11 & 12 Edw. III, 72.
[2] *Foxton* v. *Foxton*, Y.B. 20 Edw. III, II. 66.
[3] *Anon.*, Y.B. 20 & 21 Edw. I, 354–6.

§ 4. *The Statute of Marlborough, c. 9, Foreign Service, and Suit Real*

Of the Statute of Marlborough, c. 9 we have already had much to say[1]; only two cases will be considered here. The first of these is that of the *Prior of St Mary's, Bishopsgate* v. *Havering* or *Habenhache*[2]. The facts were as follows: *X* had enfeoffed *Y* of a manor to hold of *X* (for it was before the statute *Quia Emptores*) by the service of three shillings for all services, and by doing the foreign service[3] due from the manor. The plaintiff's predecessor purchased *Y*'s estate, and the defendant's grandfather purchased *X*'s. The defendant being under age his guardian by nurture (for the tenements were held in socage) had distrained the Prior to do suit of court, whereupon the Prior had brought his Replevin. The infant's guardian avowed upon the seisin of the infant's grandfather of the suit at the hand of the Prior's predecessor. The Prior suggested that the guardian could only have the wardship of what the infant's father died seised of, but the father was not seised of the suit but died claiming it. INGE, J. was evidently very much impressed by this argument. But other points arose: *Claver* (for Havering) pointed out that the statute said that a tenant in that position "non teneatur ad sectam, etc." and that the word "teneatur" betokened right rather than possession; the Prior should therefore have used the droiturel *Ne Vexes* instead of the possessory Replevin. Another interesting question was raised by SCROPE, J. who thought that the Statute of Marlborough would not apply, since although the three shillings was for all services, yet it did not include foreign service, which was, moreover, uncertain in amount. BEREFORD, C.J. ruled the contrary. The reports suggest no issue, and none is recorded.

The second case raised the following point. The statute speaks of suit service; does this equally apply to suit real, which is suit to the royal courts of the hundred and wapentake, and not to seignorial courts? The decision[4] was that the statute did not apply, with the result that if a tenement owing one suit was

[1] Above, pp. 91–100. [2] Y.B. 8 Edw. II, 18.

[3] See Pollock and Maitland, I. 238–9 for an explanation of the term.

[4] *Thornton* v. *Anon.*, Y.B. 11 & 12 Edw. III, 154.

divided among seven co-heiresses then seven suits real were due, and even if the tenements eventually came into the hands of one person again, then that person would still have to do seven suits.

§ 5. *The Statute of Marlborough, c.* 11, *and Beaupleader*

Chapter 11 of the same statute is not altogether easy to understand, although it was confirmed by Westminster I, c. 8, and by 1 Edw. III, st. 2, c. 8. The subject of *Beaupleader* occurs as early as The Petition of the Barons, 1258, c. 14, and the Provisions of Westminster, 1259, c. 5, in both of which documents it appears as a grievance of a rather uncertain nature. One thing is clear, and that is that the court did not usually tolerate scandalously bad pleading. That it took disciplinary measures to repress it is almost equally certain. The incidence of the court's reproof is not so clear; Coke[1] thought that the party had to pay the fine, but Barrington held the advocate liable[2]. It may be that we have an example of some such practice as this in a case[3] where a demandant offered an averment to oust a man from his voucher which contained matter that was inconsistent with his writ. By the strict law his writ would have abated and his case collapsed, but we are told that "the writ was not quashed, but he was amerced." Here the fine takes the slightly different form of a payment to secure exemption from a heavier penalty. It is noteworthy also that both parties might quite easily find it a grievance, the payer since it might be excessive, and his opponent since by its means the offender eluded the rigour of the law. Which of these two was the cause of the Barons' protest we cannot say, but there was certainly a good deal of hardship in the way a "miskenning" or a "stultiloquium" was redeemed. At first sight, the concluding sentence of this same chapter looks puzzling: "Be it known that by this constitution fines certain, or payments arrented from the time of the King's first passage to Brittany, are not taken away," or as BEREFORD put it: "The new law that fines be not given for pleading does not defeat rents which were anciently reserved"[4]. Here, it seems, is another

[1] 2 *Inst.* 122.
[2] Barrington, 32; so also *Bracton's Note Book*, 298 and Britton, I. 101.
[3] *Anon.*, Y.B. 33 & 35 Edw. I, 178—an anonymous note only.
[4] *Prior of Maiden-Bradley* v. *Ford*, Y.B. 33 & 35 Edw. I, 98.

example of our law's strong tendency to attach burdens and duties to land, and thus convert them from personal to real obligations. The arbitrary fine due to the owner of a seignorial court might become commuted to a regular payment of a "fine certain," or in a slightly less formal manner, the payment would still be exacted and paid, but customarily "arrented" or assessed at a fixed sum. In either case the result becomes the same in the course of time, namely, a rent[1].

§ 6. *The Statute of Marlborough, c.* 15, *and Distress*

An interesting vindication of the liberty of the subject against an overweening official, albeit in a humble sphere, is shown in a case upon the 15th chapter of the Statute of Marlborough, which makes it a serious offence for anyone, not being the king's officer, to levy a distress in the highway. An aggrieved party brought his writ[2] upon the statute, and the defendant promptly pleaded that since he was a royal bailiff the writ did not lie against him and should therefore abate without further ado. But BEREFORD was on the bench and told him plainly that the writ lay against even royal bailiffs unless they could avow. This at once revealed the root of the action, for we find the parties reaching the issue that the distress was taken "by malice and not by office." If the bailiff's plea to the writ had been successful this issue could never have been reached, and the plaintiff would have been without remedy.

§ 7. *Westminster I, c.* 40, *and the Counterpleas of Voucher*

The general principle of the Statute of Westminster I, c. 40 was undoubtedly excellent, and in working must have saved years of delay to litigants by cutting short useless vouching. Its operation was not without problems, however, and the following may be taken as typical of the difficulties which confronted the courts in applying the statute. The tenant in a plea of land[3] vouched to warranty a man and his wife, which the demandant well knew was simply done to delay his case. He therefore offered an averment as near as the circumstances of the case

[1] It may be conjectured that these rents formed part of those payments commonly called "rents of assize" in manorial accounts.

[2] *Strode* v. *Ergleys and others*, Y.B. 5 Edw. II, I. 119.

[3] *Anon.*, Y.B. 18 & 19 Edw. III, 300.

would permit to that allowed by the statute for the counterplea of voucher, saying that he would aver that neither the wife nor her ancestors were ever so seised that she or they could have enfeoffed the tenant or his ancestors of the lands in demand. The tenant at once declared that he had vouched a man and his wife and that a counterplea of only the wife's estate would not be enough to toll his voucher. But as HILARY, J. confessed, the statute speaks of when one is vouched, and says nothing of when two are vouched. The facts underlying the pleadings seem to have been that the deed in virtue of which the tenant vouched was made by, and bound, both the man and wife, but the wife had never been seised of the tenements. The law of the case was clearly summed up by WILLOUGHBY, J. who showed that "there was mischief both ways." If the counterplea were allowed to defeat the voucher of the man and wife together, then the tenant would want to vouch the man alone—and justly so for the man was seised of the land, and bound himself to warrant it; but the tenant could not bind the man alone by a deed which bound the wife as well. He would therefore suffer considerable hardship. On the other hand, if the demandant had not attempted the counterplea alleging the wife's non-seisin, then the voucher would have stood and perhaps the wife would have claimed admission under Westminster II, c. 3. This would necessitate the recommencement of the whole pleading, which would mean a very serious delay, which moreover the demandant could not have prevented by saying that the wife was never seised. This last difficulty WILLOUGHBY proceeded to avoid by saying that the court would allow the voucher, but as the demandant had not himself allowed it he would therefore not have technically admitted the seisin of the wife. The course might involve delay, but the Justice regarded it as better to delay the demandant than to disinherit the tenant. The voucher therefore stood.

§ 8. *The Statute of Gloucester*, c. 12, *and Foreign Vouchers*

Local jurisdictions could not compel the attendance of persons who were not landholders within the jurisdiction if their presence became necessary—say as warrantors—in litigation between local subjects. In such cases as this there was normally only one course: the whole plea must be removed to the King's Court, which alone had authority extending beyond the boundaries of a single liberty or shire, and of course, when once the King's Court had obtained jurisdiction, it refused to relinquish it to the end of the case. In one case, however, a local jurisdiction was able to secure special terms from the Crown, whereby the case returned to the original court as soon as possible, instead of being determined in the King's Court. The favoured jurisdiction was the City of London, and the privilege the Statute of Gloucester, c. 12[1], which enacted that when a "foreigner" was vouched in the Hustings of London, the case should be removed to the Bench, where the vouchee should be summoned and the voucher tried; but this done, the case should be sent back to the Hustings there to be determined. A case[2] occurred where the tenant in the Hustings of London had vouched to warranty a person outside the City's jurisdiction. The case therefore went to the Court of Common Pleas for the vouchee to be brought into court by process, and for any dispute concerning the voucher to be settled there. But when the case came into the Common Bench the tenant defaulted, and his wife prayed to be received according to the Statute of Westminster II, c. 3. This caused considerable debate, since it was argued that the court could only try the voucher and had no power to give a judgment that would imperil the land; wherefore there was no need for the woman to be admitted since the lands were not endangered. KELSHULLE, J. flatly stated that "judgment shall be given here as to the land" but HILARY, J. in adjudging the receipt somewhat modified this statement: "Although judgment shall not be given here as to the land," he said, "yet what is done here will lose the land elsewhere, so we admit her." Having been admitted, the wife proceeded to vouch the previous vouchee—and further dispute followed, for it was objected that by the statute they had no power in that court to consider anything but the first voucher and to send the case back to the Hustings. Finally, HILARY, J. adjudged that they could do nothing more, so he sent the case back to the Hustings, recording that the woman was admitted

[1] See also stat. 9 Edw. I.

[2] *Anon.* v. *Pokoke*, Y.B. 17 & 18 Edw. III, 420–4.

and had vouched—a course that received much criticism from WILLOUGHBY, J. who disagreed both with the receipt and the subsequent voucher.

§ 9. *Westminster II, c. 3, and Receipt*

Westminster II, c. 3 is the statute which we have found most frequently discussed in the reports, and several judgments respecting it have already been considered[1]. Here we shall illustrate only one point, viz. whether a person received to defend his right can use a plea to abate the writ. The law had been reaching the general rule that a stranger cannot abate a writ in which he is not named, but at times we do find some modification of it[2]. The rule is reasonable enough since otherwise there would be no warrant for judgment in the original writ[3]. The question is raised in a curious form when a person is admitted, although the circumstances which he put in his prayer are in fact inconsistent with the allegations stated in the writ. The court allowed the prayer but when the admittee attempted to use these facts in abatement of the writ, BEREFORD, C.J. forbade him[4]. Aid and receipt are so similar that the same solution naturally did for both, and so we find persons prayed in aid at Common Law being deprived of the right to abate the writ. SPIGURNEL, J. once said that "a woman that is received to defend her right shall not be deprived of any answers that fall in law," but *Cambridge* retorted "the statute says defend her right, not abate the writ"[5]. She could abate the count[6], but could not plead misnomer of a vill, for that would abate the writ[7].

§ 10. *Westminster II, c. 15, and Infants Eloigned*

One can see how near at least one statute came to being seriously restricted in its operation by tradition, from a case in 1339. The Statute of Westminster II, c. 15 said that in all cases where an infant can sue, he could be allowed to sue by his next friend if he himself were "eloigned," that is to say, forcibly

[1] Above, pp. 45–50, 75–7, etc. [2] *Anon.*, Y.B. 1 & 2 Edw. II, 150–2.
[3] *Ibid.* and *Neville* v. *Neville*, *ibid.* 77–8, where abatement was not allowed.
[4] *Mason* v. *King*, Y.B. 5 Edw. II, I. 103–4.
[5] *Passeley* v. *Wyveleshergh*, Y.B. 6 & 7 Edw. II (*Eyre of Kent*), II. 128.
[6] *Anon.*, Y.B. 3 & 4 Edw. II, 83–4.
[7] *Anon.*, Y.B. 19 Edw. III, 122 (45).

detained, by one who was interested in his non-appearance. This privilege was claimed in an action of Waste[1], but ALDEBURGHE and SHARESHULLE, JJ. were evidently much perturbed by the fact that so far the statute had only been applied to the assizes of *Novel Disseisin* and *Mort d'Ancestor*. Not until STONORE, J. suggested that it was most probably the defendant himself who had eloigned the infant, and that if the next friend were not allowed to plead the infant's cause the defendant would be profiting by his own tort, did the Justices finally concur in allowing his receipt. The effect of this curious decision was virtually that the court decided to apply the statute to a case it clearly covered because injustice would otherwise result. The notion that a statute had any intrinsic authority is completely alien to this attitude.

§ 11. *Westminster II*, *c.* 34, *and Dower*

Many interesting points are to be found in a case upon the Statute of Westminster II, c. 34, which says:

> If a wife willingly leave her husband and go away and live with her adulterer, she shall be barred for ever of action to demand her dower ...if she be convict thereupon, unless her husband willingly and without coercion of the Church reconcile her and allow her to dwell with him, in which case she shall be restored to her action.

The widow of the Baron de *Graystoke* brought her writ of Dower against Ralf *FitzWilliam*[2], who put forward an exception based upon the statute, saying that owing to her adultery she was not entitled to dower. The lady replied that by the provisions of the statute the exception ought to allege that she left her husband willingly, but she offered to aver that this was not the case but that the baron "came with force and arms and saddled horses and drove her away from him" while she was dwelling with him as his wife. In the course of the discussion, *Herle* made a remark that is memorable considering the early date in our legal history at which it appears: "Although she was driven away, yet there was no need for her to go to her adulterer and live with him, for nothing shows a person's will better than his own act." The

[1] *Anon.* v. *Abbot of Ramsey*, Y.B. 13 & 14 Edw. III, 16 (14).

[2] Y.B. 33 & 35 Edw. I, 532.

Common Law had not yet made the famous maxim that "the thought of man shall not be tried, for the Devil himself knoweth not the thought of man"[1]. *Herle*, on the contrary, is using the known facts of the claimant's subsequent conduct to raise the presumption that that conduct was voluntary, and thus within the statute which used the word "willingly," in spite of the undeniable fact that the baron drove his lady away. More startling still was an additional piece of evidence which *Herle* brought forward in support of the same point: "moreover we tell you that she espoused her adulterer while her husband was still living." What more cogent proof of infidelity could one want than constructive bigamy[2]? *Herle* was in advance of the court, for we read that STAUNTON, J. looked at the statute and consulted HENGHAM, and then adjudged that "...neither the eloping willingly without the dwelling, nor the dwelling without the eloping is singly the cause given by the statute, but both together"; he therefore ordered a jury from one locality to tell of the one fact, and another to tell of the other. The investigation of the lady's willingness in leaving the baron was therefore left to the jury—how they did it we do not know.

§ 12. *Westminster II, c.* 35, *and Ravishment of Ward*

An interesting example of an argument from intention being used in a difficult discussion is afforded by a case[3] upon the Statute of Westminster II, c. 35. After some controversy it was agreed that the process on a writ of Ward was the same as that laid down in the statute for a writ of Ravishment of Ward, and that the process was this: if the demandant died during the plea, then the case should be continued under a writ of re-summons by his heir if the title alleged were fee; but if the title alleged were purchase, gift, or the like, then the suit should be continued by his executor; and if the defendant died, the case should be continued against his executor, or the heir if the executor had insufficient goods to meet the liability. In the present case the defendant died and process was continued against his heir. *Grene* (for the heir) argued that the statute never gives the writ

[1] Pollock and Maitland, II. 474.
[2] Bigamy did not become a felony until stat. 1 Jac. I, c. 11.
[3] *Abbot of Croyland* v. *de Vere*, Y.B. 17 & 18 Edw. III, 472–500.

against the heir except for the insufficiency of the executor, which had not been alleged or proved in this case. WILLOUGHBY, J. discovered a serious technical difficulty; "can he recover the wardship against anyone but him who is seised of it?" he asked. Further doubts of the possibility of the statute's process were expressed by SHARESHULLE, J. who showed that one cannot sue against the heir and executor in common, and if one sues against the executor alone and he be insufficient to make satisfaction out of the goods of the deceased, then one cannot have another action against the heir. At this point *Grene* took the new line of declaring that the executors had enough to meet the claim, and demanding judgment of the writ on that account. After further discussion, HILARY, J. found another difficulty, viz. that one could not get the wardship from the heir, and the damages at another time from the executors. At this point *R. Thorpe* made the following remark:

> The statute was made with the intention that by the resummons the plaintiff should attain to his purpose, which is the recovery of the wardship, and that he cannot do against the executors when the heir is seised of the wardship. And as to the statement that the statute only gives the resummons against the heir on the insufficiency of the executors, I say that no one is a sufficient party to this judgment where the principal is to be recovered except him who is seised of the wardship, whether it be heir or executor.

This argument from the intention of the statute, although coming from so distinguished a pleader as *R. Thorpe*, did not disconcert the ingenious *Grene*; his counter-move is clever. "To this writ of resummons," he said, "the exception of non-tenure does not lie"; whence he easily deduced that the fact that the defendant was not seised made no difference, and returned to his allegation of sufficiency in the executors, and repeated the interpretation he had put on the statute. WILLOUGHBY, J. observed that Westminster II, c. 41 is another example of an action being given against one who is not seised, and expressed his agreement with *R. Thorpe's* argument. But by this time *Thorpe* had thought of something else; he pointed out that with reference to the plaintiff's death the statute makes a distinction between claims as of fee and claims as of purchase, the one being continued by the heir and the other by the executor; he now suggested that the same should apply to the defendant (although the statute does not explicitly make this provision), relying it seems on the words "eodem modo." He soon abandoned this position, however, as it was shown by WILLOUGHBY, J. that it was impossible to tell in most cases what the defendant actually did claim. *R. Thorpe* now suggested that they had begun wrong, and that the statute only applies to Ravishment of Ward (which issues in damages only) and not to Wardship, but no discussion of the point is reported, whence we may conclude that the court thought it too late to retrace its steps. Debate then took place as to whether the executors actually were sufficient to meet the claim; one side said that they were, the other said that although they had sufficient assets at the time of the testator's death they had not now, and that if the plaintiff delayed his writ so long, he did it at his own risk. The result was further prolonged discussion, into which we will not enter now. What we would direct attention to in the case, is the general method of handling a difficult statute; the discussion does not start with the statute as the principal factor, but rather centres round the Common Law, endeavouring to fit the statute into the Common Law with as little disturbance as possible. One might almost take the case as evidence of a tendency in certain quarters to regard a statute not so much as altering Common Law itself, as suggesting to the justices the lines upon which alteration was desirable, leaving to them the working out of details.

CONCLUSION

ONE cannot fail to be impressed by the strong contrast between the Common Law of England on the one hand, and the Civil and Canon Law of Rome on the other, during the period covered by this study. The stage of formal development preserved in the continental books has the inevitable effect of making our own law look singularly formless and primitive. Even a casual examination of the *Corpus* of Canon Law will afford ample evidence of the existence of a system of interpretation in the 14th century which was hardly inferior, considering its date, to that which formed the subject of the late Sir P. B. Maxwell's classic treatise. The canonists, however, were fortunate in inheriting a situation which the civilians had long ago revealed in its true perspective. That is to say, they frankly recognised that the written act of a legislator is by no means a simple affair. They discovered in practice, and openly stated in their teaching, that such a document must be interpreted somehow and by some one, if it is to form an efficient unit in an advanced legal system.

§ 1. *The Need for Interpretation*

Our common lawyers had not yet fully realised this fact, and until they did so, confusion and uncertainty were inevitable. As late as 1336 we find these words on the Statute Roll[1]:

> And every man...shall keep and observe the aforesaid ordinances and statutes...without addition, or fraud, by covin, evasion, art, or contrivance, 'ou par interpretation des paroles.'

To classify interpretation with covin and fraud clearly shows that Common Law had not yet recognised the legitimate place of interpretation in the business of government, but we have seen how circumstances were irresistibly forcing it to face the fact. Of these, the greatest was undoubtedly the gradual movement of the law courts away from the legislature—whether that legislature be the King in Council or in Parliament. When the

[1] 10 Edw. III, stat. 3.

law maker is his own interpreter the problem of a technique of interpretation need not arise. Only when he is forced to delegate the function of interpretation to a different person does the matter become urgent. This has been clearly traced through its several stages[1]. First, the legislature issues its own interpretations of its acts, or else the Judges interpret statutes in the light of their own intentions when they themselves drew them—in either case the situation is the same, for the legislator and the interpreter are one. The second stage is an attempt to continue this practice under changing conditions; the legislator and the interpreter are drifting apart, but still maintain close communication by means of informal conferences. Where the original legislator had passed away, his intentions were preserved in judicial traditions. Finally, both these expedients failed, and the courts had definitely to assume the task of interpretation, which the legislature had to relinquish.

§ 2. *The Place of Statute Law in the New Era*

Another important factor in the situation was the growing complexity of the law. The time had passed for ever when law and procedure could be modified by the simple machinery of instructions, written or even oral, privately given to the King's Justices as they set out upon their eyre. The magnitude of the business passing through the King's Courts and the technicality of the rules governing its conduct, made it necessary for future changes to be in a definite, that is, written, form, and to be published to all whose interests were affected. The informal arrangement was therefore replaced by the written statute proclaimed in the County Court. This fundamental change[2] in the machinery of government had far-reaching effects.

The first of these was the introduction of "novel ley," new law, which was put side by side with the Common Law. A law which is traditional, especially if the tradition is confined to a narrow professional circle, is easily modified in any direction which the profession as a whole finds desirable. In England the Bench was composed of the King's Judges, and the Bar of the King's Sergeants, and one can very well credit the lingering

[1] Above, Part II, Chapter II.

[2] See above, p. 56, n. 1.

tradition that much of the law which later ages regarded as immemorial custom, was in fact the result of deliberate though informal legislation carried out by the Judges and Sergeants at the behest of the King in Council[1]. But the new statute law was quite different from this. It was *written*, and English lawyers felt that the situation was unprecedented. It may be that the general nervousness had something to do with the growing rigidity of the Common Law itself. In spite of all the change between the days of Bracton and Fleta, that period as a whole must be regarded as a time of fixation of the Common Law. Even as late as the 16th century it still was felt worth while to publish Bracton's work in a very substantial folio. Be this as it may, it is clear that where once there was only Common Law, there is now "new law" as well. "Do you want the new law or the old?" is a question frequently heard from the Bench. In short, English Law is now dual, instead of a unity.

Secondly, the fixation of the Common Law gave rise to widespread attempts to misuse its machinery—now working with automatic though blind precision—for the purposes of fraud and dishonesty. It may be that this gave a strong impetus to the movement for a written statutory law. Certain it is that a large proportion of our early statutes is concerned with this subject, and the Year Books contain countless cases of the abuse of legal process for the purposes of delay and even of injustice, as well as of collusive and fraudulent litigation. At first, perhaps, it was thought that precise, written, legislation would remove the evil, but the event proved the contrary. No sooner was a statute made, than we find reported in the Year Books numerous ingenious attempts to evade or circumvent the act. Originally, perhaps, the result of legal chicanery, the new written and published statutes themselves rapidly became the cause of further artifice[2], and the battle of wits between the legislature and the smart litigant has continued until our own day.

[1] See above, p. 135. Contemporary memoranda of some of this legislation certainly exist, but there is nothing to suggest that these were published in the county as being the texts thenceforth to be applied at Westminster. In other words, they are not statutes, so much as the minutes of a more or less formal conference of Government officials.

[2] Compare above, p. 159; the Statute of Westminster II, c. 3 was one of the most important examples of this.

The third result springs from the other two. As we have seen, the statutes were a novelty which naturally demanded investigation and elucidation. The attempts to evade them clearly necessitated their interpretation. The constitutional movement outlined just now eventually compelled the judiciary to take up the task.

The new epoch inaugurated by the Edwardian period is therefore characterised by three results of the new statutory legislation: there were two sources of law instead of one; the attempts to circumvent this law bulk very largely in the Year Books; and finally the necessity of some means of interpretation was overwhelming.

We have also seen that this duty was at first undertaken by various bodies, until at the close of our period, say about 1350, it was definitely allotted to the Judiciary. This last step was of great significance. It has been suggested that our earliest practice was to assign the work of interpretation to the law-maker himself, and that the influence of Canon Law might be suspected here. But common lawyers had an independent spirit in attacking their problems, and confidently forsook the well-worn path of continental jurists by relinquishing the work of interpretation to a body outside of the legislature. Of course, only the beginnings of this departure are to be found in our period, but the rich fruit this policy bore in the 17th century demands our gratitude to the lawyers who had the courage to break with the only theory then current, and to develop English Law upon its own lines.

§ 3. *The Power of the Crown in the Courts*

In determining the attitude of mind with which the courts approached the question of interpretation, these historic factors were of considerable importance. Judges and pleaders were still, in a very real sense, royal servants, and their closeness to the monarch had important results. The deferential treatment of the prerogative in the courts is of course the greatest, but there are others. For example, the remarkable instances of the drastic expansion or restriction of statutes by the courts are easiest understood as relics of the time when the King was in his court exercising unlimited discretion. While his servants were in close touch with him they too enjoyed almost as much power, and it was hard for them to resign it upon the advent of the new statute law. Again, the determined policy of making the writ of Replevin serve the purpose of a *Contra Formam Feoffamenti*[1], in spite of the fact that two statutes stood in the way, clearly demonstrates that the Judges still cherished their old powers of moulding the law by means of decisions pronounced in court and arrangements made among themselves, carrying out their reforms by means of the royal authority which they wielded. To interpret *De Donis* retrospectively is another illustration of the same fact. Surely one of the most startling of all the phenomena described above is the occasional refusal of the courts to apply certain statutes. The fact that they offered no political or juridical theory in support of their action is still more puzzling to the modern mind. Clearly, there was no suggestion of conflict between the judicature and the legislature; rather, the two powers were still so much the personal concern of the monarch that serious conflict was impossible. Here again we have the same explanation forced upon us, namely, that these instances are relics of the wide discretion formerly exercised by the Judges in the King's name.

§ 4. *Law, Equity, and Strict Interpretation*

The wide discretionary powers described in the previous paragraph were undoubtedly necessary in view of the inexperience of the courts and of the drafters of the new statutory enactments. Reasons have also been given for the opinion that the results of this freedom of interpretation were beneficial, making as they did for symmetry and coherence, and avoiding the disastrous consequences which might have followed the blunders contained in the earlier statutes.

Towards the end of our period, however, circumstances compelled the courts to set bounds to their activities. The rapid fixation of the Common Law necessarily involved the resignation of considerable power by the courts; nor was this resignation altogether voluntary, for the growing separation of the courts from the King's immediate personal sphere will sufficiently explain the diffidence of the new school of Judges who could no longer draw upon the vast reserve of power at the disposal

[1] Above, pp. 91–100.

of the King's personal entourage. We therefore see the beginnings of a separate system of equity administered by the inner circle of the Chancery, while the remoter Common Law courts confined themselves to the old law. Inevitably they adopted the same attitude towards the new, that is, the statute law, and soon they reached the maxim, *statuta sunt stricti juris*. The coincidence of these events in the year 1342 has already been pointed out, and need not be repeated here[1].

§ 5. *The work of the Judges*

Our period closes a generation after the death of Edward I, "who was the wisest king that ever was"[2], and we may see how his judges acted in the face of his vast output of radical legislation. They blundered at times, but we believe that they made a magnificent effort to join with the great monarch in making the law straight and strong. For the greater part of the period they did not servilely follow the letter of his statutes, but loyally administered the spirit, expanding here, restricting there, and rejecting elsewhere. It would be unfair to expect very much consistency in such a situation, for to lift one plea roll and then to estimate the mass of litigation pouring through the Hall of Westminster is to realise the last main conclusion we would draw, namely, that the problem of dealing with the new statute law was urgent and demanded action at once, and that the mediaeval mind, ever anxious to get things done efficiently before speculating about them, set to work administering the statutes as well as it could, and cared little for the niceties of jurisprudence and political science. The situation was one which called for great breadth of mind and the conservative was sorely tempted to lament the "new king, new law, new judges, new masters"[3]. But the right men were on the Bench: BEREFORD and STAUNTON, HENGHAM and HILARY, each in his day played a valiant part in administering the "special," "novel" law which the great Edward had enacted. With little technical training, perhaps without even a copy of the statutes before them, they laid the foundation of the later English Law well and truly, and deserve our admiration and respect for the part they took in the greatest work of our greatest King.

[1] Above, p. 121. [2] 2 *Inst.* 156. [3] Y.B. 5 Edw. II, 1. 87.

APPENDIX I

TEXTS OF STATUTES

THE following extracts from the statutes most frequently referred to in the foregoing pages are added to save constant reference to the bulky edition of the Record Commissioners. Unless otherwise stated, the present author is responsible for the translation.

I

STATUTE OF MARLBOROUGH, C. 9

De sectis siquidem faciendis ad curias magnatum et aliorum dominorum ipsarum curiarum de cetero sic observandum est, scilicet quod nullus qui per cartam feoffatus est distringatur de cetero ad huiusmodi sectam faciendam ad curiam domini sui nisi per formam carte sue specialiter teneatur ad sectam illam faciendam: His tamen exceptis quorum antecessores vel ipsimet huiusmodi sectam facere consueverunt ante primam transfretacionem domini Regis in Britanniam, a tempore cuius transfretacionis elapsi sunt triginta et novem anni et medietas unius anni tempore quo huiusmodi constitutiones fuerant statute. Et similiter nullus feoffatus sine carta a tempore conquestus vel alio antiquo feoffamento distringatur de cetero ad huiusmodi sectam faciendam nisi ipse et antecessores sui eam facere consueverunt ante transfretacionem domini Regis supradictam. Qui autem per cartam pro certo servicio veluti pro libero servicio tot solidorum annuatim pro omni servicio solvendorum feoffati sunt, ad sectam vel aliud ultra formam sui feoffamenti non teneantur....

(Red Book of the Exchequer.)

In doing suits to the courts of magnates and other lords of courts, it shall henceforth be observed as follows, that is to say: that no one who is enfeoffed by a charter shall henceforth be distrained to do such suit to the court of his lord unless he be bound specially by the form of his charter to do that suit; except those who themselves (or whose ancestors) were accustomed to do such suit before the first passage of the lord King to Brittany (which passage was thirty-nine and a half years before these constitutions were established). Likewise, none that is enfeoffed without a charter, from the time of the Conquest, or by some other ancient feoffment, shall be distrained henceforth to do such suit unless he himself and his ancestors were accustomed to do it before the aforesaid passage of the lord King. Moreover, those who are enfeoffed by charter for a certain service, such as for the free service of so many shillings payable annually for all service, shall not be bound to suit or any thing else outside the form of their feoffment.

II

Statute of Westminster I, c. 40

Et pur ceo qe mulz de genz sont delaez de lour dreit pur fausement voucher garaunt: purveu est en brief de possession, tut a primes si com en brief de mort dauncestre, cosinage, del aiel, nuper obiit, de entrusion, e en autres briefs semblables, par les queus teres ou tenemenz seient demandez que deivent decendre, revertir, remeindre ou escheir par mort dauncestre ou de autre, que si le tenaunt vouche a garaunt e le demaundaunt le contre pleide e veille averrer par assise ou par pais ou en autre manere si com la court le Rey agardera, qe le tenant, ou son auncestre qi heyr il est, fust le primer ki entra apres la mort celui de qi seisine il demaunde, seit la verrement del demaundaunt receu si le tenaunt le veille atendre; si ceo noun, seit bote utre a autre respons sil ne eit son garaunt enpresent ke le voile garantir[1] de son gre e meintenaunt entrer en respons, sauve al demaundaunt ses excepcions encontre li sil voille voucher outre com il avoit avaunt contre[2] le primer tenaunt. De rechief en totes maneres des briefs de entre ke[3] font mencion des degrez, qe nul desoremes ne vouche hors de la lingne. Et ausi en[5] autre briefs de entre ou nule mencion nest fet des degrez, les queus briefs ne soient sostenuz fors la ou les avaundiz briefs de degrez ne poent gisir ne liu tenir de dreyt[5], et en brief de dreit, purveu est qe si le tenaunt vouche a garant e le demaundaunt le veille contrepleider, e seit prest de averrer par pays qe celi qe est vouche, ou ses auncestres, unkes naveyent seisine de la tere ou del tenement demaunde, fee, ne servise par la meyn le tenaunt ou de ses auncestres puis le tens cely de qi seisine le demaundaunt conte jesqes al tens qe le brief fu purchace et le ple meu, par quei[4] il ne poit averrer ke le tenaunt ou son auncestre seit feffe[4], seit laverrement del demaundaunt receu si le

[1] Lib. X; the Stats. Realm print *qe il voille graunter* from the Dublin Red Book, which is obviously in error. (For *qe* instead of *qi* see Y.B. 1 & 2 Edw. II, xlvii.)

[2] Lib. X; the Red Book again has the inferior reading *com*.

[3] Other MSS omit *ke*.

[4] Lib. X; *il poent averrer qe le tenaunt ou ses auncestres feoffez*—Red Book; *il poit avoir le tenant ou ses auncestres feffe*—MS Claudius D. II.

[5] The punctuation of the Stats. Realm text (and translation) obscures the fact that Entry out of the Degrees (commonly called Entry in the *Post*) is subjected to the same provision as the writ of Right.

tenaunt le voille attendre; si ceo noun, seit le tenaunt bote a autre respons sil neit son garaunt enpresent ke le voile[1] garauntir de son gre et meintenaunt entrer en respons, sauve al demaundaunt ses excepcions encountre li si com il avoit avaunt encontre le primer tenaunt. Et lavauntdit excepcion eit liu en brief de mort dauncestre e en autres briefs avaunt nomez ausi bien com en briefs qe touchent dreit. Et si le tenaunt par cas eyt chartre de garauntie de autre houme en[2] coste qe se seit oblige en nul de les avauntdiz cas [3]ou le garantie de son eyne gre[3] sauve li seit son recoverir par brief de garantie de chartre de la Chauncelerie le Rey quant il voudra purchaser, mes qe le plai ne seit por ceo delaie.

(The above text is that of *Liber X*, an Exchequer Register, reconstructed from the footnotes of the Statutes of the Realm where the text of the Red Book of the Exchequer at Dublin is collated with Liber X.)

And forasmuch as many people are delayed of their right by false vouching to warranty, it is provided that in possessory writs, especially such as *Mort d'Ancestor*, Cosinage, *Ael*, *Nuper Obiit*, Intrusion and other like writs whereby lands or tenements are demanded which ought to descend, revert, remain or escheat on the death of an ancestor or other, if the tenant vouch to warranty and the demandant counterplead it and will aver by the assize or by the country or otherwise as the King's court shall award, that the tenant (or his ancestor, whose heir he is) was the first to enter[4] after the death of him upon whose seisin he demands, then let the demandant's averment be received if the tenant will abide upon it; if he will not, let him be driven to make further answer, unless he have his warrantor present who will warrant him voluntarily and immediately enter upon the defence, saving to the demandant his exceptions against him also, if he wishes to vouch over, just as he had against the first tenant. Henceforth in all manner of writs of Entry which mention degrees, it is provided that none vouch out of the line. In other [5]writs of Entry which make no mention of the degrees (which shall not be maintained save where the aforesaid writs in the degrees cannot lie nor rightfully have place), and[5] in writ of Right, it is provided that if the tenant vouch to warranty and the demandant wish to counterplead it and be ready to aver by the country that neither he who is vouched nor his ancestors ever had seisin of the land or tenement demanded whether in fee or in service by the hand of the tenant or of his ancestors since the time of him upon whose seisin the demandant

[1] Lib. X; *qil voille*—Red Book.
[2] *De*—Red Book, Dublin.
[3] *A la garauntie de son eindegre*—Red Book, Dublin.
[4] Or, as it was usually put in pleading, "the first to abate."
[5] See n. 5, p. 171.

counts until the time when the writ was purchased and the plea moved, in such wise that he could have [1]averred that the tenant or his ancestor was his feoffee[1], let the demandant's averment be received if the tenant will abide there; if he will not, let him be driven to make further answer, unless he have his warrantor present who will warrant him voluntarily and immediately enter upon the defence, saving to the demandant his exceptions against him also, just as he had against the first tenant. And the aforesaid exception shall have place in writ of *Mort d'Ancestor* and in the other writs before named as well as in writs which touch the right. And if the tenant perchance have a charter of warranty from another man, in virtue of which he is not obliged in any of the aforesaid cases to warrant voluntarily[2], his recovery by a writ of Warranty of Charter out of the King's Chancery is saved to him when he will purchase it, but the plea shall not be delayed thereby.

III

Statute of Westminster II, c. 3

In casu quando vir amisit per defaultam tenementum quod fuit jus uxoris sue, durum fuit quod uxor post mortem viri sui non habuit aliud recuperare quam per breve de recto. Propter quod dominus Rex statuit quod mulier post mortem viri sui habeat recuperare per breve de ingressu cui ipsa in vita sua contradicere non potuit, quod in forma predicta[3] erit placitandum: si contra peticionem mulieris tenens excipiat quod habuit ingressu per iudicium, et compertum quod per defaltam, ad quod tenens necesse habet respondere si ab eo queratur, tunc necesse habet ulterius ostendere jus suum secundum formam brevis quod prius impetravit super virum et uxorem. Et si verificare poterit quod ius habet in tenemento petito, nichil capiat mulier per breve suum; quod si ostendere non poterit, recuperet mulier tenementum petitum, hoc observato quod si vir absentaverit se et noluerit jus uxoris sue defendere, vel invita uxore reddere voluerit, si uxor ante judicium venerit parata petenti respondere et jus suum defendere, admittatur uxor. Eodem modo si tenens in dotem, per legem Anglie, vel aliter ad terminum vite, vel per donum in quo reservatur reversio fecerit defaltam, vel reddere voluerit, admittantur heredes et illi ad quos spectat reversio ad responsionem si venerint ante judicium. Et si per defaltam aut reddicionem reddatur judicium, tunc habeant heredes et illi ad quos spectat reversio

[1] The Stats. Realm using another text has "infeoffed the tenant or his ancestors."

[2] The translation in the Stats. Realm strays hopelessly at this point; see Godefroy, *s.v.* Eindegré.

[3] Other MSS read *subscripta*.

post mortem hujusmodi tenencium recuperare per breve de ingressu in quod servetur idem processus sicut dictum est supra in casu ubi vir amittit tenementum uxoris; et sic in casibus predictis due concurrunt acciones, una inter petentem et tenentem, et alia inter tenentem jus suum ostendentem et petentem.

(Statute Roll.)

In cases where the husband lost by default a tenement which was the right of his wife, it was hard that the wife should have no recovery after his death save by writ of Right. Wherefore the lord King established that a woman after her husband's death may have recovery by a writ of Entry *cui ipsa in vita sua contradicere non potuit*, to be pleaded in the form below written, namely, if the tenant except to the woman's claim on the ground that he had entry by judgment, and it is found that it was upon default (which the tenant must disclose if it be demanded of him), then he shall further have to show his right according to the form of the writ which he first brought against the husband and the wife. And if he can establish his right in the tenement sought, let the woman take nothing by her writ; and if he cannot, let the woman recover the tenement sought, this being observed, that if a husband absent himself and refuse to defend his wife's right, then the wife shall be admitted if she come before judgment ready to answer the demandant and to defend her right. Similarly, if a tenant in dower, by the curtesy, or otherwise for term of life, or by gift where reversion is reserved, make default or will surrender, the heirs and those to whom the reversion belongs may be admitted to answer if they come before judgment. And if the judgment had been made upon default or render, then the heirs and those to whom the reversion belongs after the death of such tenants shall have recovery by a writ of Entry in which the same process shall be observed as has been set forth above in the case of the husband losing his wife's tenement. So in the above cases two actions concur, one between the demandant and the tenant, and the other between the tenant showing his right and the demandant.

IV

Statute of Westminster II, c. 48

De visu terre ordinatum est et statutum quod decetero non concedatur visus nisi in casu quando visus terre est necessarius; sicuti si aliquis amittat tenementum per defaultam et ille qui amisit suscitet aliud breve ad petendum idem tenementum, et in casu quando quis per aliquam excepcionem dilatoriam cassat breve post visum terre, sicut per non tenuram vel male nominando villam vel huiusmodi, si suscitet aliud breve in hoc casu, et superiori, decetero non concedatur visus terre dummodo habuerit in prioribus brevibus. In brevi de dote cum petitur dos de tenemento quod vir uxoris alienavit tenenti vel eius antecessori, cum ignorare non debeat tenens quale tenementum vir uxoris alienavit sibi vel antecessori suo, licet vir non obierit seisitus, nihilominus tenenti decetero non erit visus concedendus. In brevi eciam de ingressu cassato per hoc quod petens male nominavit ingressum, si petens suscitet aliud breve de aliquo ingressu, si tenens in priori brevi habuit visum, in secundo non habebit. In omnibus eciam brevibus per que tenementa petuntur racione dimissionis quam petens vel eius antecessor fecit tenenti et non antecessori, sicuti quod ei dimisit dum fuit infra etatem, non compos mentis, in prisona, et similibus, non jaceat decetero visus, set si dimissio facta fuerit antecessori, jaceat decetero visus sicut prius.

(Statute Roll.)

Concerning view of land it is ordained and established that henceforth view be not granted save in cases where view of the land is necessary, as if one lose a tenement by default and he who lost bring another writ to get the same tenement, and in the case where one has abated a writ by a dilatory exception after view of the land, as by non-tenure, or misnomer of vill, or such like, if he bring another writ, henceforth view of land shall not be granted in this case, nor in that above, as long as he had it in the earlier writs. In a writ of Dower when dower is demanded of a tenement which the wife's husband alienated to the tenant or his ancestor, since the tenant ought not to be ignorant of the nature of the tenement which the husband of the wife alienated to him or his ancestor, although the husband did not die seised, nevertheless shall not henceforth be granted to the tenant. Moreover, in a writ of Entry which has been abated because the demandant misnamed the entry, if the demandant bring a fresh writ upon any entry, the tenant shall not have view in the second writ if he had it in the former. Also, in all writs whereby tenements are demanded by reason of a grant which the demandant or his ancestor made to the tenant (but not to his ancestor) as having been made while he was under age, of unsound mind, in prison, or such like, view henceforth shall not lie; but if the grant was made to the tenant's ancestor view shall lie henceforth as heretofore.

APPENDIX II

SELECT CASES

THE following are a few of the more important cases upon which this study has been based. In some instances, especially in the publications of the Selden Society, the learned Editors have printed several reports of the same case which vary considerably in the details and sometimes also in the subject-matter. Where this has happened, no attempt has been made to reproduce here the critical treatment establishing the French text, the present purpose being sufficiently served by a translation of those texts which most clearly illustrate the studies in the preceding pages. Square brackets have been used to indicate words supplied by the translator to elucidate the reporter's meaning, which is often obscured from all but the technical reader by the constant use of the word "etc." The footnotes, as well as the translation, are those of the present writer.

ANON.

(Y.B. 12 & 13 Edw. III, 51)

Noticed above, pp. 40–41

In a *Replegiari* the plaintiff was nonsuited at the writ *de Secunda Deliberatione* and *Stouford* prayed that the return should not be adjudged irreplevisable[1], because, he said, the court was not apprised whether the distress was for arrears of service or not. If it was not, then they are at the common law because the statute [of Westminster II, c. 2] only mentions distress for service in arrear, *quia statutum est generale in fine*. And SHARDELOWE, J. said that in as much as he had sued a writ out of the rolls, he had put himself in the case of the statute.

DEVEREUX *v.* TUCHET

(Y.B. 3 Edw. II, 16–19)

Noticed above, pp. 53, 83

Stephen Devereux brought his writ of Entry founded upon the Statute [of Gloucester, c. 7] against William Tuchet, and demanded

[1] MS. *replevissable*.

the manor of *L.* "into which he has no entry save after [*post*] the lease which William and Lucy his wife made to Walter, Bishop of Coventry and Lichfield in fee, and which ought to revert to him according to the form of the statute made concerning such alienations[1]." And he counted that Robert Burnel gave the manor of *L.* to William and Lucy for the term of their two lives with remainder after their decease to John, father of the demandant, and his heirs.

[After argument, it was held that the parole should not demur for the nonage of the demandant.]

Herle (for the tenant)....This writ is not warranted by the statute, for the statute gives no recovery save only where a woman tenant in dower alienates in fee, and then the reversioner has immediate recovery. If you want to be aided by the statute it must be by some certain words contained in it. But the statute does not help you because you are in the remainder and therefore out of the statute. We demand judgment whether this writ ought to be answered.

Denom (for the demandant). Although the statute does not mention tenants for life, one ought to suppose that if a tenant for life alienates, the reversioner will now have his recovery for a statute [Westminster II, c. 24] says that in similar cases similar remedies shall be ordained.

BEREFORD, C.J. How will you be aided, by statute or by common law? By common law you have no writ; and if by statute, it must be by some words which it contains. But the statute does nothing for you, and only gives recovery to the reversioner when a woman, tenant in dower, alienates. Wherefore the Court awards that you take nothing by your writ.

[Extracts from another report are used in the text, above, pp. 53, 83. One manuscript continues:—]

And afterwards Stephen complained in the Chancery that his writ was abated. The Clerks of the Chancery caused BEREFORD to come, and asked him why, and he said it was not maintainable by the Statute.

Bardleby (Master in Chancery). The Statute of Gloucester says that if women holding in dower, alienate, then the reversioner shall have his recovery, and Westminster II says "quod in simili casu."

BEREFORD, C.J. Blessed be he who made that Statute! You make the writ and we will uphold it.

[1] These words summarise the allegations made in the writ of Entry in he *Post*.

Wilby *v.* Vottone

(Y.B. 32 & 33 Edw. I, 450–4)

Noticed above, pp. 41, 58

Richard Wilby, parson of the church of Yarmouth, brought the jury *Utrum* against John, son of John de Vottone and prayed recognition by the jury whether a messuage, three acres of land, and pasture for a hundred sheep in such a place were the frank almoign of the church, or lay fee. The parson's declaration was that his predecessor was seised of the same tenements as in right of his church in frank almoign in time of peace, and alienated them. And the writ was challenged because it had common of pasture in it, and *Quod Permittat* ought to be brought for common of pasture. And this notwithstanding, the writ was adjudged good. After this, the tenant said that the parson's predecessor was never seised of the common of pasture in right of the church, etc.; and as to the other tenements, we recovered them against your predecessor by a *Cessavit*; judgment.

Huntingdon. By what judgment?

Passeley. Whether the judgment was upon default or in any other manner, the tenements are forfeit for ever by the statute [of Gloucester, c. 4].

Huntingdon. If the judgment was upon default, we think we can derive some advantage, so tell us what the judgment was.

Passeley. By default.

Huntingdon. Now we demand judgment whether our church ought to be disinherited through the default, savouring of an alienation, by our predecessor, who was only guardian of the church.

Passeley. The statute speaks generally and says that if the arrears are not tendered before judgment rendered, the tenements shall be forfeit for ever; and judgment given upon default is none the less a judgment, wherefore, etc.

Huntingdon. If an infant within age had lost in a *Cessavit* upon default, it would not be prejudicial to his recovery by *Mort d'Ancestor* when he became of age. No more so here, for Holy Church is always under age.

Friskeney. The cases are not alike, for the law allows us this recovery against persons of Holy Church as well as against others[1], but it does not do so against an infant under age.

[1] The Statute of Westminster II, c. 41, only allows *Cessavit* against churchmen for the cesser of certain spiritual services; c. 21 of this statute and c. 4 of the Statute of Gloucester do not specifically mention cessers by churchmen.

Huntingdon. They have admitted that the judgment was by default; we pray judgment.

Passeley. In a writ of right brought against a parson of Holy Church who defaults after the mise of the grand assize, are not the tenements lost for ever? (implying that they were).

Hale. No, they are not, if the patron and the bishop are not prayed in aid.

Huntingdon [spoke] as before.

Friskeney. The judgment is specified in the statute, and we do not think you have power to undo that judgment which was given by common counsel.

HENGHAM, C.J. Answer: for the statute is only to be understood of cases where the writ is brought against one who can lose; but that is not the case here; wherefore, etc.

Passeley. Then we pray that he render us the arrears, or else plead according to the nature of the first writ[1].

HENGHAM, C.J. Now you say well.

Huntingdon. We are not here to plead in the nature of a *Cessavit*; we are here to recover the right of our church, and so we pray the jury.

Passeley. If we do not recover our arrears by this means [2] we shall be forclosed for ever.

Huntingdon. You have another remedy, distress.

Passeley. Perhaps you will let the lands lie uncultivated, as your predecessor did, and when we recover [seisin of them] against you by the *Cessavit*, then your successor would undo the judgment by the jury *Utrum*, and so the process would go on ad infinitum.

HENGHAM, C.J. You shall not plead in the nature of this plea before you have pleaded in the nature of the *Cessavit*.

Huntingdon. We do not know whether we ought to do any service or not, for our predecessor embezzled our charters as well as our land. Besides, I do not see how I am to plead whether I owe service or not, while I am out of the tenancy.

Upon another day *Passeley* and *Huntingdon* argued as before.

HENGHAM, C.J. The parson tells me that his predecessor has got rid of his charters, and that if it be found by the jury that he ought to do any service, he will do it willingly; so we award the jury.

[1] *Passeley* seems to have drawn this suggestion from the analogous provisions for pleading the *Cui in Vita* made by Westminster II, c. 3.

[2] That is, by exacting the forfeiture.

ANON. *v.* BRAYBROKE AND ANOTHER

(Y.B. 17 & 18 Edw. III, 390–4)

Noticed above, pp. 64, 87

A writ of wardship was brought against Gerard de Braybroke and one *A*. The grand distress was returned against Gerard, and served. *A*. came; Gerard did not.

Richemunde counted against *A*. that this same *A*. together with Gerard, who does not come, *etc*., tortiously deforced him of the wardship.

R. Thorpe. You suppose by your writ that *A*. and Gerard are deforcers in common of this wardship, wherefore one shall not answer without the other.

Richemunde. Since *A*. is in court and has heard our count and does not deny the words [of court], we demand judgment.

SHARESHULLE, J. Your writ is a *Praecipe quod Reddat* and so one cannot answer without the other; but if it were a writ of Ejectment from Wardship, or Ravishment, etc., which resemble a writ of Trespass in their nature, then one could answer without the other.

R. Thorpe. Then we pray the Proclamation against Gerard.

Richemunde. You cannot award the Proclamation in this case since the two are deforcers in common, and one of them has come.

HILARY, J. and the other JUSTICES inclined to the opinion of awarding the Proclamation against Gerard, and they looked at the process, and found that in the county where the original [writ] was brought, the sheriff had testified that Gerard had nothing, upon which the plaintiff had testified that he had assets in another county in which the distress upon Gerard was now returned.

SHARESHULLE, J. The Statute [of Marlborough, c. 7] which gives Proclamation, gives no process in any county save the one where the original [writ] was brought. You have taken your suit in another county and so the process is at common law; wherefore you cannot now have the Proclamation.

R. Thorpe. Sir, the statute says nothing more than that if the deforcer does not come at the grand distress then the Proclamation shall issue against him, and the statute says no more of one county than another; wherefore, etc.

SHARDELOWE, J. The statute gives the process in no other county but the one where the writ was brought, etc.

HILARY, J. *ad idem*. If on a writ of trespass the sheriff return that the defendant has nothing, and the plaintiff testify that he has assets in another county and thereupon have a writ, etc., although the sheriff of the other county return that the defendant has nothing, yet the plaintiff shall never have *Exigent* in that county, but must always sue the *Capias*, and that is the result of his own testification. So also in this case; wherefore since you have begun your suit at common law, you must continue it so. (And he did, by judgment.)

Anon.

(Y.B. 11 & 12 Edw. III, 374–6)

Noticed above, pp. 73–74

One John brought his writ against *W.* and *A.* his wife. *W.* made default, whereupon *A.* prayed to be received. She was received and said that one *R.*[1], formerly her husband, was seised of these tenements and gave them to one Roger and his heirs for ever with warranty to Roger, his heirs and assigns. Afterwards, Roger gave back these same tenements to *R.*[1] and this *A.*, at that time his wife, to hold to them and the heirs of their two bodies. Therefore *A.*, as Roger's assign, vouches to warranty Isabel and Sybil as daughters and heirs of Robert[1], who are within age, and prays that the parol demur until their age. And she produces both deeds.

Pole. Whereas *A.* vouches as Roger's assign, we tell you that Roger never had anything in those tenements in demesne or in service since the gift [upon which we rely]; ready to aver, etc.

Rokel. Counterplea of the voucher is given by the statute [of Westminster I, c. 40], that is to say, that neither the vouchee nor his ancestors ever had anything, etc. But to counterplead the estate of him whose assign I make myself [as a plea] against my voucher, is not maintained by any law. But perhaps the vouchee will counterplead the warranty when he comes to that stage.

Hilary, J. Now we see that if what he says is true you will not be warranted, and so it is not reasonable for you to have the voucher, especially since you have vouched persons who are under age, to delay the action. So answer, or we will oust you from the voucher.

Kelshulle. Sir, whereas he says that Roger, whose assign *A.* claims to be, never had anything, we say that he was seised, etc. Ready to aver, etc.

And the others said the contrary.

Prior of Plympton *v.* Anon.

(Y.B. 17 & 18 Edw. III, 232–4)

Noticed above, pp. 79, 126–127

The Prior of Plympton brought *Cessavit* against his tenant, who pleaded that the tenements were open to distress. At *Nisi Prius* it was found that they were not open, and the rent of twelve pence was in arrears for two years before the purchase of the writ, and the suit

[1] This *R.* is clearly the same as Robert.

by coming twice a year was in arrear one year. And in the Bench the tenant came and tendered the arrears of rent and damages.

SHARESHULLE, J. How do you tender? For mark you well, that if the land is saved by tender, he will never afterwards avow for any of the arrears previously incurred.

Pulteney. He tenders three shillings for the rent in arrears up to the present, and damages at your discretion. As to the suit, he need not tender, for *Cessavit* does not lie for it.

SHARESHULLE, J. In God's name! Will you not tender for the suit, indeed? Rest assured that *Cessavit* does lie for suit in arrear (to which SHARDELOWE, J. and the COURT agreed).

Richemunde, seeing the opinion of the COURT tendered six pence for two non-appearances found to be in arrear, and damages assessed at six pence by the COURT.

SHARDELOWE, J. What security will you find?

Richemunde. We have other land in the same vill which we will charge.

HILARY, J. We cannot know that.

Richemunde. Ask the demandant, then.

HILARY, J. No; because even if you both agree, we shall not charge any other land with the rent because the demandant is a man of religion.

Richemunde. We are ready to give security as the COURT shall award.

SHARESHULLE, J. The COURT awards that you hold your land quit by reason of your tender, and that you be in mercy. And for security we award that should it be found in this court at some future time that you again cease for two years, then the land shall forfeit for ever, so that you shall not again have the benefit of the statute [in redeeming your land] by tendering [the arrears].

BOX *v*. PALMER[1]

(Y.B. 3 Edw. II, 91–93)

Noticed above, pp. 84–85, 121

John Box brought the *Monstravit de Compoto*[2] against Palmer.

Scrope (for Palmer). The defendant has lands whereby he may be justiced: we ask judgment of this writ which is given by Statute[3]

[1] Names are from the Record which also shows that Palmer had been receiver of Box's money to trade with on Box's behalf, and refused to render account of his operations.

[2] Not simply "writ of account" as in Maitland's translation; Scrope's speech puts the difference between the two writs very clearly. See also F.N.B. 117 H.

[3] Statute of Marlborough, c. 23.

against those who have no lands or tenements by which they can be justiced.

Hedon (for Box). You have your writ of deceit[1] pending in the King's Bench whereby you can have your recovery.

Scrope. This writ is given by statute where the defendant has no lands or tenements, and we will aver that he has forty shillings worth of land: we demand judgment of the writ.

Herle. He has only two-thirds of a house and four shillings worth of rent which he took in marriage with his wife.

STANTON, J. He will have to say whether he has land or tenement in sufficiency.

Scrope. The statute is in our favour, and says nothing of sufficiency. We demand judgment.

BEREFORD, C.J. We ought to maintain ancient writs wherever they can be maintained rather than the new ones. Since he has offered to aver that he has land and tenement whereby he can be justiced, it therefore behoves you to answer.

Malberthorpe (for Box). That would be a great hardship for my bailiff might owe me two hundred pounds in arrears, and buy just two acres of land and two pennyworth of rent, and then I could never bring him to render account.

Scrope. It will be to the King's prejudice to maintain this writ of account, for as long as he has lands and tenements, the Sheriff shall answer for the issues, and that is to the King's advantage.

Herle. We are ready to aver that he has no land or tenements whereby he can be distrained to render account.

Scrope. We are ready to aver that he has land and tenements whereby he can be distrained to render account.

The averment was received; it was said that he had no land.

[From the Record it appears that he had land worth six shillings a year; eventually the defendant volunteered an account, was found in arrears, and committed to the Fleet.]

AUMEYE *v*. ANON.

(Y.B. 33 & 35 Edw. I, 78–82)

Noticed above, pp. 21, 50, 94–97, 99

John de Aumeye complained that an Abbot &c. had tortiously taken his beasts.

Herle (for the Abbot). We avow the taking &c. for that John holds of us by homage, fealty, and suit every three weeks to our court of

[1] This is Maitland's emendation for the *destente*, *de descente*, of the manuscripts.

Herdewyk in Devonshire, and by &c.; of which services one C. our predecessor was seised &c. by the hand of W., John's father. And since the homage is in arrear, the Abbot avows the taking of so many beasts &c. and for the fealty so many, and for the service so many &c. (And mark that one can be bound to do suit of court in one county for a tenement which is in another[1].)

Toudeby (for the tenant). As for the homage, we hold that we have done it, for the tenant was in the Abbot's wardship, and his mother told him that before the Abbot had the wardship he took his homage. And as to the fealty we have tendered it to him and are ready to do it.

(The questions of homage and fealty being settled.)

Toudeby. As for the suit, we do not hold by any suit, and we tell you that neither the Abbot nor any of his predecessors were ever seised of this suit before the first passage of King Henry to Brittany, which is the time set by the Statute of Marlborough for making distresses for suit, and this we are ready to aver &c.

Kingesham (for the Abbot). Then get a prohibition forbidding him to distrain you &c. which is the writ ordained for this purpose.

HENGHAM, C.J. The statute says "quod nullus distringatur pro huiusmodi secta nisi ipse vel antecessores sui facere consueverunt ante primam transfretacionem[2]" &c. and you have distrained him.

Herle. This statute ought not to help him, for we tell you that the Second Statute of Westminster which is later gives power to distrain on the strength of the seisin of an ancestor or predecessor since the date from which the writ of *Novel Disseisin* runs, from which time we and our predecessors have been seised; and this we are ready to aver, &c.

Malmesthorpe (for the tenant). Although the statute gives you power to distrain from that time, &c. that is not in contradiction to the other statute, but only delays the time at which you can lawfully do it; and this statute was made because people in pleas of distress took title on seisins so high up in times long before the statute that perchance the country could not have knowledge of it.

HENGHAM, C.J. Do not gloss the statute; we understand it better than you, for we made it; and one often sees one statute undo another.

[1] Doubtless as a result of abbreviation by various hands the French text no longer reports the argument upon this important point, which is now only briefly summarised in a Latin parenthesis stating the decision.

[2] These words are hardly more than a short summary of the actual provisions of the statute.

ANON. *v.* WALTHAM

(Y.B. 21 & 22 Edw. I, 320–325)
Noticed above, pp. 115–116

One Adam brought a writ of Formedon against John de Waltham and Maud his wife and counted how one *C.* gave these tenements to the demandant's father and mother and the heirs of their bodies, and that after [their deaths] they ought to descend to this Adam as son and heir by the form of the gift aforesaid.

Howard. Sir, we ought not to answer this writ, because it is a writ provided by the Statute [*De Donis*], and ought not to operate save after the making of the statute. We tell you that his father and mother, upon whose deaths his action would have accrued, died ten years before the statute. Judgment if this writ ought to be answered.

BEREWYKE, J. If you want to plead the statute, it behoves you to take all the words of the statute. Although his father and mother died before the statute his action by the statute nevertheless remains unless you can show that those to whom the gift was made alienated before the statute.

Howard. That answer goes to the action, but now we are not pleading there, for we only put forward an exception to the writ and not to the action, and we tell you that this writ will not serve in this case for the reason above said.

BEREWYKE, J. The statute was made to preserve and keep the will of the donor so that those to whom tenements were given by the form could not alienate. And this statute ought to operate [in this case] because it was made as to alienations to be made of tenements so given, and it does not extend to gifts made before; so your reason would have been good enough if you had said that they had alienated. On the other hand the son would have had an action before the statute to demand tenements so given after the death of his father and mother, provided that they had not alienated; *a fortiori*, then, since the statute.

Howard. This writ only lies since it was made, and we tell you as before. And whereas you say that the son would have an action before the statute where the tenements had not been alienated, that is true enough, but it would not be by this writ.

BEREFORD, C.J. As to your statement that the writ took its birth from the statute, that is true, but it was for a case which happened before the statute, and as a remedy for the hardship which occurred before this writ was provided. Although the gift were made forty years before the statute he would have remedy by the statute, because the right accrued to him at once by the form of the gift, although his action remained in suspense until after the death of those to whom the gift was made. On the other hand, when the writ of *Mort d'Ancestor* was provided it served just as well in the case when my ancestor had died previously. Moreover, when a man goes to Chancery and prays remedy for a case which has happened to him for which there was no remedy before provided, in order that he may not leave the Court in despair, the Chancellor shall agree upon the form of a writ which shall serve him in his case which before the statute was unprovided for. So your reason will not hold good.

Kyngesham. Whatever right he has by the form of the gift, his action accrues to him upon the deaths of those to whom the tenements were given. Now although the gift was made before the statute and his father and mother died after it, his action would be clear because it accrued to him since the statute. But in this case it did not accrue since, but before, by reason of the deaths [of those] to whom [the gift was] made. So we do not think he can use this writ which took its birth from so much later a time, and we pray judgment.

BEREWYKE, J. And we think the contrary.

Howard. What have they to show the form [of the gift]?

Spigurnel. A good country.

Howard. That is not enough for you have said that they were seised by the form and that the tenements ought to descend to you by reason of their purchase, and you have nothing [to show in support] of this, and we demand judgment.

BEREWYKE, J. Answer over.

Howard. Whereas they say that the tenements were given to their father and mother who were seised by the form of the gift, we tell you that they cannot say that; for before these days this same Adam who brings this writ, brought a writ of *Mort d'Ancestor* against one *P.* our feoffor whose estate we have, in respect of these same tenements, and upon that writ it was found that neither his father nor his mother were ever seised. Judgment whether they can demand anything now upon their seisin.

Spigurnel. As above.

Howard. Never seised by the form, ready.

And the others said the contrary.

THE INQUEST said that his father and mother were never seised, and so he took nothing by his writ but was [in mercy for his false claim].

Rote *v.* Anon.

(Y.B. 32 & 33 Edw. I, 480)

Noticed above, pp. 59, 118–119

Maud, who was the wife of William Rote brought her *Cui in Vita* against Benet de C.

Middleton. Benet vouches to warranty John, son and heir of G. de A., who is under age, by virtue of this charter.

Lanfar (for Maud). We pray seisin of the land, for he has vouched an infant under age; the statute says that the woman should not be delayed of her right although the tenant vouch an infant under age "quia emptor ignorare non debeat quod jus alienum emit[1]."

East. You ought never to have seisin, for the woman's recovery in this case is ordained by statute, which ought not to apply save to cases arising since the making of the said statute, and not to time before. Now we tell you that the tenements were alienated before the statute; ready to aver, etc.

Bereford, J. At common law, no one knew the law which was to be made in the future; in those days women would not have seisin.

Lanfar. Alienated since the statute; ready to aver, etc.

East. The contrary. *Ideo* [*ad patriam*].

Kellestekmur *v.* Lanbrunmur

(Y.B. 4 Edw. II, 143–7)

Noticed above, pp. 119, 136

John of Kellestekmur brought his writ of contribution against John the son of John Lanbrunmur and demanded contribution towards doing suit to the court of Henry of Pomeray in Tregony, and counted that one Richard of Kellestekmur was seised, etc., of five Cornish acres of land in the vills named in the writ, etc., which descended to the aforesaid John and John as parceners of the same inheritance, etc., which suit the aforesaid John of Kellestekmur does for himself and for the aforesaid John son of John of Lanbrunmur to the court aforesaid, etc.

Hengham[2] denied tort and force and everything that was against the provision [of Marlborough, c. 9, and said] you have counted that one Richard of Kellestekmur was seised, etc., and that the tenements to John and John as parceners; make them out to be parceners.

Miggeley. Richard of Kellestekmur had two daughters Melior[3]

[1] The actual words of the Statute of Westminster II, c. 40 are "expectet emptor, qui ignorare non debuit quod jus alienum emit."

[2] Not the famous Chief Justice, who died 18 May, 1311 (D.N.B.).

[3] Names from the Record.

and Sabine. From Melior came Richard of Kellestekmur and from Richard came John who brings this writ. From Sabine came John[1], and from John came John against whom this writ is brought.

Hengham. We tell you, Sir, that John of Lanbrunmur our father held these tenements without contributing, and died in that estate. And we are within age and ought to continue the estate of our father, whose heir we are; and so we pray our age.

Miggeley. You ought not to have your age, for you ought not to be in a better position against us than you would be against the chief lord. Now if the chief lord demanded from you this suit (towards which we claim contribution), your age would not delay you from answering; and so it should be here. Besides this, the suit we do is as much for your share of the inheritance of Richard, our common ancestor, as for ours. We pray judgment.

Hengham. As far as we are concerned, this is a writ of right, and if we are charged with contribution now we shall be so charged for ever, and we do not think that we ought to be driven to answer during our nonage to a matter which lies so high up in the right.

STAUNTON, J. Answer over.

Hengham. He demands contribution towards doing a suit, but he does not state the contribution for certain.

BEREFORD, C.J. Perhaps he spends more in doing the suit at one time than at another, and so the thing cannot be stated for certain.

[All the above is from Report I; what follows is from Report II continuing from the same point.]

Kingeshemede defended the words of court [and said] We tell you Sir, that John our common ancestor was seised in the time of King John, which is before the time of the making[2] of the statute of Marlborough on which this writ is founded, and died seised of the same tenements and the inheritance descended to Melior and Sabine as to two sisters and one heir, and partition was made between them at the same time. Wherefore, seeing that this writ is founded on the statute of Marlborough, and the statute is no warrant for this writ save in cases after the making of the statute, we demanded judgment whether he can have an action.

Miggeley. We hold that the statute was not made in defeasance of the common law, but in aid of it; we pray that we should be aided

[1] The Y.B. simplifies the descent by omitting a generation here.

[2] The MS. has "limitation." The date mentioned above, p. 92, clearly does not apply to this action, while the other manuscripts—and indeed the remainder of this very speech—make it certain that the sense requires the emendation "making." So also in the Record, which confirms this.

by this writ which is founded upon the statute, because we are now at common law.

Kingeshemede. The warrant for this plea is founded upon the statute, but the statute does not serve you except after the making of the statute. Consequently this writ upon the statute will not help you.

Miggeley. The statute was made in aid of the common law; but we are at common law; *ergo* the statute will aid us, seeing that we are not in the case of the statute, but the reverse.

Miggeley was not allowed to say this.

Then said *Miggeley*, We tell you, Sir, that such an one, our ancestor, was seised of the contribution since the making of the statute, ready, etc.

Earl of Gloucester *v.* Anon.

(Y.B. 21 & 22 Edw. I, 525)

Noticed above, p. 122

Memorandum that the Earl of Gloucester and Hereford brought a writ of right and counted upon the seisin of his ancestor in the time of King Henry [II] great-grandfather of the present King.

Warwick. If the Court says it has power to take cognisance of so remote a time we will answer willingly.

And the view was finally granted, as a favour, and against the form of the statute [of Westminster I, c. 39].

Stifrewas *v.* Wedone

(Y.B. 15 Edw. III, 44–52)

Noticed above, p. 125

Five knights made a recognisance of statute merchant to Ralph de Wedone who had execution in common against them and a *Capias* to take their bodies. He continued the suit in the roll by means of *Posteas*, in the course of which suit the knights came to terms with him and he restored to them the statute[1] which was cancelled. But notwithstanding this he sued out a writ to the sheriff to take them, and so two were taken, one being put in Newgate, and the other in the Bench.

Blaik rehearsed all this to the Justices and showed them a writ *Quod Vocatis Partibus*[2], and prayed a writ summoning Ralph de Wedone

[1] "Statute" is commonly used to describe the bond executed under the provisions of the Statute of Merchants.

[2] More often called *Audita Querela*; this writ authorises full investigation by the court where fraud, forgery, impersonation, collusion, etc., are suspected, especially in connection with bonds under the Statute of Merchants.

to answer for his falsity, and also a writ to let out upon mainprise the others who were taken, binding them to be here on the same day as Ralf.

HILARY, J. Your writ does not say that, but we will grant a writ to cause Ralf to come, and you sue in the Chancery for a writ to mainprise the others, for we cannot do it.

And then a writ was granted to the Sheriff of London to cause him to come who was in Newgate, namely Roger Stifrewas, Kt., who was one of the five knights [who made the statute]. Then the other four did not sue, so Roger proffered himself and prayed that Ralf be called.

Gayneford. The suit is made in common for all of them, and some do not come; judgment of their nonsuit.

HILARY, J. If this were an original, your challenge would lie, but it is not reasonable for Roger to be imprisoned or suffer damage through the nonsuit of the others, who are perhaps at large.

Stouford. His matter might be such that he could sue alone, but in that case he ought to have a separate writ; but this suit was commenced by all in common and cannot be lawfully continued by one only.

HILARY, J. We attach much importance to that point, but the writ before us does not agree with the statute, and so we have no warrant.

Gayneford. Then you cannot do anything, and so we pray execution of the rest of the statute which was not executed before.

And afterwards in the Hilary Term next following judgment of the nonsuit was prayed, as above.

Thorpe. This writ and suit ought to rehearse the statute which all of them made; but the complaint is individual as to the imprisonment and the recovery of their lands (unless, indeed, the lands were held in common). Consequently, although the others decline to sue, Roger who is in prison and deprived of his lands, shall not be ousted from his suit.

Gayneford. It is not for him who is grieved to have the suit, as you say, for then the suit ought to be taken for him alone.

Thorpe. I put it that even if all of them came and were willing to sue upon this writ, still each one of them would have to show his grievance separately; so, by the same reasoning, the nonsuit of the others will not oust Roger from his suit.

Pole, ad idem. This writ of *Audita Querela* comes to you from the Chancery, and gives you warrant for hearing the complaint of all of them, and of each by himself. If it chanced that none of them complained, you would do nothing; now you find by the record on the roll that Roger alone complains, upon which complaint this writ is issued, and therefore the suit shall be taken for Roger alone.

Gayneford. This writ ought to be warranted by some original, and the only original in this case is the writ of *Audita Querela.* Besides, this writ only says "to answer to the premises" (*premissis responsurus*), and does not say to whom we are to answer, and so we are without a party [against us].

Pole. That is the form in this court, and it simply means to answer to those who complain—in this case Roger alone.

Gayneford. Although according to the roll it is only Roger who complains, yet we have no day given us by the roll, but only by the writ which can only be understood as [requiring us] to answer all of them since the grievance is charged upon behalf of all of them; judgment of the writ.

Thorpe. Then it is no more than as if all had complained. I put it that even so, if they all came, they would complain in common concerning lands held in common, and have sole and several complaint in respect of their separate freeholds if such had been delivered [to the creditor under the statute], although suit were brought in common; and that if all were in court and some withdrew from the suit, the others would still have their suit.

Hilary, J. We do not award nonsuit in this case, and the writ is good enough, so answer.

And then the writ was challenged because it did not allege that the statute was delivered to Roger by Ralf. This was not allowed, because if it was cancelled, the delivery was of no consequence. And then the writ was challenged on the ground that the original only said *Audita Querela* and the writ which issued out of it, whereby the party had a day in court mentioned no certain fact to which he was to answer. This was not allowed.

Gayneford. Roger Stifrewas and the others took us by force at A.; imprisoned us, took the statute away from us, and tore off the seal; we pray judgment whether tort can attach to our person in this suit for execution.

Thorpe. The trespass which we did shall not be tried in this writ.

Gayneford. As before, [adding] without this, that we cancelled [the statute] or tore off the seal[1]; ready to aver, etc.

Thorpe. Ready [to maintain] our plaint, etc.

Gayneford prayed that his plea be entered[2].

[1] *Gayneford* puts his averment in stricter form by adding to the charge that the knights forcibly defaced the statute the complementary denial that his client, the creditor, defaced it in cancellation of the debt.

[2] Compare p. 67, above.

And note that Roger could not be let out on mainprise. Afterwards in Easter Term, *Thorpe* prayed a *Nisi Prius* for Roger.

HILARY, J. You shall not have it because the complainant is in custody, and properly so.

Thorpe. Then we pray that you receive his attorney.

HILARY, J. Certainly not, for the above reason.

Thorpe. Then let him be mainprised.

HILARY, J. That cannot be because he is taken by statute merchant, and the Statute[1] says that his body shall remain in prison until he has made satisfaction for the debt.

Thorpe. The very object of our suit is to show that satisfaction has been made; and, Sir, the mainpernors will make themselves responsible for the debt. It is a great hardship that the knight should thus be for ever in prison through the falsity of the other, because while he is in prison he will never get people to come from so distant a county.

HILARY, J. We cannot [grant mainprise].

But a day was given. Note that others in the same case were allowed mainprise in Michaelmas, Easter and Trinity Terms of the fourteenth year.

ROYAL REPLY IN PARLIAMENT, 1348

(2 *Rotuli Parliamentorum*, 203)

Noticed above, p. 126

Autre foitz le Roi, par avis des Prelatz et Grantz de la terre, fist respondre a les petitions des Communes touchantes la Lei de la terre, Qe les leis eues et usees en temps passez, ne le proces dicelle usez cea en arere, ne se purront changer saunz ent faire novel Estatut: A queu chose faire le Roi ne poait adonqes ne unqore poet entendre, par certeines causes. Mes a plus tost qil purra entendre, il prendra les Grantz et les sages de son Conseil par devers lui, et ordeignera sur cels articles et autres touchantz amendement de Lei, par lour avis et conseilx, en manere qe reson et equite serront faites a touz ses Liges et Suggitz et a chescun de eux.

The King, by the advice of the prelates and great men of the land, has already replied to the petitions of the Commons touching the law of the land that the laws had and used in time passed and the process heretofore used thereupon cannot be changed without making a new statute in that behalf, which the King cannot now or in the future undertake to do, for certain causes. But at the earliest opportunity of considering the matter he will gather round him the great

[1] 13 Edw. I, *Stat. Merc.*

men and the wise men of his council and by their advice and counsel will ordain upon these and other articles touching amendment of the law to the end that reason and equity shall be done to all and each of his lieges and subjects.

ANON. *v.* EARL OF WARREN

(Y.B. 21 & 22 Edw. I, 527–531)

Noticed above, p. 137

The Abbot of *C.* brought a new writ against the Earl of Warren which said that whereas it is not lawful for anyone to have warren except in his own demesne lands, and whereas he claims warren in the demesne of the Abbot of *C.* so that he cannot have his free chase as he ought to have, and as his predecessors used to have[1], etc.

Hyham (for the Earl). We understand that this writ which is in a new form ought not to be answered, because no new writ ought to be allowed unless the common [law] is deficient. And since he may have his recovery at common law (by *Replegiari* if the Earl should seize his greyhounds, or by writ of trespass if he came into the Abbot's demesne lands with force and arms) we demand judgment.

Scoter. This writ cannot be abated unless he tells us of another writ to serve our case; but you will not give us recovery by any other writ demanding our free chase, because we are seised of the soil. We demand judgment whether you ought not to answer to this writ.

Warwick. Sir, he says that he cannot have his free chase; but, Sir, to have a chase is properly of bucks and does, and to have a warren is properly of hares, coneys and partridges. Now there are neither bucks nor does there, so he has not been disturbed in his chase, and we demand judgment of the writ.

HERTFORD, J. Can he not have a chase in a warren? Of course, he can.

Hyham. There are three reasons why we should not answer to this writ. The first is that every writ brought in the King's Court ought to be founded upon the common law or upon the special law; but by the common law no such writ is provided. So it ought to be formed upon the special law. But it is not provided by the special law, because the words "*cum nulli liceat*" should take their rise in the statute and the King's prohibition. But the King has not prohibited this matter, nor is there any statute provided in this case. So this writ is not formed upon the statute, and therefore it is formed neither on the common law nor on the special law. The second

[1] The reporter has thought it sufficient to summarise only the preamble of the Abbot's writ.

reason is that each new writ ought to be provided by the common counsel of the land, but this writ is not by the common provision, and so it cannot be maintained. The third reason is that every writ ought to be purely of right, or of possession, or of trespass. But this writ is not of right because of the word "*consueverunt*[1]"; nor is it possessory, for it says "*debet*[2]"; nor is it trespass, for the writ makes no mention of damages[3]. So we demand judgment.

METINGHAM, J. So according to you it is neither on the lines nor in the spaces.

Louther. The statute says let no man depart from the Chancery in any new case until he has been provided with a remedy for his case[4]; and since this writ is given and provided for us by the Chancery and the Court, we demand judgment; and so our writ is provided by the statute.

Kyngesham. As to your charge that our writ is not in the right, we tell you that it is, and the "*consueverunt*" has relation to the royalty, which is of the right[5], and we demand judgment if our writ be not good enough.

[At this point the report abruptly concludes.]

[1] The allegation of the predecessors' enjoyment of the franchise—of their seisin, in fact—gives the writ a possessory character, in *Hyham's* opinion.

[2] The claim that he "ought" to have the demand naturally lies in the right.

[3] Damages are the distinguishing feature of trespass writs.

[4] Westminster II, c. 24.

[5] A chase is by royal grant, and therefore seisin must be proved in claiming it. See above, p. 144.

INDEX

PRINTED IN ENGLAND BY J. B. PEACE, M.A., AT THE CAMBRIDGE UNIVERSITY PRESS

www.ingramcontent.com/pod-product-compliance
Lightning Source LLC
LaVergne TN
LVHW091045080826
845145LV00002B/637